FOR PALEST

For Palestine

Essays from the Tom Hurndall Memorial Lecture Group

Edited by Ian Parker

https://www.openbookpublishers.com

©2023 Ian Parker (ed.). Copyright of individual chapters is maintained by the chapter's authors

Digital material and resources associated with this volume are available at https://doi.org/10.11647/OBP.0345#resources

ISBN Paperback: 978-1-80511-025-5
ISBN Hardback: 978-1-80511-026-2
ISBN Digital (PDF): 978-1-80511-027-9
ISBN Digital ebook (EPUB): 978-1-80511-028-6
ISBN XML: 978-1-80511-030-9
ISBN HTML: 978-1-80511-031-6
DOI: 10.11647/OBP.0345

Front cover image by Tom Hurndall, Figure in front of tank at Rafah, Gaza (April 2003).

Cover design by Jeevanjot Kaur Nagpal.

Fig. 1 Anonymous, Tom Hurndall sitting in the Al Ruweished Refugee Camp at the Jordan/Iraq border, photo taken on his Olympus camera, March 2003.

Contents

The Sixteen Tom Hurndall
Memorial Lectures

The First Lecture took place in November 2005, with Dr Salman Abu Sitta (founder of the Palestine Land Society) on 'Prospects for peace in Palestine'.

The Second Lecture was in November 2006 with Richard Kuper (Jews for Justice for Palestinians, London) on 'Human rights and the Israeli-Palestinian conflict'.

The Third Lecture was in January 2008 with Ilan Pappe (University of Exeter) on 'The dispossession of Palestine: Sixty years on'.

The Fourth Lecture was in December 2008, with Kamel Hawwash (Chair of the Britain-Palestine Twinning Network, the Birmingham-Ramallah Twinning initiative and the Midlands Palestinian Community Association) on 'Can Palestinians regain the initiative for ending the occupation?'

The Fifth Lecture was in November 2009, with Avi Shlaim (Professor of International Relations, University of Oxford) on 'Israel's offensive in Gaza: Rhetoric and reality'.

The Sixth Lecture was in November 2010, with Karma Nabulsi (University of Oxford) on 'Overcoming fragmentation: Palestinian refugees and the Right of Return'.

The Seventh Lecture was in October 2011, with Haneen Maikey (Director of alQaws Centre for Sexual and Gender Diversity in Palestinian Society, Jerusalem) on 'Queer politics and the Palestinian struggle: Ten years of activism'.

The Eighth Lecture was in April 2013, with Eyal Weizman (Professor of Visual Cultures and director of the Centre for Research Architecture at Goldsmiths, University of London) on 'The fields and forums of political action'.

The Ninth Lecture was in April 2014, with Daniel Machover (Head of Civil Litigation, Hickman & Rose Solicitors, London) on 'Are some or all Palestinians victims of Israeli apartheid?'

The Tenth Lecture was in March 2015, with Rania Masri (Associate Director of the Asfari Institute for Civil Society and Citizenship, American University of Beirut) on 'Dismantling racism and colonialism: Challenges for the BDS movement'.

The Eleventh Lecture was in March 2016, with Adam Hanieh (Senior Lecturer in Development Studies at SOAS, University of London) who spoke on the title 'Palestine in the shadow of regional turmoil'.

The Twelfth Lecture was in March 2017, with Penny Green (Professor of Law and Globalisation, Queen Mary University of London) speaking on 'Evicting Palestine: Israel's criminal urban planning programme'.

The Thirteenth Lecture was in March 2018, with Miriyam Aouragh (Senior Lecturer and Leverhulme Fellow at CAMRI, University of Westminster) speaking on 'Resisting cybercide, strengthening solidarity: standing up to Israel's digital occupation'.

The Fourteenth Lecture was in March 2019, with Salma Karmi-Ayyoub (a criminal barrister in London) speaking on 'Israel's Nation State Law and its consequences for Palestinians'.

The Fifteenth Tom Hurndall Memorial Lecture was in November 2020, with Tim Llewellyn (a former BBC Middle East correspondent) speaking on 'How Britain's mainstream media bends to the winds'.

The Sixteenth Tom Hurndall Memorial Lecture was in December 2021, with Lara Sheehi (clinical psychologist, secretary of the Society for Psychoanalysis and Psychoanalytic Society) speaking on 'Psychoanalysis under occupation'.

Acknowledgements

We are grateful to Manchester Metropolitan University (MMU) for allowing the Memorial Lecture to take place on its premises, to the many people who helped with planning, logistics and with chairing the lectures over the years, and, of course, to the distinguished guest speakers who gave their time to travel to Manchester to speak without a fee to support this cause. The chapters in this book follow, in the order they were given, the topics that were presented, with some amendments to the texts in some cases to situate the lecture. In some cases we have included new pieces of writing by the lecturers that reflect the contents of their lectures. These contributions provide diverse perspectives on the struggle that Tom lived and died for, and they also remind us of the history of struggle to put and keep Palestine on the political agenda. They are of a time and a place, academic pieces written for a particular context, with a commitment to history and truth. The Tom Hurndall Memorial Lecture Group (THMLG) has no institutional funding. The organising group brings together colleagues from MMU, the University of Manchester, the University of Salford and the University of Central Lancashire. There is a blog page with details of upcoming lectures at https://hurndallmemoriallecture. wordpress.com/ and a Facebook page at https://www.facebook.com/ groups/113162458703983.

Many thanks to the Hurndall family for the photographs of Tom Hurndall, and those taken by him that we have included in the book. References to the 'ISM' in the photo captions are to the 'International Solidarity Movement', a group of volunteers dedicated to the use of non-violent protests against the Israel Defence Forces, IDF, in the West Bank and the Gaza Strip. References to Rafah are to the part of the Gaza Strip bordering Egypt, and the site of a separation wall erected by Israel and of a no-go or sterilised strip created by Israeli troops through the evacuation and/or demolition of homes between the border and Rafah City. In March and April 2003, when the photos were taken, the ISM was seeking to prevent demolition by protests and/or occupation of the houses affected. Rachel Corrie, a member of the ISM, had been killed by an IDF bulldozer the previous month.

Fig. 2   Israeli-controlled territories, Wikimedia (2018), public domain,
https://commons.wikimedia.org/wiki/File:Israeli-controlled_territories.png.

Contributors

Miriyam Aouragh, who gave the thirteenth Hurndall Memorial Lecture in 2018, is a Dutch-Moroccan anthropologist. She is a Reader at the Communication and Media Research Institute, University of Westminster. She is the author of the book *Palestine Online* (2012) and the forthcoming *Mediating the Makhzan* as well as the author of a number of scholarly publications (https://camri.ac.uk/blog/staff/dr-miriyam-aouragh/). She often engages as a public intellectual in activist movements and debates concerning racism, imperialism and capitalism. Her research and writings focus on anti-racism, cyber warfare, grassroots digital politics and (counter-) revolutions. Aouragh's intellectual approach and political investment is inspired by the notion that "each one's liberation is bound up with the other".

Wala AlQaisiya was a doctoral student at Durham University, Department of Human Geography, and is currently a Teaching Fellow at LSE, London. Their research raises the question on meanings of queer(ying) spaces within the current Palestinian context and their relevance in relation to de-colonial geographies and imaginaries.

Penny Green, who gave the twelfth Hurndall Memorial Lecture in 2017, is Professor of Law and Globalisation, Head of the School of Law and Founder/Director of the International State Crime Initiative (ISCI) at Queen Mary University of London. Professor Green has published extensively on state crime, state violence, mass forced evictions/displacement and resistance to state violence. She has a long track record of researching in hostile environments and has conducted fieldwork in the UK, Turkey, Kurdistan, Palestine/Israel, Tunisia and Myanmar. Professor Green's most recent projects include a comparative study of civil society resistance to state crime in Turkey, Tunisia, Colombia, Myanmar, PNG and Kenya; Myanmar's genocide of the Rohingya;

and forced evictions in Palestine/Israel. Her books include *State Crime: Governments, Violence and Corruption* (2004) and *State Crime and Civil Activism* (2019). In 2015 she and her ISCI colleagues Thomas MacManus and Alicia de la Cour Venning published their seminal work on the Rohingya *Countdown to Annihilation: Genocide in Myanmar* and in 2018 published *Genocide Achieved: Genocide Continues*.

Adam Hanieh, who gave the eleventh Hurndall Memorial Lecture in 2016, is Professor of Political Economy and Global Development at the Institute of Arab and Islamic Studies, University of Exeter. His current research focuses on global political economy, development in the Middle East, oil and capitalism. He is the author of three books, most recently *Money, Markets, and Monarchies: The Gulf Cooperation Council and Political Economy of the Contemporary Middle East* (2018), which was awarded the 2019 International Political Economy Group (IPEG) Book Prize of the British International Studies Association.

Ghaith Hilal is an architect, designer, and Palestinian queer activist, based in Ramallah, Palestine. Ghaith has been an active member of alQaws' West Bank leadership since 2007, and a board member since 2009, during which he wrote articles on queer organising in Palestine in both Arabic and English.

Kamel Hawwash, who gave the fourth Hurndall Memorial Lecture in 2008, is a British-Palestinian Professor of Engineering based at the University of Birmingham, originally from Jerusalem. He is Chair of the Palestine Solidarity Campaign (PSC), a founding member of the British Palestinian Council (BPC) and a founding member of the National Campaign for Rebuilding the PLO.

Richard Kuper, who gave the second Hurndall Memorial Lecture in 2006, was a founder member of Jews for Justice for Palestinians in February 2002. At the time of preparing this lecture for publication, he is web editor of Jewish Voice for Labour.

Salma Karmi-Ayyoub, who gave the fourteenth Hurndall Memorial Lecture in 2019, is a barrister specialising in criminal law. She provides legal consultancy and advice services to individuals, non-governmental organisations and solicitors' firms on issues related to criminal and human rights law. From 2009 until 2012 she headed an international litigation project at the Palestinian human rights organisation, Al Haq, where she is currently a legal consultant focusing on issues related to corporate responsibility for human rights violations. Salma is Chair of the legal charity, Lawyers for Palestinian Human Rights. Her articles have appeared in *The London Review of Books*, *Huffington Post* and *The Nation*, among other publications.

Tim Llewellyn, who gave the fifteenth Hurndall Memorial Lecture in 2020, was the BBC's Middle East Correspondent based in Beirut from 1976 to 1980, and again from 1987 to 1992, based in Nicosia. He continued broadcasting on Middle East matters for the BBC as a freelance commentator and contributor until 2004, after which he became a vocal critic of the BBC's coverage of Israel and Palestine and more or less disappeared from the BBC airwaves. He is the author of *Spirit of the Phoenix: Beirut and the Story of Lebanon*, published by IB Tauris in 2010.

Daniel Machover, who gave the ninth Hurndall Memorial Lecture in 2014, is a solicitor and partner at the London criminal justice and human rights law firm, Hickman and Rose. His expertise is in vindicating the rights of people who have suffered at the hands of the state, in inquest and public inquiry work and in representing individuals and organisations in complex civil litigation cases. Daniel's work for victims of crimes at the hand of state agents has led to the prosecutions of police officers and prison officers, while his work for victims of state crimes abroad (war crimes, torture and crimes against humanity) has placed him at the forefront of the movement for universal criminal jurisdiction.

Haneen Maikey, who gave the seventh Hurndall Memorial Lecture in 2011, was a Palestinian queer community organiser, co-founder and the executive director of alQaws. Haneen is author of 'The History and Contemporary State of Palestinian Sexual Liberation Struggle' (in *The Case for Sanctions Against Israel*, ed. Lim A., 2012); along with different articles about queer organising in Palestine and Pinkwashing.

Rania Masri, who gave the tenth Hurndall Memorial Lecture in 2015, is a political activist, organiser, and university lecturer. Her publications centre on issues of environmental justice, social movements, anti-war, and, of course, the liberation of Palestine. She can be reached via twitter @rania_masri and email at raniazmasri@gmail.com.

Karma Nabulsi, who gave the sixth Hurndall Memorial Lecture in 2010, is a Tutor and Fellow in Politics at St Edmund Hall at the University of Oxford, and the Library Fellow. Her research is on eighteenth- and nineteenth-century political thought, the laws of war, and the contemporary history and politics of Palestinian refugees and representation. Their chapter was also published in 2003 in *Government and Opposition*, 38 (4), pp. 479–96, https://doi.org/10.1111/1477-7053. t01-1-100025.

Ilan Pappe, who gave the third Hurndall Memorial Lecture in 2007, was born in Haifa in 1954. He taught in Israeli universities until 2006, when he was forced to leave Israeli academia. He joined the University of Exeter in 2007. He is the Director of the European Centre for Palestine Studies at the University of Exeter. He is the author of twenty books, among them *The Ethnic Cleansing of Palestine* (2007) and *On Palestine*, with Noam Chomsky (2010).

Ian Parker, who wrote the first section of the Introduction about the Lecture Series, is Honorary Professor of Education at the University of Manchester.

Amelia Smith is a recognised name within the human rights and global issues sector. As a columnist and author of features she works closely with communities facing the most serious challenges within the UK, Egypt, Syria and the MENA region. She has edited two non-fiction books about Egypt and the Arab Spring and interviewed scores of political prisoners and their families. Her work has been translated into many languages.

Avi Shlaim, who gave the fifth Hurndall Memorial Lecture in 2009, is an Emeritus Professor of International Relations at the University of Oxford and a Fellow of the British Academy. His books include *War and Peace in the Middle East: A Concise History* (1995); *The Iron Wall: Israel and the Arab World* (2014); *Lion of Jordan: The Life of King Hussein in War and Peace* (2007); and *Israel and Palestine: Reappraisals, Revisions, Refutations* (2009).

Lara Sheehi, PsyD (she/her), who gave the sixteenth Hurndall Memorial Lecture in 2021, is an Assistant Professor of Clinical Psychology at the George Washington University's Professional Psychology Program. She teaches decolonial, liberatory and anti-oppressive theories and approaches to clinical treatment, case conceptualisation, and community consultation. She is the president-elect of the Society for Psychoanalysis and Psychoanalytic Psychology (APA Division 39), and the Chair of the Teachers' Academy of the American Psychoanalytic Association. She is co-editor of *Studies in Gender and Sexuality* and co-editor of *Counterspace in Psychoanalysis, Culture, and Society*. Lara is on the advisory board to the USA–Palestine Mental Health Network and Psychoanalysis for Pride. She is co-author with Stephen Sheehi of *Psychoanalysis Under Occupation: Practicing Resistance in Palestine* (2022).

Salman Abu Sitta, who gave the first Hurndall Memorial Lecture in 2005, is Founder and President of Palestine Land Society, London, which is dedicated to the documentation of Palestine's land and People: website www.plands.org. He is the author of several books on Palestine, including the compendium *Atlas of Palestine 1917–1966*, English and Arabic editions, the *Atlas of the Return Journey*, the *Atlas of Palestine 1871–1877* and *Mapping my Return: A Palestinian Memoir* (in English and Italian), the first Nakba memoir in English for southern Palestine. He has written over 400 papers and articles on the Palestinian refugees, the Right of Return, the history of al Nakba and human rights. His Palestinian address to Balfour is available at https://www.youtube.com/watch?v=rz45l_qHdRw.

Annapurna Waughray, who contributed the second section of the Introduction, 'I Am not Afraid to Look' about Tom Hurndall (a section that was originally designed to appear on the MMU website; management decided that it was not suitable for publication as a report on the lecture), is Professor of Human Rights Law in the Manchester Law School at the Manchester Metropolitan University.

Eyal Weizman, who gave the eighth Hurndall Memorial Lecture in 2013, is Professor of Spatial and Visual Cultures and founding director of the Centre for Research Architecture and the international investigative project, Forensic Architecture. He is the author of *Hollow Land* (2007),

The Least of All Possible Evils (2012), and *Forensic Architecture* (2017). After a hugely acclaimed exhibition at the ICA, *Forensic Architecture* was shortlisted for the 2018 Turner Prize. They have exhibited around the world, and in 2019, their work was included in the Whitney Biennial.

Foreword

On behalf of Tom, my sincere thanks to the highly respected speakers whose erudite lectures, representing many facets of the plight of Palestinians, are collated in this book. They are amongst the best of writers, lawyers, historians, academics, educationists, media experts, medical practitioners and activists of conviction who dedicate themselves to a cause that millions of us across the world care deeply about. With their vast knowledge and often moving first-hand experience, they express what it means to be a Palestinian living under an interminable and brutal occupation. I hope everyone looks forward to reading this book and is left with even greater curiosity.

My warmest thanks to Ian Parker for the truly colossal task of collating these brilliant essays, the outcome of sixteen memorial lectures. Thank you for your energy and perseverance, for understanding what drove Tom, how determined he was to see with his own eyes and to record his rational thoughts.

To everyone involved in the publication of this book, you have helped give expression to the essence of what drove Tom and his growing sense of injustice. Thank you.

Extract from Tom's diary, 2nd November 2001: 'What do I want from this life? What makes me happy isn't enough; all those things that satisfy our instincts complete only the animal in all of us. I want to be proud. I want something more. I want to look up to myself and when I die I want to be smiling about the things I've done, not crying for what I haven't. I guess I want to be satisfied I know the answer to this question. Everyone wants to be different, make an impact, be remembered.'

A year after Tom's death, the family carried out our own investigation and justice campaign after a cover-up by the Israeli Defence Forces. Following a military trial in Israel there was a partial justice. The soldier received an eight-year sentence for Tom's manslaughter. It was an unprecedented outcome, and a case that made legal history in bringing the IDF to account for its killing of an unarmed civilian.

Jocelyn Hurndall, Tom's mother

Fig. 3 Tom Hurndall, Tank and observation post at Rafah, Gaza, April 2003.

Introduction

This book comprises a series of scholarly lectures that remember and honour the life and death of a photography student in Manchester, Tom Hurndall. The lectures have usually taken place in the institution where Tom studied, Manchester Metropolitan University, though the process of setting up and continuing the series has not always been easy. The lectures have been organised under the auspices of the Tom Hurndall Memorial Lecture Group. Many people have been involved in keeping the lecture series going over the years, and we acknowledge them here in a two-part introduction by two of the recent organisers. The first part is devoted to the history of the lecture series, drawing attention to the institutional and political issues that are raised by such a project; the second describes Tom's life and death. We conclude the introduction with a list of the internationally-respected lecturers, providing the dates and titles of their contributions from 2005 to 2021.

I. The Tom Hurndall Memorial Lecture

In 2005 an annual public lecture was established in Tom's name at Manchester Metropolitan University to remember his decision to bear witness through his photographs, his determination to tell the truth of what he saw, and his bravery and selflessness in doing so.

The Annual Tom Hurndall Memorial Lecture was initiated by a small group in Manchester Metropolitan University (MMU) under the leadership of Jules Townshend in the Department of History, Politics and Philosophy. Jules guided the lecture series; inviting speakers and arranging the first five lectures at MMU. The first lecture took place in November 2005, with Dr Salman Abu Sitta from the Palestine Land Society, and the second lecture was in November 2006 with Richard Kuper from Jews for Justice for Palestinians. The third lecture took place

 https://doi.org/10.11647/OBP.XXX.01

in the University of Manchester in January 2008 with Ilan Pappe from the University of Exeter. We were back in MMU for the fourth lecture, with Kamel Hawwash, Chair of the Britain-Palestine Twinning Network, the Birmingham-Ramallah Twinning initiative and the Midlands Palestinian Community Association. Avi Shlaim from the University of Oxford gave the fifth lecture in November 2009, and this lecture included a contribution from Tom's mother, Jocelyn Hurndall.

When Jules Townshend retired, he passed the baton to Ian Parker, then based in the Department of Psychology at MMU, who organised the next four lectures with help from the team, and with continued support from Manchester Palestine Solidarity, represented by Linda Clair, who sold Palestinian goods at the event. Chris Roberts from the Institute for Population Health at the University of Manchester had worked with Jules on the first five lectures together with Paul Kelemen from the Department of Sociology, and continued on the organising team. The sixth lecture was in November 2010 with Karma Nabulsi from the University of Oxford, the seventh lecture was in October 2011 with Haneen Maikey, Director of alQaws Centre for Sexual and Gender Diversity in Palestinian Society, Jerusalem, the eighth lecture was in April 2013 with Eyal Weizman from Goldsmiths, University of London, and the ninth lecturer was in April 2014 with Daniel Machover of Hickman and Rose Solicitors in London.

Ian Parker left his post at MMU at the beginning of 2013, before the eighth lecture, and so much of the responsibility for the later lectures needed to be devolved to members of the group, now named the Tom Hurndall Memorial Lecture Group. The tenth lecture was organised by Anandi Ramamurthy, then at the University of Central Lancashire in the Department of Media; this was in March 2015, with Rania Masri from the American University of Beirut. The eleventh lecture was in March 2016, arranged once again by Ian Parker, with Adam Hanieh from SOAS, University of London.

By this time, new members of staff from within MMU had been mobilised to support the lecture series, with a decision to obtain financial support from different departments, and Annapurna Waughray from the Manchester Law School in MMU arranged the twelfth lecture in March 2017 with Penny Green from Queen Mary, University of London. Then Christian Klesse, who had been on the team for some years, working with Adi Kuntsman, both from the Sociology Department, arranged the thirteenth lecture in March 2018 with Miriyam Aouragh from the University of Westminster.

Meanwhile, Anandi Ramamurthy had been working with colleagues in the Department of Photography at MMU, Tom Hurndall's home department when he was a student, to set up a permanent marker of Tom's presence in the university. Over the course of several years a competition was arranged (with generous support for the prize and for installation from the Lipman-Miliband Trust). A design was chosen, and the long process of working with MMU to establish the piece of sculpture commemorating Tom's life took up much time and energy. MMU management stipulated that the reference to Tom's death in Gaza should be removed from the plaque next to the sculpture, and they then wanted the sculpture site moved from the central campus, the All Saints campus where Tom had studied and where most of the lectures had been given, to the new Brooks Building in the Birley Fields campus. These issues, to date, have not been resolved. We have continued, since 2018, to press MMU to install the sculpture. We arranged the fourteenth lecture in March 2019 with Salma Karmi-Ayyoub, a criminal barrister in London.

The COVID-19 pandemic posed additional challenges throughout 2020, though we were also very fortunate in gaining agreement from the Department of History, Politics and Philosophy to host the lecture. This was a step forward in gaining institutional recognition for the lecture and for acknowledging Tom Hurndall as a student at the university. We held the fifteenth lecture online, chaired by the Head of Department, Steve Hurst, in November 2020, with Tim Llewellyn, a former BBC Middle East correspondent as speaker, and the sixteenth lecture also took place online in 14 December 2021 with Lara Sheehi, secretary of the Society for Psychoanalysis and Psychoanalytic Society in the United States.

You can read these lectures, now gathered together in this book, not only as a series of reflections and interventions from different standpoints, but also as a record of an evolving analysis in solidarity with the Palestinian people that carry the traces of the years in which they were given.

We have organised these lectures over the years against opposition from fervent supporters of the Israeli State, and in the face of repeated attempts to have the lecture series excluded from MMU premises. The ethos of the series, and now this book, is that the process of building international solidarity with Palestinians takes many forms, and that scholarly debate is one important aspect of that solidarity. A commemoration and discussion inside the university is, both supporters and critics of the Israeli State well know, a way of legitimising the existence of the Palestinian people and the organisations that represent them. Speakers in the lecture series who are also involved in active solidarity with Palestinians, as Tom Hurndall was, have been clear that open debate is part of a wider struggle for justice. The problems we have faced are, however, nothing to the years of exploitation and oppression suffered by the Palestinians.

What should be clear from this brief account of the history of the lecture series is that the Tom Hurndall Memorial Lecture Group has been a rather *ad hoc* affair with changing personnel, and that the institutional circumstances have always been difficult. The memorial sculpture may yet enable Tom Hurndall's life to be permanently marked in the collective historical memory of MMU, and the team is committed to keeping Tom's memory alive in the annual lectures. If at all possible, this should be with active institutional support from MMU. This book is part of the process of making Tom Hurndall visible in MMU, in Manchester, and in supporting the struggle of the Palestinian people, a struggle for which Tom gave his life.

II. 'I am not afraid to look'

These are the words of Tom Hurndall, a twenty-one-year-old Manchester Metropolitan University photography student, in Gaza, Palestine in April 2003.

In February 2003, on the eve of the invasion of Iraq, Tom travelled from Manchester to the Middle East to bear witness to what he saw in Iraq and then Palestine.

On 11 April 2003 he was shot in the head in Rafah, Gaza by an Israeli army sniper while attempting to rescue two children trapped by

Israeli sniper fire. He was left in a coma and died aged twenty-two on 13 January 2004 in a London hospital without regaining consciousness.

Tom was born in London, the eldest of four children. In September 2002, following a gap year in Jordan and Egypt, Tom started a degree in photographic journalism at Manchester Metropolitan University.

In February 2003, shortly after the huge protest in London against the invasion of Iraq, he travelled via Jordan to Iraq with the 'Human Shields', an organisation of civilians whose opposition to the proposed war and belief in the principle of non-violent direct action led them to volunteer to be an unarmed presence in Iraq itself, as human shields.

Tom's stated purpose was to document and provide coverage of what he saw and found. He sent photographs and articles back to Manchester for publication in MMU's award-winning student magazine *PULP* (which was closed in 2010).

'I am here to photograph', he wrote in an article for *PULP*, but 'too modest to describe myself as a photo-journalist' (although his photographs are astonishingly beautiful). 'I am a twenty-one year old student of Manchester Metropolitan University and I am studying [for] a photography course.' He was someone who looked, asked questions, wanted to understand: what type of people are human shields, what was inner Iraq really like, what was the real consensus among the Iraqi people about regime change, weapons of mass destruction, oppression, and war; and what was the British government proposing to do with hard-earned taxes.

In an article for *PULP* in February 2003, Tom wrote of the Human Shields: 'It occurred to me that I had never been part of a group of people that I respected so much. Few if any conformed to their tree-hugging image, none were political extremists, and only a couple had ever before been any form of activist. It struck me that these were absolute representatives of those who attended the march the week before in London, except that they had the courage to take the protest one step further and still keep it peaceful. In that way and through that courage I felt proud to be associated with them and guilty for my differing motives for being there,' adding, 'When I return to Manchester, any suggestion of their "stupidity" would result in a probably violent rebuttal from myself. These people were heroes in my eyes.'

Tom sent two more articles to *PULP* from Iraq before travelling to Jordan at the beginning of March 2003, where he photographed conditions in the Al Ruwaished refugee camp and made efforts to send his material back to the UK. At the end of March 2003 he decided to go to Hebron to cover the International Solidarity Movement (ISM) in the Palestinian Territories, not least because 'I want to see what is going on with my own eyes.' He planned to be back within two to three weeks and to publish a photo-essay called 'In the Middle', adding 'if I don't get shot by Iraqis, Israelis, Palestinians or Americans.'

By early April 2003 he was in Israel and had made contact with the ISM—civilian volunteer peace activists engaged in non-violent unarmed resistance to the Israeli occupation of Palestine—with whom he travelled on 6 April 2003 to Rafah in the Gaza Strip. Within twenty-three hours of arriving in Rafah he had been 'shot at, shelled, tear-gassed, hit by falling brick/plaster, "sound-bombed", almost run over by the moving house called a D10 bulldozer, chased by soldiers and a lot else besides...'

Between 7 and 11 April 2003 he worked alongside ISM in Rafah, bearing witness to what he saw there, taking photographs of what was happening in Rafah, while wearing the uniform of bright-orange fluorescent jacket and trousers, known by everyone to signify that he was an unarmed peace volunteer: 'I am not afraid to look; that is what I am doing over here now'.

On 11 April 2003 the jacket and trousers were ignored by the Israeli Defence Force (IDF). Around 4pm, while trying to rescue two Palestinian children trapped by IDF sniper fire coming from nearby Israeli watchtowers, Tom was shot in the head by an Israeli sniper.

Tom was left in a coma and died in hospital in London nine months later, on 13 January 2004, at the age of twenty-two, without ever regaining consciousness.

The sniper who killed Tom was roughly the same age as him: It was Wahid Taysir Hayb, a decorated Bedouin Arab Israeli army sniper in an IDF reconnaissance unit.

In October 2003 after months of struggle by Tom's parents to establish the truth of what happened that day, Israel ordered an IDF investigation into Tom's killing to be opened. As a result, Taysir Hayb was convicted of manslaughter, obstruction of justice, and false testimony, and in August 2005 was sentenced to eleven and a half years in prison.

Facts about Tom's time in the Middle East between 21 February and 11 April 2003, accounts of his experiences and all quotes here are taken from *The Only House Left Standing: The Middle East Journals of Tom Hurndall*, which was published by Trolley Books Ltd in 2012, with a foreword by renowned journalist and war reporter Robert Fisk.

1. The Key to Peace:
The Return of the Refugees[1]

Salman Abu Sitta

Millions of people around the world saw the forty-minute slow, savage, deliberate murder of a twelve-year-old boy, Durra, huddled behind his distraught father, who was waving desperately for the killers to stop shooting. Or they have seen other images like this. Within the frame of a camera, the world witnessed the unfolding of the second Palestinian Nakba replayed yet again: an unarmed civilian population in their homeland facing a foreign army descending upon their shores from as far as Moscow and New York, armed to the teeth, supported by Western money and political clout. This is the story of Palestine played over and over again, without the moral power of human rights, and without the military power of international law ever coming to their rescue.

There is nothing like it in modern history. A foreign minority attacking the national majority in its own homeland, expelling virtually all of its population, obliterating its physical and cultural landmarks, planning and supporting this unholy enterprise from abroad, and claiming that this hideous crime is a divine intervention and victory for civilisation.

This is the largest ethnic cleansing operation in modern history. The population of 530 towns and villages were expelled at gunpoint. They had been driven out by the horror of at least thirty-five reported massacres. According to Israeli files recently released, 89% of the

---

1   This chapter is taken from an article on the Palestine Land Society website which includes detailed maps of the areas and populations Dr. Abu Sitta describes, and is available at http://www.plands.org/en/articles-speeches/speeches/2005/the-key-to-peace-the-return-of-the-refugees.

    https://doi.org/10.11647/OBP.XXX.02

villages have been depopulated by Israeli military assaults, and 10% by psychological warfare. That leaves only 1% who left of their own accord.

The refugees were the majority (85%) of the Palestinian inhabitants of the land that became Israel. Their land is 92% of Israel's area. Thus, Israel was created on a land it does not own. There are 5.25 million refugees, who represent two thirds of the Palestinian people; the equivalent of which would be 160 million homeless in America. Of the refugees, only 3.8 million are registered with the United Nations Relief and Works Agency, UNRWA; this accounts for 75% of all refugees. We should also remember that the figures frequently quoted by the press are a gross underestimate.

Ethnic Cleansing

In spite of five major wars, occupation, and oppression, 88% of refugees remain in historical Palestine and within a hundred-mile radius of it. This is an indication of the bond that binds these refugees to their homeland. 12% of these refugees are equally divided between other Arab and foreign countries. While they have been struggling to return home ever since 1948, aided by the full moral weight of international law, Israel and its supporters have been concocting plans to complete their ethnic cleansing operation. No less than forty plans have been proposed, all of which are similar in their objectives but vary in detail. They are all based on the notions that:

- Palestinians are not people, but a bunch of Arabs who can live anywhere;
- there is no Palestine, only Eretz Israel;
- Palestinians do not deserve their land like the Israelis do; and
- Israel could help these Palestinians to relocate elsewhere as a humanitarian gesture.

Needless to say, these are patently racist ideas.

In her 1996 book, *Refugees into Citizens: Palestinians and the End of the Arab-Israeli Conflict*, Donna Arzt proposes what appears to be a humanitarian plan; that is, to settle Palestinians anywhere in the world, except in their home. She proposes to ship one and a half million people to diverse locations and to force the others to stay in exile. Perhaps nobody learnt anything from the Nazi Holocaust. It is a sad reflection on the moral character of those who, more than any others, should have learnt lessons from past tragedies. In today's world, ethnic cleansing is a war crime. Forcible resettlement is a war crime. In fact, settling the occupier's people in the occupied territory is a war crime. To expel Palestinians is a war crime; to prevent their return home is a war crime; to resettle them elsewhere is a war crime; to replace them with the occupiers is also a war crime.

Why should the refugees not return to their homes, as they have done in Kosovo, Timor, Kuwait, and countless other places? International law is solidly behind them. The United Nations General Assembly Resolution 194, calling for their Right to Return, has been affirmed by the international community over 100 times in fifty-two years. This right is a basic right; it supersedes any political agreement, has no statute of limitation and cannot be negotiated away by proxy or by any representation.

The Right of Return is enshrined in the Universal Declaration of Human Rights (Article 13) and in the sanctity of private ownership which cannot be extinguished by sovereignty, occupation or passage of time.

The Right of Return

Who can deny this solid right? Israel and the US do, but not the rest of the world. Israel also gives practical obstacles as an argument against return. Let us examine them one by one. It is often claimed that the country is full, and that there is no space left for the Palestinians. Nothing is further from the truth. Of course, even if that were true, the right of return is not diminished. If an occupier expels an owner of a house at gunpoint, he is not entitled to keep the house just because he has filled it with his cousins and friends.

Let us examine Israel's demography. We can divide Israel demographically into three categories: Areas A, B and C. (The maps defined at the Oslo II Accord are available at this link: https://en.wikipedia.org/wiki/West_Bank_Areas_in_the_Oslo_II_Accord.)

Area A has a population of 3,013,000 Jews (as of the end of 1997) and its area is 1,628 sq. km, which is the same area, largely in the same location, as the land which the Jews purchased or acquired in 1948. Its area is 8% of Israel. This is the total extent of Jewish ownership in Israel. This area has the heaviest Jewish concentration, however, most Jews still live in the same neighbourhood from 1948.

Area B has a mixed population. Its area, which is 6% of Israel, is just less than the land of those Palestinians who remained in Israel. A further 10% of the Jews live there. Thus, in a nutshell, 78% of the Jews live in 14% of Israel.

That leaves Area C, which is 86% of Israel. This is largely the land and the home of the Palestinian refugees. Who lives there today? Apart from the remaining Palestinians, the majority of the Jews who now live there live in a few towns. 860,000 urban Jews live in either originally Palestinian towns or newly established towns. The average size of a new town in Area C is comparable to the size of a refugee camp. In fact, Jabaliya Camp in Gaza is larger than two new towns in the north of Area C and larger than three new towns in the south of Area C. If Jabaliya Camp were a town in Israel, its rank in terms of size would be in the top 8% of Israeli urban centres.

Who, then, controls the vast Palestinian land in Area C? Only 200,000 rural Jews exploit the land and heritage of over 5 million refugees packed into refugee camps and denied the right to return. Those who derive their livelihood from agriculture equate to only 8,600 Kibbutzniks, assisted by 22,600 Jewish employed workers and 24,300 foreign workers from Thailand.

The refugees in Gaza are crammed in at a density of 4,200 persons per sq. km. If you are one of those refugees, and you look across the barbed wire to your land in Israel, and you see it almost empty, at five persons per sq. km (almost one thousand times lower density than Gaza), how would you feel? Peaceful? Content? This striking contrast is the root of all the suffering. It can only be ended with the return of the refugees. This minority of rural Jews, holding five million refugees hostage, is obstructing all prospects of a just peace.

What do those rural Jews do? We are told that they cultivate the (Palestinian) land and produce wonderful agriculture. We are not told that three quarters of the Kibbutzim are economically bankrupt and that only 26% of them produce most of the agriculture. We are not told that the Kibbutz system is ideologically bankrupt; there is constant desertion, and there are very few new recruits. Irrigation takes up about 60–80% of the water in Israel, two thirds of which is stolen Arab water.

Agriculture in the southern district alone uses 500 million cubic meters of water per year. This is equal to the entire water resources of the West Bank now confiscated by Israel. This is equal to the entire resources of upper Jordan including Lake Tiberias, for which Israel obstructed peace with Syria. The total irrigation water, a very likely cause of war, produces agricultural products worth only 1.8% of Israel's Gross Domestic Product (GDP). Such waste, such extravagance, such disregard for the suffering of the refugees, and such denial of their rights is exercised by this small minority of Kibbutzniks, who could be accommodated in only three of the sixty refugee camps scattered in the Middle East. When the refugees return to their land, they will be able to resume their agricultural pursuits, and no doubt this would take up the slack in GDP. More importantly, peace will be a real possibility.

Scenarios of Return

Let us consider two scenarios, which, if applied, are likely to diffuse much of the tension in the Middle East. Let us imagine that the registered refugees in Lebanon (362,000) are allowed to return to their homes in Galilee. Even today, Galilee is still largely Arab. Palestinians there outnumber the Jews one and a half times. If the Lebanon refugees return to their homes in Galilee, the Jewish concentration in Area A will hardly feel the difference, and the Jews will remain a majority in all areas, even when they are lowest in number, as in Area C. To illustrate this, we have plotted all existing built-up areas today and the location of the depopulated villages (with maps at http://www.plands.org/en/articles-speeches/speeches/2005/the-key-to-peace-the-return-of-the-refugees). There is not the slightest interference, which shows that original villages can be rebuilt on the same spot.

Furthermore, if the 760,000 registered refugees in Gaza are allowed to return to their homes in the south, which are now largely empty, they can return to their original villages, while the percentage of the Jewish majority in the centre (Area A) will drop by only 6%. The number of rural Jews who may be affected by the return of Gaza refugees to their homes in the south does not exceed 78,000, or the size of a single refugee camp. This is a glaring example of the miscarriage of justice

One of the manifestations of such injustice is that Russian immigrants are freely admitted to live on Palestinian land simply because they claim to be Jews. The striking fact is that they number almost the same as Lebanon and Gaza refugees combined. Those refugees are denied the right to return while those Russian immigrants are taking their place, their homes, and their land.

So much for the claim of the physical 'impossibility' of the return. The vacant nature of Palestinian land is so problematic that Israel is trying to find people to live in this territory. None other than Sharon and Eitan, both hardcore Zionists, started a scheme in 1997 to sell the refugees' land to builders to construct apartments that American or Australian Jews can buy without being Israeli. Kibbutz farmers who rented this land from a 'Custodian of Absentee Property' (i.e., from a refugee) received 'compensation' up to 25% of its sale value.

This made the bankrupt farmers rich overnight. City dwellers who did not share this wealth were in uproar, and the 'Ronen Committee' was formed to submit a moderating proposal to limit this sudden wealth. There was a debate in the Knesset about it. This illegal activity — selling land that is in custody — prompted the United Nations (UN) to issue resolutions affirming the entitlement of the refugees to receive any income from their property for the last fifty years and calling on all states to present all documents and information they may hold on the refugees' property. In September 1998, and again in 2000, the Arab League passed a resolution to call on the UN to send a fact-finding mission to report on the status of the refugees' land and appoint a custodian to protect their property. But, to date, land continues to be sold without international intervention.

It is often said that Israel opposes the return of the refugees on the basis that this will change the Jewish character of the state. What do they mean by the phrase 'Jewish character'? Do they mean the legal, social, demographic, or religious character? Let us examine these one by one. First, what is the legal meaning of the Jewish character? In the words of a noted Jurist, Thomas Mallison: 'The Jewish character is really a euphemism for the Zionist discriminatory statutes of the State of Israel which violate the human rights provisions [...]. The UN is under no more of legal obligation to maintain Zionism in Israel than it is to maintain apartheid in the Republic of South Africa' (https://www.un.org/unispal/document/auto-insert-196128/).

Not only is this immoral, it is also illegal under enlightened Human Rights law, and is abhorrent to the civilised world. In March 2000, the reports of Treaty-Based Committees, such as Human Rights Committee, Committee on the Elimination of Racial Discrimination, Committee on Economic, Social and Cultural Rights and Committee against Torture, have all condemned Israeli practices and characterised, for the first time so clearly, the exclusive structure of Israeli law as the root cause of all of its violations of international law. How, then, can the international community accept the premise of a 'Jewish character' as a basis for the denial of the right to return home?

The 'Melting Pot'

If supporters of Israel's occupation mean a 'social' Jewish character, this idea is clearly a misnomer. Would anyone believe there is much in common between a Brooklyn Jew and an Ethiopian Jew? Or between a Russian claiming to be a Jew and a Moroccan Jew? We know that the gulf between the Ashkenazi and the Haredim can never be bridged. The Sephardim (or Mizrahim) are allocated the lower rungs of the social ladder. Jerusalem and Tel Aviv are being polarised along sectarian lines. Israel has long given up on the idea of a melting pot.

There are thirty-two languages spoken in Israel. Prof. Etzioni Halevi of Bar Ilan University, a specialist on Jewish national identity, says 'we are not a single people, language is different, attire is different, behaviour and attitude are different, even the sense of identity is different' (see https://www.deiryassin.org/byboard29.html). If you take into account the Palestinians and non-Jewish Russians (42% of them), you get 30% non-Jews in Israel and 70% Jews. How can one call this a homogeneous society?

If by the 'Jewish character' they mean the numerical superiority of Jews, they have to think again. The Palestinians who remained in their homes now represent 26% of all Jews. They are everywhere. In Area A (which has the highest concentration of Jews), they constitute 11% of inhabitants. In the mixed Area B, they constitute 21% of inhabitants. In Area C, they constitute 70% of the inhabitants on average, but they are double the number of inhabitants in the Little Triangle and 1.5 times the number of the inhabitants in Galilee. How could Israel ignore their presence? Will Israel plan another massive ethnic cleansing operation? That is very unlikely. If attempted, there would be a sea of blood. They are there to stay, and their number is set to increase. In the year 2010, Palestinians in Israel will constitute 35% of inhabitants, and they will be equal to the number of Jews in 2050, or much earlier when immigration dries up. So what is the value of chasing an elusive target while innocent people wait in the refugee camps?

In Palestine in 2005 (in Israel, the West Bank and Gaza), Palestinians already made up 47% of the whole population. The Israeli notion of numerical superiority is therefore impractical and short-sighted, as is the notion of an exclusive and homogeneous Jewish society. Neither has any chance of success. On the contrary, maintaining those racist policies will continue to alienate most of the world and will accumulate a great deal of anger that may one day explode with disastrous results.

   If they mean the religious Jewish character, who says that this is in danger? For one thousand years, the Jews did not find a haven for their religious practice anywhere better than the Arab world.

One must therefore conclude that the cliché 'Jewish character' is meant to justify keeping the land and expelling the people. The refugees are not only those in the camps and in exile. There are other refugees, citizens of the State of Israel, who are still not allowed to return home. The Palestinians who remained in their homes after the Israeli invasion of 1948 were locked up as virtual prisoners of war under martial law, a situation which lasted for eighteen years, until 1966. The military governor had the power to detain anybody, and to prohibit the population from travelling anywhere. No exit or entry to villages was allowed.

We know that all expelled refugees were declared 'absent', and their land and property were confiscated by the Custodian of Absentee Property, which turned it over to the Development Authority, which in turn put it under the management of the Israel Land Administration (ILA). The ILA today controls 92.6% of Israel's area, which is essentially Palestinian property. But those who remained, and did not happen to be in a particular place on a particular day, were also registered as 'absent' and their land was confiscated. They now number 250,000. They are internal refugees, although they are Israeli citizens. They are dubbed 'present absentees', an oxymoron in itself, and a term that clearly describes the fallacy of Israeli legal formulation.

Israel created a web of fictitious legal formulations to confiscate Palestinian property. It would confiscate land for public interest, public security, absorption of immigrants or any contrived purpose. Land was confiscated under the pretext that it is 'uncultivated'; it is uncultivated because the owner is expelled and not allowed to return. If the owner is there and cultivates his land, the area is declared 'closed' by military order and no one is allowed to enter. After three years, the land is then declared 'uncultivated', and is subsequently confiscated. The confiscated land is restricted for the benefit of Jews only. Laws prohibit the use, lease, and mere presence of non-Jews on this land. This is the institutional racism that is repeatedly condemned by human rights groups.

With population growth and land scarcity, Israeli Palestinians had to build new houses on their land, which then developed into villages. These villages are not shown on Israeli maps, and are not provided with utilities, health or education services, nor even connected to roads. They are the so-called 'unrecognised villages'. There are over forty such villages in the north of the territory.

In the southern district of Beer Sheba, the situation is much worse. Half of the population of 130,000 in Beer Sheba lives in forty-five unrecognised villages. Their property rights are completely denied. They are plagued by a fascist military force called Green Patrol. This patrol evicts people from their land, shoots flocks and dogs, pulls down houses, ploughs over crops, uproots fruit and olive trees, sprays crops with toxic materials and demolishes dams.

The most cruel of the racist Israeli policies are practised in Beer Sheba. Despite overwhelming evidence of brutality, charges against Green Patrol have been dismissed.

Where does all of this lead us? There is no question that the Israeli racist practices, denial of human rights and contempt for international law, are the root of all evil and should not be allowed to continue. At the moment, Israel is shielded from punishment and censure by its military force and political protection, blindly provided by the US Congress and Administration, to the detriment of the USA's own interests.

Against this massive power stands the determined struggle of the civil population of Palestine. Now, they are supported by an astonishingly huge world-wide constituency. Demonstrations are held across the world to express outrage towards and condemnation of Israel.

There are hundreds of societies and Non-Governmental Organisations (NGOs) which condemn this injustice and oppression. Many of these societies have made inroads with their own parliaments. All of these efforts are directed towards implementing international law and human rights.

Israel and the US are isolated in this huge arena of global public opinion, and in the United Nations. How long can this go on?

US Policy

US policy in the Middle East has two pillars: the first is to secure oil supplies and the second is the unquestioning support of Israel. In 1930, Arab states favoured the US by giving them oil concessions in preference to Britain and France, whose colonial past did not make them acceptable partners. The US appeared to be a 'clean' country, both honest and diligent. That is, until the creation of Israel in 1948 and the unashamedly expedient political policies of President Truman, who prioritised his own electoral interest above that of his country.

Eisenhower and Kennedy restored the balance. It was reversed again by Johnson and successors. Since then, the US administration supplied Israel with a huge arsenal of weapons, $135 billion of taxpayers' money, which is more than the aid granted to Sub-Saharan Africa, all of Latin America and all of the Caribbean combined. This is in addition to unqualified and singularly biased political support.

The anger and outrage felt by the Arabs towards the US support of Israel's occupation of Arab lands seriously damaged US-Arab relations, and on some occasions threatened the oil supply. Thus, Israel demolished the goodwill which had been a feature of the Arab-American relationship since the beginning of the last century. So far, the US has succeeded in maintaining two opposed policies: hurting Arab interests and getting their oil.

This obviously cannot go on. It is clear from the groundswell of indignation in the Arab world that their rulers must now follow a policy of reciprocal action. Good relations could prevail only if respect for national interests, not to speak of respect for international law, were reciprocated.

Israel pursues a policy of unattainable objectives. Its dream of numerical superiority is short-lived. Its practice of apartheid and racism is doomed. Its denial of human rights will not remain uncensured. Finally, its total dependence on its military might, and on US singular obedience to its every whim, is the epitome of short-sightedness. If Israel is to survive where it has been planted, it should uphold the common principles by which its neighbours live: each on the territory he owns, not on the territory he occupies by force. The rights of each party must be respected.

As for the Palestinians, they have endured their own holocaust (Nakba) of 1948, suffered wars, occupation and oppression. But they still exist; they have survived. There is no way that they could disappear, no matter how much Israel wishes them to do so.

The example of the Intifada in 2000 shows that the Palestinians cannot simply continue to look across the barbed wire and see their homes occupied by Russians and Ethiopians while they rot in refugee camps. They must return home. This is in the Israelis' best interests in the long run. This is in the long-term interest of the US. This is in the interest of peace and stability in the Middle East. This is what the whole world has affirmed year after year since 1948.

The Palestinians are determined to win their freedom and recover their basic rights. Justice will no doubt prevail. The question is: how many boys will die like Durra before this happens?

Fig. 4 Tom Hurndall, A 'human shield' who travelled with Tom on the roof of a
power station, February 2003.

2. Human Rights in the Israeli-Palestinian Conflict

Richard Kuper

The events in Gaza and on the West Bank, appalling as they are, are not the only, or even the most terrible, infringement of human rights to be found on the planet. One only has to think of the genocide in Darfur, or the torture camp at Guantanamo. Why does the fate of the Palestinian people, and peace in the Israel-Palestinian conflict, matter so profoundly?

Singling out Israel

Individuals will have personal reasons for singling out any cause they choose to support. You might identify with those who are suffering or see their oppressors as like 'us', or feel responsible historically in some way for that particular cause, and wish to make amends. And while we might hope that all oppressions would be universally condemned on the simple grounds that people shouldn't treat others the way they do, we know this doesn't cut much ice in the real world. There are too many valid causes and we inevitably select from these, hoping perhaps that success in one will have a knock-on effect. But shouldn't we be consistent? Isn't Israel singled out above all possible justification? Doesn't this encourage antisemitism? Isn't Israel demonised? The answer is, sometimes, yes. Solidarity movements generally tend to exaggerate the purity of their own side and the sheer bloody nastiness of the oppressors.

Sometimes this exaggeration does overstep all reasonable, and sometimes indeed acceptable, boundaries. In the case of Israel, it is

   https://doi.org/10.11647/OBP.XXX.03

especially important to get the criticism right. Not just because those striving for justice in the region are up against powerful geo-political interests that give Israel a great deal of support; but, because of Israel's particular history, getting it wrong can and is used to mobilise sympathy and support in favour of 'plucky little Israel', 'outpost of Western values', and this despite action after action that, in the case of some other state, would call down universal condemnation. We need to remember that the immediate circumstances giving rise to the establishment of Israel is a history of European antisemitism culminating in a genocide in which a full third of Jews worldwide were exterminated. It was a genocide in which, it must be said, the world basically stood by. This has to be taken on board if we want to understand the extraordinary depths of emotion that surround so many discussions about the Israeli-Palestinian conflict.

I would go further and say that we need to understand the fear of antisemitism among Jewish communities in the world today, nor must we downplay its existence. The fact that cries of antisemitism are sometimes used to silence critics of Israeli policies should not lead us to dismiss all cries of antisemitism as phoney. They are not. Antisemitism, like all other forms of racism, is a plague in Western societies and a plague on civilised values. But I am not concerned here with a strategy for opposing racism in general, or antisemitism in particular. I merely want to alert you to the need to be alert in solidarity work for those things which undermine the struggle morally, and allow debate to be diverted from the realities of the situation on the ground into emotive highways and byways. There is no need to exaggerate, no need to demonise, no need to make false comparison; and we simply need to think carefully about the language of struggle that we deploy. So I want to reflect on this 'singling out Israel' issue.

Double Standards

My own reasons for concern are perhaps worth recording. I grew up in apartheid South Africa in the 1950s and Zionism promised an alternative life for young and idealistic Jews like myself who found apartheid anywhere between uncomfortable and unbearable, and who saw little possibility of doing anything meaningful about it. A disproportionate number of Jews, to their credit, were deeply involved in the anti-apartheid struggle; but others organised an alternative social world around the goal of making 'aliyah' (lit: rising up) to Israel and found warmth and comfort in the egalitarian ideals of the kibbutz or in the challenge of building a new society from the ground up, of 'making the desert bloom'. Of course, we 'knew' there were some Arabs in Israel; we also knew that many had left, egged on, we believed, by vindictive Arab leaders who promised that they would return triumphant to their lands once the Jews had been thrown into the sea. Unwittingly, we cast Arabs into the same mould as the apartheid regime we abhorred cast the blacks; as alien, foreign, other, an existential threat. It didn't strike us as odd in the slightest that a people who had had nothing to do with the Holocaust in Europe should somehow be expected to pay the price they had been forced to pay.

I came to England and became a committed socialist. But it nonetheless took me a long time to recognise the double standards I was operating in my personal life with regard to the Israeli-Palestinian conflict; and my commitment today to the Palestinian cause has no doubt elements of atonement within it. I most certainly single out Israel, in part at least because I turned a blind eye to aspects of it when I should have known better, and because I expected more of it. My personal trajectory may not be intrinsically interesting. But what is interesting is that so many people converge on the Israeli-Palestinian conflict as a focus of their attention and commitment.

Indeed, Norman Geras, writing on 13 January 2006 in his blog, makes this a reason for inherent suspicion:

> It doesn't just happen that a whole lot of individuals converge on one cause. There have to be reasons. The movement today to institute boycotts of one kind and another against Israel, but not against other states whose human rights records are worse, and often vastly worse than Israel's — I just name Sudan here to get this point comprehensively settled — didn't come about simply through a lot of different individuals homing in, for a multitude of personal reasons, on the justified grievances of the Palestinians. Either there are good reasons [...] [o]r there are not such good reasons — and then there is at least a prima facie case for thinking some prejudice against the country or its people may be at work.

Now I happen to think there are good reasons (even if they're not good enough for Norman Geras, whose comments postdate an earlier attempt of mine to look at the issue of 'Singling out Israel'!).

The points I had previously made, and which Geras found inadequate, were the following:

First, Israel singles itself out and presents itself as special. It sees itself as a state based, as its Declaration of Independence declares, 'on the precepts of liberty, justice and peace taught by the Hebrew Prophets'. In the words of Isaiah, 'We are a light unto the nations'. Israel is constantly lauded as the only 'democratic country in the Middle East' with the 'most moral army in the world'. It invites evaluation in terms of its own founding principles and it constantly reaffirms its commitment to these values. It claims to be defending Western values and presents itself as an outpost of these principles. What better criteria to judge it by?

Second, Israel *is* special, in that it controls a number of religious sites that are of especial significance to three world religions. They have been contested over the generations and the millennia. In recognition of this reality, UN Resolution 181 of 1947, on which Israel's legitimacy is based, called for the creation of a special international zone, encompassing the Jerusalem metropolitan area. Since then, religious concerns and motivations have deepened, and there are literally hundreds of millions of Christians and Muslims, in particular, who have grave concerns about their holy places. You don't need to be religious yourself to appreciate the profound part that religious sentiment has played historically, and indeed increasingly continues to play, in today's world. All of this sits uneasily with Israel's 1980 'annexation' of East Jerusalem and declaration that 'a united Jerusalem' is 'the eternal capital of the Jewish state', an annexation that the UN Security Council Resolution 478 of 1980 unanimously rejected as a violation of international law.

Third, the United States clearly finds Israel special, in that it has been far-and-away the largest single recipient of US foreign aid since the 1960s. From 1949 to 1996, the total of US foreign aid to all of the countries of sub-Saharan Africa, Latin America and the Caribbean combined was $62.5 billion, almost exactly the same amount given to Israel alone in this period! Total aid to Israel was approximately one third of the US foreign-aid budget until the Iraq invasion, and still remains at a very high level. The extent to which the US has singled out Israel as its most loyal ally in the region is indeed extraordinary. Insofar as one believes that the US plays a dominant role in the international system, its choice of which countries to support is of legitimate concern. When the US, often standing alone, vetoes resolution after resolution concerning Israel in the UN Security Council, on the issue of Gaza on 13 July 2006 and again on 11 November 2006, Israel is singled out. Israel is singled out, too, by the US as being the only country allowed to possess nuclear weapons with no demands being made for their control.

Fourth, Israel singles itself out in a different way with regard to the Jews of the world. It presents itself as their real home, as opposed to the multiplicity of countries in which Jews have settled and integrated. Integration can never be permanently successful, antisemitism is ever-present and persecution is always just around the corner. In that sense, there is always an implicit accusation of disloyalty made against Jews who do not give Israel their whole-hearted support. And Jews who speak out against the actions of the Israeli government as 'Not in Our Name' are often accused from within the Jewish community of 'self-hatred' or worse.

To these four points I would now like to add two more.

Fifth: Israel presents itself as a bastion of 'Western values' in general terms as already mentioned, but, since 11 September 2001, also in the 'war against terror', a battle that Israel claims to have been fighting for decades. Days after 9/11 Sharon called Arafat 'our Bin Laden', despite Arafat's opposition to Bin Laden's opportunistic adoption of the Palestinian cause. And indeed, Israel is treated differently in many ways, as though it were the frontline in some division of the world between the West and 'the Other', Europeans and Muslims or whatever terms some supposedly fundamental divide the future clash of civilisations is cast in.

The sixth point is the occupation. What other country has been in occupation of another people's land for such a long period, in defiance of international law; what country has refused to define its borders and accept, or indeed even acknowledge, the green line and print it on its maps, as the Israeli government has failed to do over past decades? Perhaps China's domination of Tibet has some parallels, though the PRC bases its claims to Tibet on the theory that Tibet became an integral part of China 700 years ago. It is a disputed history perhaps, but very different from the Israel-Palestine situation.

It is my contention that each of these points, taken alone, gives a valid reason for 'singling out' Israel. Taken together, I believe the case is overwhelming. Double standards do indeed predominate in any discussion of Israel, but rarely in the way its supporters claim. Throughout much of Europe and much of the Muslim world, it looks as though Israel is indeed singled out for favour, for support, for exemption when others are condemned. It is time to stop singling Israel out in this way, and to hold it accountable to the same values and criteria it claims to be embodying: values that are liberal, democratic, non-discriminatory and just.

Human Rights and International Humanitarian Law

So, having identified what I believe to be ample grounds for this focus on Israel, I now want to single out Israel in a very precise sense, contrasting its high-flown rhetoric and its actual practice in respect of human rights, particularly in regard to war. Let me say at the outset that I am not a lawyer. But I can also say that these issues are too important to be left solely in the hands of lawyers. What I say will be informed by my reading of legal texts and issues, and I believe it will stand up to scrutiny at the legal level. I know it will stand up to scrutiny at the human and moral level, at the level of ordinary everyday understanding. And should it be found wanting on some nice legal point here or there, I hope it is the law which will change over time, not our reactions to what appear to me self-evident violations of human rights. I therefore make no claims to originality in what I am going to say. Rather, the reverse. I hope I can document everything by references to documents and interpretations which command general agreement. I am indebted in particular to the International Humanitarian Law Research Initiative, based at the Harvard School of Public Health, to B'Tselem, the Israeli information centre for human rights in the occupied territories, to ACRI, the Association for Civil Rights in Israel and to Human Rights Watch. (Perhaps I should add in thanks to the dozens of other organisations that also contribute to monitoring human rights in Israel-Palestine: the Palestine Centre for Human Rights, Physicians for Human Rights,

Rabbis for Human Rights, MachsomWatch, the Israeli Campaign Against House Demolitions, Yesh Din, and the rest.)

I believe that the various charges add up to a simple one—that the Israeli army, far from acting as 'the most moral army in the world', as it claims to be, acts with impunity in the occupied territories, where violence on a daily scale, including torture and illegal killings, goes not only unpunished but generally unremarked upon. The Law of Occupation, according to the International Humanitarian Law Research Initiative, is one of the oldest and most developed branches of International Humanitarian Law (IHL). Among other things, it regulates the relationship between the Occupying Power and the population of the occupied territory (including refugees and stateless people), providing protection to the latter against potential abuse by the former. The definition of occupation is very practical: does the foreign military force exercise actual control over a territory? There is no need for a declaration of intent by the occupying forces, nor are their motives for occupation relevant.

Occupation does not and cannot confer sovereignty over any of the occupied territory to the Occupying Power. This can come about only by a freely entered-upon agreement between equal partners. On the contrary, the Occupying Power has duties: it is responsible for ensuring public order and safety in the occupied territories, and should not interfere with the social and political fabric of society unless absolutely prevented from doing so.

The law of occupation is codified largely in the 1949 Fourth Geneva Convention, specifically designed to protect civilians in times of war. It focuses on the treatment of civilians at the hands of the adversary, whether in occupied territories or in internment. Adopted on 12 August 1949, it entered into force on 21 October 1950; and Israel ratified it with effect from 6 July 1951.

The Convention prohibits, among other things, violence to life and person, torture, taking of hostages, humiliating and degrading treatment, sentencing and execution without due legal process, and collective punishments of any kind, with respect to all 'protected persons'. It calls for them to be humanely treated at all times, with no physical or moral coercion, intimidation or deportation. Article 147 specifies 'grave breaches' of the Convention as including wilful killing; torture or inhuman treatment; wilfully causing great suffering or serious injury to body or health; unlawful deportation or transfer or unlawful confinement of a protected person; wilfully depriving a protected person of the rights of fair and regular trial; taking of hostages and extensive destruction and appropriation of property, not justified by military necessity and carried out unlawfully and wantonly. Israel, I believe, is in daily breach of its obligations under international law. Putting it into cautious legal language, some of these breaches probably amount to war crimes.

a) Let us start with the simple issue of humane treatment (all Articles referred to below are Articles of the Fourth Geneva Convention, available at https://ihl-databases.icrc.org/en/ihl-treaties/gciv-1949). Article 27 states: 'Protected persons are entitled, in all circumstances, to respect for their persons, their honour, their family rights, their religious convictions and practices, and their manners and customs. They shall at all times be humanely treated, and shall be protected especially against all acts of violence or threats thereof and against insults and public curiosity.'

In reality, almost everything that follows here has a bearing on this general rubric of 'humane treatment'. Let me introduce it here with a few instances of violations:

- Every day tens of thousands of Palestinians are subjected to a checkpoint system involving body searches, humiliation and inconvenience. These checkpoints are routinely justified as part of Israel's necessary security system, to prevent terrorists infiltrating into Israel. What is not generally known is that of the more than 600 barriers, road blocks and physical checkpoints in existence on the West Bank at more or less any point in time, no more than twenty-six are between Israel and the occupied territories; the rest are all internal.

- In report after report, Machsom [Checkpoint] Watch and B'Tselem chronicle incidents of violence, at times gross violence, against Palestinians that are unnecessary and without justification. Claims of police or army brutality generally remain uninvestigated and have become the norm.

This is made abundantly clear, too, in the testimony of former soldiers now in the organisation Breaking the Silence.

- From September 2000 to September 2006, sixty-eight pregnant Palestinian women gave birth at Israeli checkpoints, leading to thirty-four miscarriages and the deaths of four women, according to the Palestinian Health Ministry's September report.

- The Family Unification Law forbids Israelis married to, or who will marry in the future, residents of the Occupied Territories from living in Israel with their spouses. This law does not apply to spouses who are not residents of the Occupied Territories and is inherently racist in its formulation.

b) More specifically, on the issue of torture or brutality, Article 31 states: 'No physical or moral coercion shall be exercised against protected persons, in particular to obtain information from them or from third parties.' Article 32 prohibits the use of 'any measure of such a character as to cause the physical suffering or extermination of protected persons', a prohibition that applies not just to murder, torture, etc., 'but also to any other measures of brutality whether applied by civilian or military agents'.

Violations:

- According to a 2003 report by the Public Committee Against Torture in Israel and other human rights organisations [Back to a Routine of Torture: Torture and Ill treatment of Palestinian Detainees during Arrest, Detention and Interrogation September 2001–April 2003], there is evidence of systematic and routine torture of Palestinian prisoners causing 'severe pain or suffering, whether physical or mental'. Violence, painful tying, humiliations and many other forms of ill treatment, including detention under inhuman conditions, are a matter of course.

  The report claims that the activities of Shin Bet or General Security Services (GSS) are rubber stamped by the bodies which are supposed to keep the GSS under scrutiny:

- The High Court of Justice had not accepted a single one of the 124 petitions submitted by the Public Committee Against

Torture against prohibiting detainees under interrogation from meeting their attorneys during times of Intifada.

- The State Prosecutor's Office transfers the investigation of complaints to (you've guessed it!) a GSS agent to follow up.

- The Attorney General grants wholesale, and with no exception, the 'necessity defense' approval for every single case of torture.

The result is a total, hermetic, impenetrable and unconditional protection that envelops the GSS system of torture, and enables it to continue undisturbed, with no supervision of scrutiny to speak of. The achievements of the HCJ [Israeli High Court of Justice] ruling of 1999, which was to put an end to large-scale torture and ill treatment, limiting it to lone cases of 'ticking bombs', have worn thin... (2003 report by the Public Committee Against Torture in Israel and other human rights organisations)

Ha'aretz reported on 8 November 2006 that:

In the past year alone, about 40 allegations of serious torture of Palestinians have been submitted to Attorney General Menachem Mazuz. [...] [He] has not deemed any of the complaints as warranting a criminal investigation against the interrogators.

c) With regard to collective punishment Article 33 states: 'No protected person may be punished for an offence he or she has not personally committed. Collective penalties and likewise all measures of intimidation or of terrorism are prohibited.'

Violations:

- The Family Unification Law (see above), is a form of collective punishment.

- The sweeping nature of restriction of movement in the form of closure, siege and curfew constitutes a form of collective punishment. After the outbreak of the Second Intifada in 2000, Israel imposed a total closure on the occupied territories and has prohibited Palestinian movement between the occupied territories and Israel and between the West Bank and Gaza, unless they have a special permit. Since 2000 Israel has issued no new entry permits.
  Israel also imposes internal closures on specific towns and

villages. Since October 2000, most Palestinian communities in the West Bank have been closed off by staffed checkpoints, concrete blocks, dirt piles or deep trenches. During curfews, residents are completely prohibited from leaving their homes. As B'Tselem has put it:

The sweeping nature of the restrictions imposed by Israel, the specific timing that it employs when deciding to ease or intensify them, and the destructive human consequences turn its policy into a clear form of collective punishment. Such punishment is absolutely prohibited by the Fourth Geneva Convention.

- House demolitions are carried out under the emergency regulations (DER 119) of the British mandate which provide for an authority to demolish a house as a response against persons suspected of taking part in or directly supporting criminal or guerilla activities. Recently, application of DER 119 has become limited to instances in which an attack was launched from a specific house or cases in which an 'inhabitant' of the house was suspected of involvement in an offense. The term 'inhabitant', however, has been broadly defined to include persons who do not necessarily reside in said house regularly, and often is applied to family homes in which a suspected offender previously resided. *The regular occupants' knowledge of the offense has been deemed irrelevant by the Israeli authorities.* This is clearly a form of collective punishment.

  Had I more time I would deal with issues like imprisonment without due process as well as deportations and destruction of personal property, all covered by relevant clauses of the Fourth Geneva Convention. Instead, let me move rapidly to one of the central questions of the occupation: — that of the colonies or, as the more anodyne English word has it, 'settlements'.

d) Settlements: Article 49, para 6 states:

The Occupying Power shall not deport or transfer parts of its own civilian population into the territory it occupies.' And the Hague Regulations prohibit the occupying power to undertake permanent changes in the occupied area, unless these are due to military needs in the narrow sense of the term, or unless they are undertaken for the benefit of the local population.

Settlement activities were relatively slow to begin after the occupation, and there were only thirty settlements by 1977. But six years later, after Ariel Sharon became first Minister of Agriculture, then Minister of Defence, in the Likud government of Menachem Begin, the number soared to over a hundred. Similarly, the number of settlers, small to begin with and only topping fifty thousand in 1982, had doubled a decade later. Then, between 1993 and 2000, the number of settlers on the West Bank (excluding East Jerusalem) increased by almost 100 percent. (These were of course the Oslo years, with the biggest single increase during 2000 at the height of the peace negotiations.) There are, as of 2006, close to four hundred and fifty thousand in all, including substantial settlements in East Jerusalem, numbering at least one hundred and eighty thousand.

In B'Tselem's words,

> The establishment of the settlements leads to the violation of the rights of the Palestinians as enshrined in international human rights law. Among other violations, the settlements infringe the right to self-determination, equality, property, an adequate standard of living, and freedom of movement. [...]
>
> Despite the diverse methods used to take control of land, all the parties involved — the Israeli government, the settlers and the Palestinians — have always perceived these methods as part of a mechanism intended to serve a single purpose: the establishment of civilian settlements in the territories.

B'Tselem's conclusions, again in its own words, are as follows:

> Israel has created in the Occupied Territories a regime of separation based on discrimination, applying two separate systems of law in the same area and basing the rights of individuals on their nationality. This regime is the only one of its kind in the world, and is reminiscent of distasteful regimes from the past, such as the Apartheid regime in South Africa.

Peace Now Settlement Watch has published 'Breaking the Law in the West Bank — The Private Land Report — Nov. 2006', the summary of which begins:

> This report by the Peace Now Settlement Watch Team is a harsh indictment against the whole settlements enterprise and the role all Israeli governments played in it. The report shows that Israel has

effectively stolen privately-owned Palestinian lands for the purpose of constructing settlements and in violation of Israel's own laws regarding activities in the West Bank. Nearly 40 percent of the total land area on which the settlements sit is, according to official data of the Israeli Civil Administration (the government agency in charge of the settlements), privately owned by Palestinians. The settlement enterprise has undermined not only the collective property rights of the Palestinians as a people, but also the private property rights of individual Palestinian landowners.

Summary: Grave Breaches of the Convention

Article 147 specifies 'grave breaches' of the Convention as including wilful killing; torture or inhuman treatment; wilfully causing great suffering or serious injury to body or health; unlawful deportation or transfer or unlawful confinement of a protected person; wilfully depriving a protected person of the rights of fair and regular trial; taking of hostages and extensive destruction and appropriation of property, not justified by military necessity and carried out unlawfully and wantonly.

I have given a mere hint of the evidence for the *prima facie* breach of Article 147. Comprehensive records of all of these acts have been documented by reliable Israeli human rights organisations (as well, of course, by many reliable Palestinian organisations) and can be easily found on the internet.

What Does Israel Say about This?

Israel, after all, is not some two-bit banana republic, but fiercely proud of its allegiance to democracy and the rule of law.

Israel's official position is that the Fourth Geneva Convention is not applicable. That claim is based on an extremely narrow interpretation of Article 2 of the Convention, claiming that the Convention only applies where a legitimate sovereign is evicted from the territory in question. According to this argument, since neither Egypt nor Jordan were recognised as legitimate sovereigns of the Gaza Strip and West Bank respectively prior to 1967, the Convention is not applicable.

This argument has however been rejected by the entire international community, including the United States (and by many Israelis), since

Article 2 explicitly sets out the conditions of application and is clearly intended to apply when an occupation begins during an armed conflict between two or more High Contracting parties. It makes no distinction regarding the status of the territory in question.

Irrespective of the nature of the war in 1967, Israeli conquest of the Occupied Territories was the direct result of just such an 'armed conflict' between High Contracting Parties to the Convention.

Israel has also argued that it has voluntarily applied the 'humanitarian' provisions of the Fourth Geneva Convention. This is disingenuous as the document is in its entirety a 'humanitarian' document and, as a signatory, Israel is bound by the entire document, not just the parts it chooses to apply. Furthermore, the Israeli Supreme Court recognises the situation as one of 'belligerent occupation' and has recently applied the Convention on the basis that 'the parties agree that the humanitarian rules of the Fourth Geneva Convention apply to the issue.'

Israeli governments have sometimes claimed that the settlements are the result of the initiatives of private citizens, not state policy. This is a transparent lie, since government after government has implemented a consistent and systematic policy intended to encourage Jewish citizens to migrate to the West Bank. Tools used to this end are the granting of financial benefits and incentives to citizens, raises in the standard of living of these citizens and encouragement of migration to the West Bank. Indeed most of the settlements in the West Bank are defined as national priority areas. In 2000, for instance, the average *per capita* grant in the Jewish local and regional councils in the West Bank was approximately sixty-five percent higher than the average *per capita* grant inside Israel.

Israel argues it has valid claims to title in the occupied territories based on 'its historic and religious connection to the land', 'its recognised security needs', and the fact that it came under Israeli control 'in a war of self-defense, imposed upon Israel'. Nothing in the Convention leads credence to any of these arguments which are irrelevant in terms of international law.

However, in June 2000, the Israeli government well and truly demonstrated the cynicism of its claim, in which it had persisted since occupying the territories in 1967, that the territories are 'disputed'. In their last-ditch legal attempt to prevent the government from removing them, the Gaza settlers took their case to the Israeli Supreme Court. *The government asserted that it was, indeed, in belligerent occupation of the territories, and had always been so.* Therefore Israeli settlements in them could only ever have been temporary and could be removed by the government. The Supreme Court decided in favour of the government by a 10:1 majority. It said that its decision applied to the West Bank as well as Gaza.

The Concept of 'Military Necessity'

Israel often uses the concept of 'Military Necessity' to justify its actions: Article 27 of the Fourth Geneva Convention allows the Parties to the conflict to 'take such measures of control and security in regard to protected persons as may be necessary as a result of the war.'

But, military necessity is not what any occupying army says it is. Military necessity is, strictly, a legal concept rather than a military one, an exception to the applicability of International Humanitarian Law only as and when it is so stated in the law. So, for instance, military necessity can never justify actions that are prohibited in absolute terms under the law, e.g., acts of torture or other inhumane treatments.

A decision on the legality of the actions and policies of the occupying power must be made considering all information reasonably available, and after ascertaining that there is no feasible alternative, military necessity incorporates clear conditions: the occupying power must be facing an actual state of necessity; there must be an immediate and concrete threat; and the measures adopted must be proportionate.

The Wall

The hollowness of the Israeli justification was made very clear when the legal situation with regard to the Wall/barrier/security fence was clarified by the International Court of Justice in an advisory opinion issued on 9 July 2004. No overview of human rights in the territories would be complete without a look at the Wall which provides the starkest image possible of the realities of the occupation. A complex structure, part twenty-five-foot-high wall, part ditch and barbed wire, part an intrusion-detecting fence, part path/road and smoothed strip of sand to detect footprints, the barrier, when completed, will be over twice as long as the green line it is supposed to protect.

Only about one fifth of the route follows the Green Line itself; in some areas it will run far inside the West Bank in order to capture key Israeli settlements such as Ariel (twenty-two kilometres inside the West Bank), the Gush Etzion bloc (with fifty thousand settlers) near Bethlehem and the Maaleh Adumim settlement east of Jerusalem. 'Despite Israel's contention that the wall is a "temporary" security measure', comments Human Rights Watch, it captures settlements that Israel has vowed to hold onto permanently; for example, when PM Sharon said that the Ariel bloc of settlements 'will be part of the State of Israel forever'.

According to realistic estimates, the barriers will result in the isolation of tens of thousands of Palestinians from the rest of the West Bank and from each other. Strictly speaking, I could have used aspects of the Wall story to illustrate any and all of the breaches of the Fourth Geneva Convention alluded to above, but there has actually been, in July 2004, a legal ruling by the International Court of Justice (available online at https://www.icj-cij.org/en/case/131). This is the highest instance of international law, so it is worth looking at in its own right.

The ICJ ruling settled definitively many issues that Israel had long disputed:

- It emphasised that East Jerusalem, the West Bank and Gaza are occupied territories.

- It ruled that both the Hague Regulations and the Fourth Geneva Convention were applicable to the Occupied Palestinian Territory (OPT).

- It ruled that the International Covenant on Civil and Political Rights (ICCPR), the International Covenant on Economic, Social and Cultural Rights (ICESCR), and the Convention on the Rights of the Child (CRC), the main foundation of international human rights law as opposed to international humanitarian law, are all applicable within the OPT; and that the construction of the barrier violated various provisions of each of these conventions.

- It ruled the construction of the barrier to be in violation of international law. The ICJ called upon Israel to immediately cease construction and dismantle the barrier, as well as to make restitution or pay compensation to those injured by the barrier.

- The ICJ noted the possibility that Israel would use the barrier as a means to incorporate the settlements which 'would be tantamount to annexation' and thus infringe the right of the Palestinian people to self-determination. It ruled that the barrier violated various provisions of international humanitarian law, especially relating to the destruction and seizure of property in occupied territories.

- It ruled: 'The wall, along the route chosen, and its associate regime gravely infringe a number of rights of Palestinians residing in the territory occupied by Israel, and the infringements resulting from that route cannot be justified by military exigencies or by the requirements of national security or public order.'

- It ruled that Israel's construction of the barrier was not justified either by the right to self-defence enshrined in Article 51 of the United Nations Charter or by a state of necessity.

It Is Time to Draw This to a Conclusion

It is my belief that it is necessary and desirable to 'single out Israel', but in doing so, I have chosen to focus on universalist human rights themes. We can, and must, debate the origins of these human rights violations: the extent to which they are simply the kind of thing that happens in all prolonged occupations, the extent to which they arise from Israel's demographic obsession with having a Jewish state and the racist fear this generates about Palestinian population growth as a 'ticking bomb'; the old Zionist dream of a greater Israel, wanting Judea and Samaria but not wanting the Palestinians, and so on. But in this talk I have merely wanted to focus on what Israel is currently doing and, by implication, the need to mobilise opposition to it.

I'd like to conclude by returning to the situation in Gaza: According to B'Tselem: 'On October 30 [2006], Israel's Prime Minister Ehud Olmert reportedly told the Knesset Security and Foreign Affairs Committee that in the past three months, the Israeli military has killed 300 "terrorists" in the Gaza Strip in its war against terror groups'.

B'Tselem points out that this includes 155 people, including 61 children, who did not even take part in any fighting and 'sends a dangerous message to soldiers and officers, according to which unarmed Palestinian civilians are a legitimate target. The statement contains within it a twisted logic whereby the fact that someone was killed by the military proves that he or she is a terrorist.' Since the commencement of Israel's Occupation Forces operation in Beit Hanoun on 1 November 2006, the number of additional dead has reached 77.

Uri Avnery, asking if the Beit Hanoun massacre was done on purpose or by accident, says this:

> The ammunition used by the gunners against Beit-Hanoun — the very same 155mm ammunition that was used in Kana — is known for its inaccuracy. Several factors can cause the shells to stray from their course by hundreds of meters. He who decided to use this ammunition against a target right next to civilians knowingly exposed them to mortal danger. Therefore, there is no essential difference between the two versions.

The truth is that the Israeli army and its soldiers on the ground are acting with impunity. There may be rules of engagement, there may be high moral standards, but in practice they are all too often ignored and no sanctions are applied to those ignoring them.

And Tom Hurndall's murder showed all too well how the system works...

Fig. 5 Tom Hurndall, Israeli soldier communicating with ISM volunteers on the
Rafah border, April 2003.

3. New-Old Thinking on Palestine

Ilan Pappe

There is a famous Jewish maxim that people tend to look for a lost key where there is light and not where they lost the key. There is a sense that the diplomatic efforts to end the Israel/Palestine conflict were a search for the key where there was light, but not where it was lost. In this chapter, I will attempt to explain why this was a shot in the dark and why it is still going on, despite its obvious failure. In the second part I will suggest a better location for the lost key and a different pathway towards a solution.

Oslo Accords

The efforts of the Oslo peace accords, which has now been dead for many years, began in the immediate aftermath of the 1967 June War. It was an accord directed from Washington and highly influenced by both mainstream scholarly ideas of 'conflict management' and Israel's major concerns. From the very start, the Palestinians were ignored as significant contributors to the peace agreements. These efforts were based on a certain perception of the origins of the Israel/Palestine conflict and the reasons for its continuation. This perception re-graded the 1967 June War as the starting point for the conflict and hence framed the conflict as a dispute over the future of the occupied West Bank and the Gaza Strip. Such a perception reduces Palestine geographically to the West Bank and the Gaza Strip (22% of historical Palestine) and the Palestinians to the people living in those two areas. More profoundly, this approach is based on the assumption that the conflict in Israel/Palestine is between

    https://doi.org/10.11647/OBP.XXX.04

two national movements with equal right to the place that need external help to find a compromise.

This paradigm of parity stems from the academic background of many of the Americans involved in the peace process. According to this view, an outside mediator should have adopted a business-like approach to the conflict over Palestine (in its reduced geographical and demographic definition). This paradigm is based on two principles. The first is that everything visible is divisible or, put differently, partition is the best solution for conflicts such as the one raging between Israel and Palestinians. The second principle is that partition should reflect the balance of power and would, most importantly, be accepted by the stronger party of the divide. This meant not only that Israel since 1967 in all the peace plans was offered more and the Palestinians less; the proposition was also accompanied by a certain didactical logic: if the weaker party declines the offers of partition, then a lesser deal will be offered to it. Hence the Palestinians were offered half of Palestine in 1947, around twenty percent after 1967 and subsequently just over ten percent of their homeland.

Since 2007, this approach has been abandoned, at least temporarily, by the main outfit that is supposed to carry it on: the 'Quartet' (made up of the EU, UN, US and Russia). Before 2007, however, it dominated the peace efforts from the days of the shuttle diplomacy in the 1970s (when the then American Secretary of State, Henry Kissinger, was moving between Amman and Jerusalem trying to find a formula which would divide the West Bank and the Gaza Strip between Israel and Jordan), through the Autonomy talks following the Israeli-Egyptian peace agreement, up to the Madrid conference of 1991 that introduced the Palestinians as partners for the partition of the occupied 1967 territories. In 1993, this approach was the basis for the Oslo Accords, an agreement that has disastrously deteriorated the quality of life of the occupied people of the West Bank and the Gaza Strip. However, the principle of partition and the didactic approach were less manifest in the Declaration of Principles signed on the White House lawn on 13 September 1993.

In an article in *Ha'aretz* on 4 September 2018, Amira Hass explained in detail how Oslo was the fruit of Israel's cunning scheme to perpetuate the occupation rather than to end it. Hass claimed that the 'Bantustans', the fragmented West Bank and the Gaza Strip, are the result of ingenious Israeli planning that was carried out by deceiving the world and creating a situation that absolved Israel of any legal and economic obligations to these enclaves. Hass pointed to another fact that indicates that the Oslo process enacted a further partition and fragmentation of Palestine. The negotiations with the Palestinians were entrusted to the Civil Administration. This body had managed the occupation since 1981 and was bound to continue the occupation by all means possible. One of their practices, typical to any colonial regime, was 'divide and rule'. Therefore, while the Oslo Accords promised to protect the integrity of the West Bank and the Gaza Strip as one unit, the Civil Administration did all it could to keep them apart, in the name of the accord.

The accord left the decision about the status of the Palestinians in the occupied territories in the hands of this Civil Administration. This power of registration allowed Israel to treat the Gaza Strip as a different administrative unit after 1993. On top of this, Israel made it almost impossible for people to move between the two enclaves. The accord does not mention the word 'occupation', Hass commented, nor the right of the Palestinians for self-determination; while the Palestinians, and probably most of the international representatives involved in the accord, assumed that Palestinian self-determination and the end of the occupation was the main goal of the Oslo Accords.

The separation is accompanied by a particularly cruel water policy. The separation of the Gaza Strip and the West Bank included a partition of the water resources, which allocated to the people in Gaza a very limited aquifer that soon dried out and led to the salination of the soil. Further proof of Israel's real intentions behind Oslo is the increased policy of house demolition pursued since the accords. This, again, formed part of the systematic destruction of the infrastructure that rendered the prospect of an independent state *de facto* impossible.

The separation of the West Bank into Areas A, B and C enabled Israel, through the definition of Area C as one under exclusive Israeli military control, to annex informally 60 percent of the West Bank. The rest were bisected by apartheid roads open only to settlers and new settlements, all part of a plan that accompanied the 1993 alleged Israeli commitment to reconcile with the Palestine Liberation Organisation (PLO).

So, one important reason for the failure of this approach was that there was never a genuine wish by Israel to accept a 'two states' solution based on the Palestinian right of self-determination and independence. However, even if there was some ambivalence displayed by Israel (due to a struggle between a kind of peace camp that wanted to move towards a two-states solution and a right-wing coalition vehemently opposed to the idea), it seems that in the beginning of this century such an ambiguity faded away and the Israeli political system shifted to the right with a clear anti-two states agenda.

More importantly, there emerged a new political consensus that since the peace process is dead, what is needed is a unilateral Israeli policy of annexation, fragmentation, ethnic cleansing and strangulation. The purpose of these unilateral actions is to ensure Israel's supremacy in historical Palestine and beyond. This approach is different from the one adopted by the governments which ruled Israel in the first thirty years of occupation. While all Israeli governments since 1967 could not envisage an Israel without the West Bank (and some without the Gaza Strip as well), they disagreed on how best to ensure this geographical achievement that had been won in the June War of 1967. Until the turn of this century, the governments of Israel were obsessed with the demographic question; hence the principal methodology for keeping the West Bank as part of Israel included territorial compromises and active ethnic cleansing in areas such as the Greater Jerusalem region, in order to have the land without the people.

Israeli political leaders are not deterred by the demographic reality in twenty-first-century Israel and Palestine. The vision of a Jewish state in which most of the Palestinians do not have equal rights is a reality into which many of the Israeli Jews were born and which they accept as morally valid and politically feasible (and this was finally institutionalised through the Nationality Law passed at the end of 2018). Any Palestinian resistance is framed today in Israel as terrorism, and any criticism from the outside is branded as antisemitism.

This approach and policy dimmed the dividing line between Israel and the occupied territories. Although there are still differences in the judicial status of Palestinians on both sides of the Green Line, these seem to disappear quickly. The facts on the ground, i.e., an ongoing Jewish colonisation of the West Bank, which includes not just small settlements, but proper urban sprawl, render any idea of a sovereign independent Palestinian state impossible. As mentioned before, 'Dawlat Filastin', the

State of Palestine, which is how the Palestinian authority refers to Area A in the West Bank, is merely eleven percent of the West Bank (which is less than three percent of historical Palestine), and is under total Israeli control.

Thus, in 2019, we were faced with an international community that still sponsors the two-state solution, a fragmented Palestinian leadership losing its legitimacy by the day that also adheres to this solution, and diminishing Israeli support for this kind of solution. The real peace effort has been dead for all intents and purposes for a long time. We waited, without holding our breath, for Donald Trump's 'Deal of the Century' that was supposed to reignite the process. We now have quite a clear idea of what that would have entailed: in essence, an American blessing of Israeli unilateralism. The plan was very clearly stated by major figures in the government that ruled Israel in 2018, and which was always likely to have a similar composition after the April 2019 elections. It included an Israeli annexation of Area C (as noted, 60 percent of the West Bank) as a major step to be followed by enhanced autonomy in Areas A and B for the Palestinian Authority. The next step is to try to depose Hamas and install the PA instead, either by force or thorough political agreements.

Trump was not going to offer anything that the American administrations have not offered before. He was in any case more honest about America's role in the Israel/Palestine question. The previous administrations pretended to be honest brokers in the conflict, but in essence unconditionally adopted the Israeli point of view and disregarded the Palestinian one. In the past, the official position of the State Department was that the Israeli annexations of Jerusalem and the Jewish colonies in the West Bank were illegal, but in practice nothing was done to stop them from expanding. Trump seemed to be more candid when he admitted openly that the US is not an honest broker and that his first priority is to give *carte blanche* to the Israelis to do what they deem right in the Palestine question. Trump's policy would have been the same as previous ones, but without the charade.

In fact, we knew that it was more likely that Trump would desert any meaningful effort to intervene in the Israel/Palestine question. It also seemed very unlikely that another international actor, be it the EU or China, would take America's place. The result is stagnation in the peace process and the continuation of Israeli unilateral policies aiming at solidifying Israeli control all over historical Palestine. The imbalance of power is such that currently one can see no internal or external actors who can change this course of action or improve this dismal reality.

An Alternative Way Forward

This is a good time for reflection on an alternative way forward in the long run, without forgetting for a moment to deal with the catastrophic situation on the ground. The situation on the ground worsens precisely because the old plan is not working and there is no alternative to replace it. The number of political prisoners in the West Bank has increased, as has the killing and the demolishing of homes and villages such as Han al-Ahmar. The Judaisation is expanding, the brutal settlers' harassment reaching new heights of intimidation and violence. The situation in the Gaza Strip is even worse. The UN predicted that in 2020 the Strip would be unsustainable, and therefore, we have to be conscious of the need for short-term action and long-term thinking. In many ways, the BDS (the Boycott, Divestment and Sanctions) movement represents the need to engage urgently with that reality, while strategising for the future. The movement was founded around 2005 in response to a call from the Palestinian civil society to the international community to take a more vigorous position towards the Israeli policy in Palestine. It identified three basic rights which Israel violates with regard to the Palestinians: the right of the Palestinian refugees to return; the right of the Palestinians who live in the occupied West Bank and the besieged Gaza Strip to be freed from military rule; and the right of the Palestinian minority of Israel to equal citizenship in the state. One can only hope that this strategy, which has so far been effective, will eventually stop at least some of the atrocities on the ground.

Meanwhile, we should make up for the wasted half-century, in which everyone was looking for the key to where the light is and not where we lost it. For that to happen, we have to recognise the need to revisit the history of the Zionist project in Palestine and adopt a new dictionary that would fit the realities on the ground and the chances for reconciliation in the future.

The new approach is based on a historical analysis that goes back to the early days of Zionism (whereas the dominant view in the West depicts 1967 as the departure point of the conflict). The new approach also frames the conflict as one between a settler-colonial movement, Zionism, and the native population, the Palestinians (and not between two national movements).

We make a distinction between settler colonialism and classical colonialism. The settler colonialists are Europeans who were forced to leave Europe due to persecution or a sense of existential danger and who settled in someone else's homeland. They were at first assisted by empires, but soon rebelled against them as they wished to re-define themselves as new nations. Their main obstacle however was not their empires, but the native population. And they acted according to what the great scholar of settler colonialism, Patrick Wolfe, called 'the logic of the elimination of the native'. At times this led to a genocide, as happened here, at times to apartheid, as occurred in South Africa. In Palestine, the presence of the native population led to the ethnic cleansing operation of the 1948 Nakba and ever since. The settlers also saw themselves as the indigenous and perceived the indigenous as aliens.

The paradigm explains well what lay behind the ethnic cleansing operations in 1948. Regardless of the quality of the Palestinian leadership, the ability or inability of the Arab world to help, or the genuine or cynical wish of the Western world to compensate for the Holocaust, Zionism was a classical settler-colonial movement that wanted a new land without the people who lived on it. Hence, long before the Holocaust, the Zionist settlers acted upon the logic of the elimination of the natives and 1948 provided the opportunity for partial realisation of the vision of a de-Arabised Palestine.

However, in 1948, 'only' half of the indigenous population was expelled, and Israel succeeded in taking over 78% of the coveted new homeland. (A homeland demanded by the secular Jewish settler movement, Zionism, by using a sacred religious text, the Bible, as a scientific proof for their right to national sovereignty in the land, and hence the Palestinians were the usurpers who took it over. The first setters who came in between 1882 and 1914 could have not made it in Palestine without the help of the local Palestinians, but in their diaries and letters back home they described their local hosts as the foreigners who usurped our ancient homeland and destroyed it.) The inability to get rid of all the Palestinians and the takeover of most, but not all, of the land is an incomplete process that explains the Israeli policy towards the Palestinians ever since 1948.

This is the background for the harsh policy towards the Palestinians left within Israel, the 1948 Arabs as they are named by the Palestinians or the Israeli Arabs as they are referred to by Israel. Until 1956, this community was subjected to further ethnic cleansing operations, dozens of villages were expelled, in which there lived people regarded as citizens of the Jewish state whose Declaration of Independence promised to protect them, yet who were expelled by the settler state.

Then they were put under harsh military rule that robbed them of any normality in their life, where soldiers could arrest, shoot or banish them at will. The settler-colonial state saw its Arab citizens as aliens with a potential of becoming hostile aliens at any given moment.

The settler-colonial paradigm also explains the Israeli policy leading to the June 1967 War, as well as its policy during the early years of the occupation of the West Bank and the Gaza Strip. The occupation was not a defensive response to an all-Arab attack, but rather an Israeli solution to the incomplete nature of the 1948 operations.

The paradigm of settler colonialism also offers an explanation for the major decisions that Israel took after the war, decisions that expose why there was no chance from the beginning for any peace process based on a two-state solution. More than anything else, for me, it exposes the Israeli perception of the West Bank and the Gaza Strip as two huge mega-prisons that by now a third generation of hundreds of thousands of Israelis is involved in policing and maintaining as a way of life that to them appears normal and acceptable, while the rest of us look on with disgust, horror and dismay at the brutality and inhumanity imposed on millions of Palestinians incarcerated there, whose only crime is being Palestinians. Nowhere else in the world do such mega-prisons exist, and yet Israel has been excused for this inhuman monstrosity it created in 1967 and continues to maintain today.

The settler state needed the remaining 22%, as the borders of 1948 were deemed indefensible and, moreover, the ancient biblical sites in the West Bank were deemed the heart of the ancient land of Israel without which the new nation-state would not thrive. Ever since 1948, important sections of the Israeli political and military elite planned takeovers of the West Bank and the Gaza Strip. The plans moved into a more practical stage when, in 1963, the principal politician objecting to such a takeover, David Ben-Gurion, was removed from political life. In 1963, a group of senior officers and officials drew up the 'Shaham plan', which would ultimately be implemented in 1967, to abolish the military rule imposed on the Palestinians inside Israel and instead impose it on those Palestinians living in the West Bank and the Gaza Strip after their planned occupation.

As early as four years before the actual takeover, it was clear that with the coveted new territory, the settler state would have new demographic problems. Like all settler-colonial movements before them, space and people were the two main factors troubling the future of a settler colony. The more territory one holds, the more natives there are. The issue was how to eliminate them, and the answer and methods depended on the capacity, circumstances, and the ability of the indigenous population to resist.

In the immediate aftermath of the June 1967 War, the decision as to how to engage with the new territory while solving the new demographic challenge rested with the thirteenth government of Israel. It was the most consensual government that Israel ever had or will have. Every shade of Zionism and Jewish orthodox anti-Zionism was represented in this unity government. This explains its ability to carve out a strategy that is still adhered to today. It is based on several decisions. The first of these was the decision not to officially annex the new territories, but also never to give them up as part of the space of the future Jewish state. This is how the geographic (spatial) issue was resolved. As for the population, after some hesitation and quite substantial forced transfer of populations, the decision was made not to ethnically cleanse the population. The status of the population was to have some official connection with the previous powers, namely Jordan and Egypt, but basically, the Minister of Defence defined the new inhabitants of the greater Israel, as citizenless citizens. A worried Minister of Foreign Affairs, Abba Eban, inquired how long people could live in such a condition. 'Oh', Dayan answered, 'for at least fifty years'.

The next decision was not to engage in a peace process, with the help of the Americans, that aimed to obtain international — and if possible Arab, and later on even Palestinian — legitimisation of or at least consent for Israel's wish to have the territory without the people, and its demands that this should be the basis for a future peace process. It was taken for granted that there would be genuine public debate in Israel about the future of the territories and some friction with the US, but it was felt that at the end of the day, the Israeli interpretation of what consituted peace and what constituted a solution would prevail. Nothing that happened in the next fifty-two years indicates that these politicians were wrong to set their hopes on Palestinian fragmentation, Arab impotence, American immunity and global indifference.

The approach of having the land without the people and calling this arrangement peace was devised in June 1967. The Labour Party, still dominating Israeli and Zionist politics, always believed that some land could be conceded for the sake of demographic purity, and were thus enchanted by the colonialist idea of partition, which alas quite a few Palestinians fell for over the years. Partitioning of the new occupied territories into a Jewish West Bank and Gaza Strip and a Palestinian West Bank and Gaza Strip was the way forward.

The first partition map was presented by Yigal Allon, one of the leaders of the Labour government. The Jewish space would be determined, he said in June 1967, by colonisation. He drew a strategic map that left only densely populated Palestinian areas out of the Jewish West Bank and Gaza Strip. The problem for the thirteenth government and those that followed it, the Golda Meir and Rabin governments, was that the new messianic movement, Gush Emunim, had a different map of colonisation, one based on the Bible and the nationalistic imagination of Israeli archaeologists, who wanted to settle Jews precisely on densely populated Palestinian areas. As early as 1974, this twin effort from above and below defined the West Bank as a partitioned space between a Jewish West Bank and a Palestinian one. The former was growing all the time, while the latter was shrinking all the time.

The other constituent element of the settler-colonial policy after 1967 was the question of how to rule and police the citizenless citizens. In the last fifty-two years, the settler state has employed two models for ruling millions of citizenless citizens. Both of these models are mega-prison models, with only one difference from a real prison: that a prisoner can leave the prison and become a refugee with no right of return.

The open prison model is based on allowing freedom of movement inside the Palestinian areas and controlled movement outside the

Palestinian areas and between the West Bank and the Gaza Strip. It gives no growing space for the Palestinians, nor any new villages or towns built on land coveted for present or future Jewish settlements. There is no resistance to the geopolitical reality imposed by Israel, and a certain level of autonomy in the running of municipal affairs. The first open prison was run between 1967 and 1987. Life was constantly monitored by the army and, from 1981 onwards, by an organisation called the Civil Administration, and ruled by a set of regulations that gave the military unlimited power in the lives of citizenless citizens. They were arrested without trial, expelled, their houses and business demolished, wounded and killed at the discretion of soldiers, quite often of lower ranks.

This form of rule prevailed first between 1967 and 1987, and then for a second time between 1993 and 2000. It has prevailed for Areas A and B in the West Bank since 2004. Every new open prison model is worse for 'the inmates' than the last. Privileges granted in the first term are reduced as long-term punishment for resisting the model. Remember, this is the world of jailer and warden. Thus, the second open prison, which one might call the open prison model of the Oslo Accords, and which created mini prisons in Areas A, B and C and the Gaza Strip, is far less open that its predecessor. This didactic approach of teaching the Palestinians lessons that will make them docile and disempower them to the point of submission is ingrained in the Israeli perception, and supported by Israeli orientalists.

The first Palestinian resistance to the open prison model was in the First Intifada in 1987. As a punishment, the open prison model was replaced with a maximum-security prison. Between 1987 and 1993, this included short-term punitive actions; mass arrests without trial, wounding and killing of demonstrators, massive demolition of houses, shutting down of business and the education system and, most importantly, further expropriation of land for the sake of Jewish settlements.

The Palestinians were offered a sophisticated open prison model in Oslo (regardless of how Palestinians and the wider world saw the accord). This is why the end of the occupation is not mentioned in the accord and there is no promise to end the intensive Israeli involvement in the lives of Palestinians, even if the latter were to implement every other Israeli demand of the accord.

However, this model also included a long-term, didactic punishment. From 1994 there was no longer freedom of movement within Palestinian areas, let alone outside of them, and the Judaisation of the West Bank increased. The Gaza Strip was encircled with barbed wire in 1994, and the privilege granted in the open prison model for Gazans to work in Israel was also withdrawn. A further permanent punishment was the allocation of more water to the Gush Qafif settlements, and of the decision to cut the Gaza Strip into two parts controlled by Israel.

While life under the first open prison model was unacceptable to the Palestinians, the second model was far worse, objectively, and even more importantly, because it was presented as part of a peace process. The years devoted to Oslo and its implementation had created a life under conditions far worse than those in the prior model.

The second uprising yet again generated a punitive maximum-security model: far worse in its short-term punitive actions and long-term punishments. There was now massive use of military power, including F-16 fighter jets and tanks, against the civilian population, in particular during the 2002 Defence Shield operation. The urbicide that had been witnessed in Syria, Iraq and Yemen recently was a prelude to the use of such power in the third model of the maximum-security prison imposed on Gaza after Hamas took over in 2006.

In 2007, the two models clearly transpired in Israel's approach to ruling the West Bank and the Gaza Strip, still loyal to the thirteenth government's main decision in 1967 not to annex, not to expel and not to withdraw. The only aspect discarded was the attempt to present this approach as a temporary measure pending peace, or to describe the open prison model as a 'peace plan'. Even the Israeli public and politicians grew tired of this charade and adopted what Prime Minister Ehud Olmert called 'unilateralism'. Where there is collaboration there is an open prison model, in Areas A and B, with long-term punitive actions: hundreds of checkpoints and an apartheid wall meant to humiliate millions of people into submission in the belief that this will discourage a third uprising. The checkpoints are the recruiting ground for a cruel network of informants that is expected to attack the dignity and self-respect of a whole nation that miraculously still succeeds in remaining human and steadfast. There were also closures of whole towns and villages, with only one exit controlled day and night by the army or, recently, by private companies.

Where there is resistance, as in the Gaza Strip, the maximum-security prison has turned into a ghetto, with Israel rationing food and calories, undermining the health and economy to the point of creating a human catastrophe, as acknowledged by the UN's prediction of the de-development and unsustainability of the Gaza Strip for years onwards.

The military punishment is none other than a set of war crimes and an incremental genocide of the Palestinian people in the Gaza Strip. This is achieved by dehumanising the Palestinians, and their children, depicting them as soldiers in an enemy's army that can legally be targeted by the Israeli army as enemy forces (this was the same doctrine used in the Nakba: a village was an army base, a neighbourhood an army outpost, and those who lived in them were enemy soldiers, not men, women and children).

All the Zionist parties of Israel in one form or another subscribe to these two models as the only possibility. The dominant political powers in Israel wish to import this twin model into Israel proper vis-à-vis the Palestinians in Israel, and they might succeed in doing so. The recently passed nationality law is an indication that this is indeed their future policy.

The only way of stopping this is first to recognise the settler-colonial nature of Israel and as a result to understand that what is needed is not peace but decolonisation, not just of the areas occupied in 1967, but of the whole of historical Palestine, which includes implementation of Palestinian refugees' right of return.

Secondly, we should revisit the two-state solution as an open prison model and think hard about how one might create one democratic state for all, taking into account two things: 1. that the representative bodies of the Palestinians, until today, still subscribe to the two-state solution, and 2. that there is already one settler apartheid, Israel, all over historical Palestine. We need a Palestinian change of mind, and international endorsement and BDS of such a way forward, and then we might actually succeed in generating a change from within Jewish society. When all of these elements are finally in place, there will be a hope for this torn country and its people.

Fig. 6 Tom Hurndall, Destruction in Rafah, Gaza, April 2003.

4. Can Palestinians Regain the Initiative for Ending the Occupation?

Kamel Hawwash

Those of you who have visited Palestine recently will testify to the fact that the Palestinian people feel isolated from the outside world. This isolation is most strongly felt at the moment in the Gaza Strip, a prison for its one and a half million inhabitants, a completely immoral and unjustifiable act by Israel. However, the Palestinians are also aware of the solidarity they enjoy from the thousands of people who visit Palestine to see the situation for themselves. In the specific context of Gaza these 'international' visitors risked their lives to break the siege of the Strip, as it happened in 2008 when boats sailed from Cyprus to Gaza in defiance of the Israeli blockade of the Palestinian territory. In 2008, I chaired a meeting in Birmingham at which Palestinian visitors from Ramallah and Clare Short MP spoke about the situation in the West Bank and Gaza; Clare gave a first-hand account of her recent boat trip and the truly desperate situation she saw there.

Clare survived to tell the tale but sadly James Miller, Rachel Corrie and, of course, Tom Hurndall did not return. All three were murdered by Israel Defence Forces. I pay tribute to these departed friends and to those that continue to work for peace and justice for the Palestinian people. I would also like to remember the late Palestinian Poet Mahmoud Darwish, who died on 9 August 2008, the year I gave this lecture.

 https://doi.org/10.11647/OBP.XXX.05

After being invited to give this lecture, I spent some time wondering about what the theme would be. I considered talking about the multitude of initiatives from the Madrid Conference to Oslo, bringing us all the way to Annapolis. I also considered talking about the role of international solidarity with the Palestinian people. But both of these topics are really about how the Palestinians have tried to end the occupation and how ordinary people around the world have tried to help them achieve this. I then thought that it may be interesting for an audience in Britain to hear about a study that I have been involved in which has sought to identify alternative strategies for ending the occupation. I finally settled on the title of this lecture, 'Can Palestinians regain the initiative for ending the occupation?'

This title assumes that the Palestinians had the initiative to end the occupation, lost it and are now looking at ways to regain this initiative. I believe that it can be argued that the Palestinians have had periods when they had the initiative, albeit under very difficult circumstances, to end the occupation, and other periods when they lost it. The creation of the Palestine Liberation Organisation (PLO) brought to the fore the issue of the Palestinians and the injustice that befell them when Israel was created by force on their land in 1948, resulting in their dispossession and the creation of the refugee problem. In 1988 the Palestinian Declaration of Independence accepted the creation of Palestine on the 1967 borders, with East Jerusalem as its capital. In 1987 the First Intifada broke out and this was largely non-violent. In 1991 the Palestinians joined the Madrid Peace Conference, as part of a joint Palestinian-Jordanian delegation.

In 1993 Yasser Arafat signed the Oslo Accords with Yitzak Rabin, laying the ground, as he and many thought, for a final resolution of the Israel/Palestine issue. The Second or Alaqsa Intifada started in September 2000. The Arab Peace Plan was launched in 2002. Finally, the Annapolis Conference took place in November 2007.

Now, different people will view these events differently in terms of whether the Palestinians had the initiative at a particular stage. However, it would be difficult for anyone to argue that the Palestinians currently have the initiative for ending the occupation. I will be exploring this next.

Where Are We Now?

So, where are we now? Well, we will look at the situation on the ground soon but I was interested in two interviews with Ehud Olmert, Israel's recent Prime Minister, which made me wonder if he was beginning to see sense. On 29 November 2007, he said that Israel was 'finished' if it forced the Palestinians into a struggle for equal rights. If the two-state solution collapsed, he said, Israel would 'face a South African-style struggle for equal voting rights, and as soon as that happens, the state of Israel is finished'. Israel's supporters abroad would quickly turn against such a state, he said: 'The Jewish organisations, which were our power base in America, will be the first to come out against us because they will say they cannot support a state that does not support democracy and equal voting rights for all its residents'.

It is legitimate to ask, then, what as the incumbent Prime Minister are you going to do about it? What has he done to create the conditions that would move Israel away from an apartheid-like system? Well, let us again look at the situation on the ground. I read with some interest, surprise and a little disbelief Ehud Olmert's interview with *Yediot Ahronoth*, which was reported in *The New York Times* on 29 September 2007. This, on the face of it, is groundbreaking. 'What I am saying to you now has not been said by any Israeli leader before me', Mr. Olmert told the newspaper *Yediot Ahronoth* in the interview on the occasion of the Jewish new year, observed from Monday evening till Wednesday evening. 'The time has come to say these things.'

He said that traditional Israeli defence strategists had learned nothing from past experiences and that they seemed stuck in the considerations of the 1948 war of independence: 'With them, it is all about tanks and land and controlling territories and controlled territories and this hilltop and that hilltop', he said. 'All these things are worthless.' He added, 'Who thinks seriously that if we sit on another hilltop, on another hundred meters, that this is what will make the difference for the State of Israel's basic security?'

Over the last year, Mr. Olmert has publicly castigated himself for his earlier right-wing views and he did so again in this interview. On Jerusalem, for example, he said: 'I am the first who wanted to enforce Israeli sovereignty on the entire city. I admit it. I am not trying to justify retroactively what I did for 35 years. For a large portion of these years, I was unwilling to look at reality in all its depth.' He said that maintaining sovereignty over an undivided Jerusalem, Israel's official policy, would involve bringing 270,000 Palestinians inside Israel's security barrier. It would mean a continuing risk of terrorist attacks against civilians like those carried out by Jerusalem Palestinian residents with front-end loaders.

'A decision has to be made', he said. 'This decision is difficult, terrible, a decision that contradicts our natural instincts, our innermost desires, our collective memories, the prayers of the Jewish people for 2000 years.' The government's public stand on Jerusalem until now has been to assert that the status of the city was not under discussion. But Mr. Olmert made clear that the eastern, predominantly Arab, sector had to be yielded, 'with special solutions' for the holy sites. On peace with the Palestinians, Mr. Olmert said in the interview:

> We face the need to decide but are not willing to tell ourselves, yes, this is what we have to do. We have to reach an agreement with the Palestinians, the meaning of which is that in practice we will withdraw from almost all the territories, if not all the territories. We will leave a percentage of these territories in our hands, but will have to give the Palestinians a similar percentage, because without that there will be no peace.

But what has the man who led Israel for some years actually done, rather than said?

Current Situation

The following quote and statistics provided by Dr Mustapha Barghouti, General Secretary of the Palestinian National Initiative at a press conference on 26 November summarise the position since Annapolis. Dr. Barghouti said 'Annapolis has widened the gap between the quest for a peace agreement and the building of a Palestinian State. It was a one-way negotiation, with efforts shown only by the Palestinian side. Israelis didn't negotiate. They imposed their reality on the ground', he added. 'A country without a capital, infiltrated by settlements, containing the biggest open-air jail in its body — Gaza — suffering from daily war crimes and where its refugees have no right of return: this is what they are trying to sell us', said Mustafa Barghouti.

He then cited the following statistics since Annapolis: 3,063 attacks have been carried out in Palestine (1,700 in the West Bank and 1,363 in Gaza); 543 Palestinians have been killed (65 in the West Bank and 478 in Gaza. More than 71 were children.); 2,362 Palestinians have been injured (1,125 in the West Bank and 1,237 in Gaza. More than 138 were children.); 770 Palestinian prisoners were released while Israel imprisoned 4,945 more (4,351 from the West Bank; 574 from Gaza, including 351 children). There were, in 2014, an estimated 10,500 Palestinian prisoners in Israeli jails; Gaza continues to be under siege. Since the beginning of the siege in 2006, more than 260 patients have died as hospitals have run out of medical supplies, and treatment abroad is barred. 160 types of medicine have already run out in Gaza due to the blockade. Supplies of another 130 will run out soon and at least 90 items of medical equipment, including 31 dialysis machines, are out of order; Checkpoints have risen from 521 to 699; At least 30 people (including children) died at a checkpoint, in the West Bank or Gaza; 74% of the main West Bank routes are controlled by checkpoints or blocked entirely; In September 2008, the weekly average of flying checkpoints was 89; 2,600 houses for settlers are currently under construction, 55% of which are on the eastern side of the Wall; In 2008, tenders for settlement construction increased by 550%; Today, there are 121 Israeli settlements and 102 outposts in the West Bank in which 462,000 settlers are living; Settlements are built on less than 1.5% of the Occupied Palestinian Territory land but due to the extensive infrastructure, they take up more than 40% of the land; After Annapolis, the Israeli government gave a preliminary green light in August for the new illegal settlement of Maskiot in the Jordan Valley; House evictions are currently taking place in Jerusalem. The Al Kurd family, who have lived in their house in Sheikh Jarrah for 50 years, was violently evicted by the Israeli occupation forces on 9 November 2006. For two weeks, they lived in a tent without water, heating or electricity, then Abu Kamal, the father of five, died. Suffering from diabetes, his health conditions worsened due to the pressure of the eviction.

The Israeli apartheid policy remains. The amount of water available for Palestinian consumption is 132 mcm, 132 million cubic metres, while Israelis enjoy 800 mcm. The domestic water consumption of Palestinians is 60 litres/day/person (although the WHO recommends a minimum of 100 litres/day) while the Israelis consume 220 litres daily. Palestinians pay 5 shekels per water unit and 13 shekels per electricity unit, while Israelis pay 2.4 shekels (water) and 6.3 (electricity). The building of the Wall continues. 409 km (57%) of the apartheid Wall had been constructed by 2014, while 66 km (9%) was under construction. When completed, the total length of the Wall would be 723 km, twice the length of the Green Line, and 14% of the Wall would be on the Green Line, while 86% would be inside of the West Bank.

As you can see from these statistics, the situation in Palestine has deteriorated markedly since the Annapolis Conference. Olmert gave the impression that he realised that the Palestinians exist and have rights and that Israel cannot have security or peace without a settlement that is acceptable to them. But his government continued along the path of entrenching the occupation and of making the lives of Palestinians so miserable that they would leave of their own accord.

Since Annapolis, the Palestinian Leadership has embarked on a programme of regular meetings with the Israeli Leadership encouraged, cajoled and pressured by the American Administration, which announced that there would be an agreement between Israel and the Palestinians by the end of 2008.

The PLO Chairman and Palestinian National Authority (PA) President, Mahmoud Abbas has made it clear that he will continue to negotiate, but these sterile negotiations have not resulted in even the outline of a peace agreement by the end of 2008. He has also made it clear that he will continue negotiations with the new Israeli Government when it is elected. Will he continue to negotiate for the foreseeable future? What is the incentive for Israel to negotiate seriously, and is it really interested in reaching an agreement with the Palestinians?

Background to the Palestine Strategy Study Group

Those questions and others have been the subject of discussion amongst a group of Palestinians, which became known as the Palestine Strategy Study Group (PSSG). I will now focus on the work of this group. In 2007, I received an invitation to a workshop joining a group of Palestinians from the West Bank and the Diaspora at the Dead Sea, Jordan. The approach came from an International Peace and Security think-tank, the Oxford Research Group (ORG), based in London. The approach seemed interesting because the proposal was to bring together a group of Palestinian politicians, academics, businessmen and activists from different political backgrounds and different regions of the world. Prior to this, most initiatives were about 'dialogue' between Palestinians and Israelis and have singularly failed to produce a positive outcome. The title of the project was 'Regaining the Initiative: Exploring Palestinian Strategic Options'. The opening paragraph to the concept proposal read:

> The failure in securing national independence and establishing a viable state has led Palestinians to be suspicious of Western motivations and interventions. The West demands that Palestinians meet certain conditions before attaining statehood. These include, among others, ending all forms of armed resistance, recognizing Israel as a Jewish state, reforming the Palestinian security system and building effective institutions of governance. To most Palestinians, however, such demands are seen to be unjust. While Palestinians in the end want a functioning state and a prosperous economy, most of them argue that it is virtually impossible to do so while under a military occupation. The aim of the project is to initiate a new strategic framework for action, internally and externally, that begins by emphasising this reality. The central question to be answered by a group of leading Palestinian strategists and activists is: how to end occupation and prevent post-independence domination? The output of two planned workshops is a document reached through the consensus of the participants. This document could then be presented as a gift to the Palestinian nation in the occupied territories and in the diaspora on the eve of commemorating the 60th anniversary of the Nakba.

The project was funded from a grant that the ORG had secured from the European Union.

The First Workshop

The overwhelming majority of the participants were from the West Bank as Gazans were not allowed to travel because of the siege and a number of invitees were not allowed to travel from the West Bank, particularly from Nablus. I was one of only three people from Europe.

I arrived at the venue on the Jordanian side of the Dead Sea not knowing what to expect. I was joined by some twenty other participants and we spent three intensive days, firstly analysing where we were as

Palestinians and then looking to possible future scenarios. The essential question was 'how do we end the occupation?'

We analysed the current reality of the situation against four dimensions, Palestinian, Israeli, Regional and International. We considered our strengths and weaknesses, risks and opportunities and considered the factors under Palestinian control that were helpful or unhelpful to the objective of ending the occupation.

We then considered possible future scenarios revolving around the negotiations. What if the negotiations succeeded and what does success mean? And what if the negotiations failed, again whatever that meant? Clearly, neither complete success nor failure was possible. Bear in mind that George W. Bush had by now indicated that he was confident of a deal between Palestinians and Israelis by the end of 2008, before he left office.

We also identified the priorities for the Palestinians as reforming the Palestine Liberation Organisation, internal reconciliation, strategies for ending the occupation and mechanisms for bolstering Palestinian staying power and resistance.

The group discussed what the final product of our deliberations would be. Are we producing an initiative *à la* Geneva Document or a report or academic document? There was general agreement that this would be a report that set out the strategic options for Palestinians, and not a specific initiative. It was agreed that there would be a follow-up meeting in March/April 2008 and this took place in Turkey, again to allow as many invitees to attend as possible.

The second meeting focused more on the strategic options for ending the occupation and it was important for the group to identify strategic options not only for ending the occupation, but also for raising the cost of the occupation, as this would force Israel to re-think its strategy. It is argued that Israel left the Gaza Strip not because it believed in returning the land to its owners, but because the Palestinian resistance made the cost of continuing with this occupation prohibitive. It was a one-sided decision by Israel to 'disengage' from Gaza rather than part of a negotiated settlement. It is important to note here that Mahmoud Abbas was the PA President and PLO Chairman then, but Israel did not meet his request to coordinate the withdrawal with him.

The work of the PSSG continued after Turkey through meetings in Palestine and email correspondence. The outcome was the document entitled 'Regaining the Initiative: Palestinian Strategic Options to End Israeli Occupation', which was published in August 2008.[1] This fifty-page document does not specify a detailed action plan but rather sets out a possible way forward to inform a strategic debate by Palestinians and their supporters.

However, the PSSG suggests that these may be among the main headings for a coordinated action plan; action to promote Palestinian national unity: national reconciliation, power sharing, reform of the PLO; action to formulate coordinated Palestinian strategy: goals and tools; action to realign the solidarity movement; action to mobilise and empower the Palestinian people.

When the strategic aim is to compel Israel to participate in genuine negotiations to establish a Palestinian State on terms acceptable to Palestinians: action to clarify Palestinian negotiation requirements, benchmarks and time limits; action to orchestrate national resistance: changed configuration of the PA; action to prepare strategic alternatives to a negotiated agreement; action to communicate the above to Israeli decision-makers and the Israeli public (there are no better alternatives to a negotiated agreement for Israel: all the alternatives are worse for Israel); action to elicit regional and international support; action to change perceptions and policies in the United States; action to ensure that the Palestinian discourse forms the framework for discussion about the Palestinian future (if negotiations fail, the responsibility is seen to lie with Israel, not with the Palestinians).

When the strategic aim is to re-orientate Palestinian strategy because Israel has failed to negotiate a genuine two-state outcome: action to block Israel's preferred alternatives to a negotiated agreement; action to promote Palestinian alternatives to a negotiated agreement action to elicit regional and international support for the new strategy; action to ensure that the Palestinian discourse forms the framework for discussion about the Palestinian future where Palestinians will retain the strategic initiative.

---

1   https://content.ecf.org.il/files/M00715_RegainingTheInitiative2008English.pdf

The PSSG contends that Israel is not a serious negotiating partner and that its strategic calculations are wrong. It argues that Israel will not come to a negotiated settlement that is acceptable to Palestinians because it perceives that there are other alternatives to a negotiated settlement: to prolong the negotiations indefinitely by pretending that 'progress has been made' and that suspensions are temporary; a pseudo provisional 'two-state agreement' with a strengthened but severely constrained PA; a unilateral separation dictated by Israel; control of the occupied territories by Egypt and Jordan.

For the Palestinians none of the above would be acceptable as they would fail to meet our national aspirations and could in fact undermine our national identity and rights. The basis of the negotiations with Israel since 1991 have been United Nations Resolutions which call for an end to the occupation of the West Bank, Gaza and East Jerusalem, captured by Israel in 1967, and an implementation of Resolution 194 regarding the refugees' right to return and compensation. The PSSG suggests that 'if Israel refuses to negotiate seriously for a genuine two-state outcome, Palestinians can and will block all four alternatives by switching to an alternative strategy made up of a combination of four linked reorientations to be undertaken singly or together'. Those are:

> First, the definitive closing down of the 1991 negotiation option so long abused by Israel; Second, the reconstitution of the Palestinian Authority so that it will not serve future Israeli interests by legitimising indefinite occupation and protecting Israel from bearing its full burden of the costs of occupation (it may become a Palestinian Resistance Authority); Third, the elevation of 'smart' resistance over negotiation as the main means of implementation for Palestinians, together with a reassertion of national unity through reform of the PLO, the empowerment of Palestinians, and the orchestrated eliciting of regional and international third-party support. The central aim will be to maximise the cost of continuing occupation for Israel, and to make the whole prospect of unilateral separation unworkable; Fourth, the shift from a two-state outcome to a (bi-national or unitary democratic) single state outcome as Palestinians' preferred strategic goal. This reopens a challenge to the existence of the State of Israel in its present form, but in an entirely new and more effective way than was the case before 1988.

Since its publication, the report has generated a number of articles both in the Arab and English media. The discussion has ranged from welcoming it as a timely initiative to dismissing it as yet another initiative that is not very different to others. Much of the discussion generated has been about the potential shift from a two-state to a one-state solution to the Palestinian problem. This is an important issue but should not be seen as the most significant outcome from this initiative.

I believe that one of the most important outcomes is the sheer fact that a forum was established where a group of Palestinians were able to analyse the current situation and to look for ways in which Palestinians can regain the initiative for realising our legitimate rights rather than continuing along the path of the current sterile negotiations, which any independent-minded analyst can see failing to achieve them. We can identify and implement strategies that will raise the cost of the occupation and therefore put pressure on Israel to negotiate seriously. Israel's policy of indefinite negotiations and the creation of facts on the ground will backfire as serious discussions are now taking place about a single state of some form as the choice of Palestinians.

Palestinian alternatives to a negotiated agreement are difficult but possible. They are preferable to a continuation of the status quo. The reorientation of Palestinian strategy cannot be blocked by Israel. Israel's alternatives to a negotiated agreement are delusory: Palestinians can and will block all of them. The outcome for Israel will be worse. Palestinians should not be deterred by the past, but should look with confidence to the future.

The main conclusion of the strategic review conducted by the PSSG is that Palestinians have more strategic cards than they think, and Israel has fewer. Over the longer term, Israeli military power is of limited use — and will even be a liability — if we learn how to play our cards properly. No political arrangement based on force alone endures. Israel is wrong to think that the longer the game goes on, the more strategic opportunities it will have.

It is the other way round. It is hoped that Israel swiftly comes to acknowledge the strategic logic set out in this report and acts accordingly in its own best interest. But, if Israel does not do this, then we Palestinians are ready to retain the strategic initiative whatever the eventuality, and to shape our future according to our own wishes, not those of others. We are currently exploring ways of developing the work of the PSSG further, particularly in examining in more detail some of the issues that still require this.

The Palestinians must regain the initiative to end the occupation but we will need help from ordinary people around the world to end it. There is a growing understanding across the world of the injustice that still exists in the twenty-first century, where a people have been dispossessed of their land and have been scattered all over the world and Israel is seen as a threat to World Peace, as reported in a European Union poll in 2003. It continues to defy International law and Human Rights Conventions. Its brutal and immoral siege on Gaza continues unabated. Its President, Simon Peres, a suspected war criminal, was awarded an honorary knighthood by the Queen, and the European Parliament voted on its proposed EU-Israel Association Agreement, which enables far greater Israeli participation in European Community programmes. It really beggars belief that a state that is a serial breaker of International Law and Human Rights Conventions, and one that has laid a siege to one and half million people, is rewarded with an upgrading of its status in Europe. Fair-minded people everywhere should be in contact with their MPs demanding that they vote against it.

This, however, demonstrates the task ahead if the Palestinian people are to be free.

Fig. 7 Tom Hurndall, Peace Volunteer badges before coach journey to Baghdad,
February 2003. All rights reserved.

5. Reflections on the Israeli-Palestinian Conflict

Avi Shlaim

In this chapter I argue that the state of Israel is legitimate, but only within its original boundaries, and that the Palestinians are the main victims of the conflict, victims of Israeli colonialism. The history of the region over the last sixty years can be convincingly explained in terms of the strategy of the 'iron wall', first expounded by Ze'ev Jabotinsky, which advocates negotiation only from a position of unassailable strength. The basic deal of 'land for peace' expressed in UN Resolution 242 was sound, but never effectively implemented and Yitzhak Rabin, the only Israeli prime minister prepared to negotiate, was murdered. The recent, brutal onslaughts on Gaza give little grounds for optimism.

These are reflections about a subject which has preoccupied me for the best part of four decades. Most of these reflections are included in one form or another in my book *Israel and Palestine: Reappraisals, Revisions, Refutations*, published by Verso in 2009. The volume gathers a number of essays published in the previous twenty-five years on the theme of the Israeli-Palestinian conflict. Some of these essays are scholarly articles with footnotes; some are more polemical comment pieces for newspapers; others are review essays which originally appeared in the *London Review of Books*.

The paperback edition of this book was reviewed by Rafael Behr in *The Observer* on 3 October 2010. Behr perfectly encapsulates the book's main topic:

> Several times in *Israel and Palestine*, his collection of essays on the Middle East, Avi Shlaim refers to Zionism as a public relations exercise. It sounds

  https://doi.org/10.11647/OBP.XXX.06

glib. But Shlaim [...] isn't talking about sales and marketing. He means a configuration of history that casts one side of a dispute as victim and the other as aggressor in the eyes of the world. In Zionism's case, the story told is of Israel restored to the Jews, carved from empty desert, 'a land without a people for a people without a land'. By extension, Arab hostility to Israel's creation was irrational cruelty directed against an infant state. It is a romantic myth requiring a big lie about the indigenous Palestinian population. Their expropriation was, in Shlaim's analysis, the 'original sin' that made conflict inevitable. He also sees the unwillingness of Israeli leaders to recognise the legitimacy of Palestinian grievance as the reason why most peace initiatives have failed. There was a time of greater pragmatism, when ordinary Israelis at least were ready to swap land for peace. But that trend was crushed by a generation of turbo-Zionists from the Likud party. Instead of trading occupied territory for normal diplomatic relations with the Arab world, they aggressively colonised it, waging demographic war to shrink the borders and diminish the viability of any future Palestinian state. Palestinian leaders are not spared Shlaim's criticism. He singles out Yasser Arafat's decision to side with Saddam Hussein in the first Gulf war, for example, as a moral and political blunder. But most of the essays are about the cynical manoeuvrings of Israeli politicians. As a collection it is plainly one-sided; Shlaim does not aim at a comprehensive overview of the conflict so much as a running rebuttal of Israel's version of it; an insurgency in the public relations war.[1]

I plead guilty to the charge of being one-sided. My sympathy is with the Palestinians because they are the victims of this tragic conflict, the victims of a terrible injustice. Injustice is by definition one-sided: it is inflicted by one party on another. I am a politically-engaged writer and I believe in justice for the Palestinians. By justice I mean an end to the occupation and the establishment of an independent Palestinian state in Gaza and the West Bank with a capital city in East Jerusalem. The Palestinian state I envisage would be alongside Israel, not instead of Israel. In short, I am a supporter of a two-state solution. If this makes me one-sided, then so be it.

What I propose to do is not to try to summarise the book, but to offer you some reflections on the Israeli-Palestinian conflict from an historical perspective. Everything to do with Israel is controversial, so

---

1   https://www.theguardian.com/books/2010/oct/03/avi-shlaim-israel-palestine-reappraisals-revisions-refutations.

let me pre-empt misrepresentations by stating where I stand. I have never questioned the legitimacy of the Zionist movement or that of the State of Israel within its pre-1967 borders. What I reject, and reject uncompromisingly, is the Zionist colonial project beyond the 1967 borders.

I belong to a very small group of Israeli scholars who are known collectively as 'the new historians' or 'the revisionist Israeli historians'. The original group included Simha Flapan, Benny Morris, and Ilan Pappe. We were called the new historians because we challenged the standard Zionist version of the origins, character, and course of the Arab-Israeli conflict. In particular, we challenged the many myths that have come to surround the birth of Israel and the first Arab-Israeli war.

The first thing to say about 'old history' is that it is a nationalist version of history. The nineteenth-century French philosopher, Ernest Renan, wrote that 'Getting [...] history wrong is part of being a nation'. Nationalist versions of history do indeed have this feature in common: they tend to be simplistic, selective, and self-serving. More specifically, they are commonly driven by a political agenda. One political purpose they serve is to unite all segments of society behind the regime. The other common purpose is to project a positive image of the nation to the outside world. Conventional Zionist history is no exception — it is a tendentious and self-serving version of history.

The late Edward Said was not himself a historian, but he attached a great importance to the 'new history', to critical historiography about Israel's past. The educational value of the 'new history', he thought, is three-fold: first, it educates the Israeli public about the Arab view of Israel and the conflict between the Arabs and Israel; second, it offers the Arabs an honest version of history, genuine history which is in line with their own experience, instead of the usual propaganda of the victors; third, the 'new history' helps to create a climate of opinion, on both sides of the divide, which is conducive to progress in the peace process. (One of the thirty essays in my book is on 'Edward Said and the Palestine Question'.)

There are two aspects to the Arab-Israeli conflict: the inter-communal and the inter-state. The inter-communal aspect is the dispute between Jews and Arabs in Palestine; the inter-state aspect is the conflict between the State of Israel and the neighbouring Arab states. The neighbouring

Arab states intervened in this conflict on the side of the Palestinians in the late 1930s and they have remained involved one way or another to this day. In the late 1970s, however, President Anwar Sadat of Egypt began the trend towards Arab disengagement from the conflict.

The Zionist movement was remarkably successful in the battle to win the hearts and minds of people. Zionism is arguably the second greatest PR success story of the twentieth century — after the Beatles! Zionist spokesmen skilfully presented their movement as the national liberation movement of the Jews, disclaiming any intention of hurting or dispossessing the indigenous Arab population. The founding fathers of Zionism promised that their movement would adhere to universal values like freedom, equality, and social justice. Based on these ideals, they claimed to aspire to develop Palestine for the benefit of all these people, regardless of their religion or ethnicity.

A huge gap, however, separated the proclaimed ideals of the founding fathers from the reality of Zionist treatment of the Arab population of Palestine on the ground. This gap was filled by Zionist spokesmen with hypocrisy and humbug. Even as they oppressed and dispossessed the Palestinians, the Zionists continued to claim the moral high-ground. In the face of overwhelming evidence to the contrary, they persisted in portraying Zionism as an enlightened, progressive, and peace-loving movement and its opponents as implacably hostile fanatics. One of the achievements of the 'new history' is to expose this gap between rhetoric and reality.

From the early days of the Zionist movement, its leaders were preoccupied with what they euphemistically called 'the Arab question'. This was also sometimes referred to as 'the hidden question' — the presence of an Arab community on the land of their dreams. And from the beginning, the Zionists developed a strategy for dealing with this problem. This was the strategy of the 'iron wall', of dealing with the Arabs from a position of unassailable military strength.

In 2000 I published a book under the title *The Iron Wall: Israel and the Arab World*. It covered the first fifty years of statehood, from 1948 to 1998. This is a fairly long history book but I can summarise it for you in a single sentence: Israel's leaders have always preferred force to diplomacy in dealing with the Arabs. Ever since its inception, Israel has been strongly predisposed to resort to military force, and reluctant, remarkably reluctant, to engage in meaningful diplomacy in order to resolve the political dispute with its neighbours. True, in 1979 Israel concluded a peace treaty with Egypt and in 1994 it concluded a peace treaty with Jordan, but the overall pattern remains one of relying predominantly on brute military force.

The architect of the iron wall strategy was Ze'ev Jabotinsky, an ardent Jewish nationalist and the spiritual father of the Israeli Right. In 1923 Jabotinsky published an article titled 'On the Iron Wall (We and the Arabs)' with an analysis of 'the Arab question' and recommendations on how to confront it. He argued that no nation in history ever agreed voluntarily to make way for another people to come and create a state on its land. The Palestinians were a people, not a rabble, and Palestinian resistance to a Jewish state was an inescapable fact. Consequently, a voluntary agreement between the two parties was unattainable. The only way to achieve the Zionist project of an independent Jewish state in Palestine, Jabotinsky concluded, was unilaterally and by military force. A Jewish state could only be built behind an iron wall of Jewish military power. The Arabs will hit their heads against the wall, but eventually they will despair and give up any hope of overpowering the Zionists. Then, and only then, will come the time for stage two, negotiating with the leaders of the Palestine Arabs about their rights and status in Palestine.

The iron wall was a national strategy for overcoming the main obstacle on the road to statehood. The Arab revolt of 1936–1939 seemed to confirm the premises of this strategy. The point to stress is that this was not the strategy of the right, or of the left, or of the centre. Based on a broad consensus, it became the national strategy for dealing with the Arabs from the 1930s onwards. Regardless of the political colour of the government of the day, this was the dominant strategy under successive Israeli prime ministers from David Ben-Gurion, the founder of the state, to Binyamin Netanyahu, the current incumbent.

In my book I argue that the history of the state of Israel is the vindication of the strategy of the iron wall. First the Egyptians, in 1979, then the PLO, in 1993, then Jordan, in 1994, all negotiated peace agreements with Israel from a position of palpable weakness. So the strategy of 'negotiations from strength' worked. The disappointment is that, in Israel's entire history, only one prime minister had the courage to move from stage one, the building of military power, to stage two, negotiations with the Palestinians. That prime minister was Yitzhak Rabin and the transition occurred during the secret talks in the Norwegian capital between Israeli and PLO representatives which produced the 1993 Oslo Accords.

In the rest of what I have to say, my reflections will revolve around four major landmarks in the history of the Israeli-Palestinian conflict: the 1948 war for Palestine; the June 1967 war; the 1993 Oslo Accords; and the Gaza war of December 2008.

The War for Palestine

The first Arab-Israeli war was, in fact, two wars rolled into one. The first phase, from the passage of the UN partition resolution on 29 November 1947 to the expiry of the British Mandate over Palestine on 14 May 1948, was the war between the Jewish and Arab communities in Palestine and it ended with a crushing defeat for the Palestinians and in the decimation of their society. The second phase began with the invasion of Palestine by the regular armies of the neighbouring Arab states on 15 May 1948 and it ended with a ceasefire on 7 January 1949. This phase, too, ended with an Israeli triumph and a comprehensive Arab defeat.

The main losers in 1948 were the Palestinians. Around 730,000 Palestinians, over half the total population, became refugees and the name Palestine was wiped off the map. Israelis call this 'the War of Independence' while Palestinians call it the *Nakba*, or catastrophe. Whatever name is given to it, the war for Palestine marked a major turning point in the history of the modern Middle East.

The debate in Israel between the 'new historians' and the pro-Zionist 'old historians' initially revolved round the fateful events of 1948. There are several bones of contention in this debate. For example, the old historians claim that the Palestinians left Palestine of their own accord and in the expectation of a triumphal return. We say that the Palestinians did not leave of their own accord; that the Jewish forces played an active part in pushing them out. Another argument concerns Britain's intentions as the Mandate over Palestine approached its inglorious end. The old historians claim that Britain's main aim in the twilight period was to abort the birth of a Jewish state. On the basis of the official British documents, we argue that Britain's real aim was to abort the birth of a Palestinian state. There is another issue in dispute: why did the political deadlock persist for three decades after the guns fell silent in 1949? The old historians say it was Arab intransigence; we say it was Israeli intransigence. In short, my colleagues and I attribute to Israel a far larger share of the responsibility for the root causes of the Israeli-Palestinian conflict than the orthodox Zionist rendition of events.

It seems to me undeniable that the creation of the State of Israel in 1948 involved a monumental injustice to the Palestinians. And yet I maintain that the State of Israel within its original 1949 borders is legitimate. Some people say that this is inconsistent: how can a state built on injustice be legitimate? My answer to my critics is twofold. First of all, there was the all-important United Nations resolution of 29 November 1947, which called for Mandatory Palestine to be divided into two states, one Arab and one Jewish. This resolution constitutes an international charter of legitimacy for the creation of a Jewish state. Secondly, in the first half of 1949, Israel negotiated, under UN auspices, a series of bilateral armistice agreements with all its neighbours: Lebanon, Syria, Jordan, and Egypt. These are the only internationally recognised borders that Israel has ever had, and these are the only borders that I still recognise as legitimate.

My graduate students at Oxford challenge me relentlessly on this point. In the first place, they claim that the UN partition resolution was unfair to the Palestinians because it was their country that was being divided. My reply is that this argument confuses fairness with legality. The partition resolution may well have been unfair but since it was passed by a two-thirds majority of the votes in the General Assembly, it cannot be regarded as illegal. A further argument that my students deploy is that even if Israel was legitimate at birth, its occupation of the rest of Palestine since June 1967 and the apartheid system it has installed there undermines its legitimacy in the eyes of the world. This argument is much more difficult to counter. By its own actions, by maintaining its coercive control of the occupied Palestinian territories, and by its callous treatment of innocent Palestinian civilians, Israel has torn to shreds the liberal image it enjoyed in its first two decades of its existence.

The June 1967 War

The second major watershed is the June 1967 war, popularly known as the Six-Day War. The main consequence of that war was the defeat of secular Arab nationalism and the slow emergence of an Islamic alternative. In Israel, the resounding victory in the Six-Day War reopened the question of the territorial aims of Zionism. Israel was now in possession of the Sinai Peninsula, the West Bank, and the Golan Heights. The question was what to do with these territories and to this question two very different answers were given. The moderates favoured the restoration of the bulk of these territories to their owners in return for recognition and peace. The secular and religious nationalists, on the other hand, wanted to hold on to these territories, and especially to the West Bank, which they regarded as an integral part of the Land of Israel.

The United Nations had its own solution to the conflict: Security Council Resolution 242 of November 1967, which proposed a package deal, the trading of land for peace. Israel would give back the Occupied Territories with minor border modifications and the Arabs would agree to live with Israel in peace and security. One feature of Resolution 242 which displeased the PLO was that it referred to the Palestinians not as a national problem but merely as a refugee problem. Resolution 242 has been the basis of most international plans for peace in the region since 1967.

History shows that this formula is sound. Whenever it was tried, it worked. In 1979, Israel gave back every inch of the Sinai Peninsula and it received in return a peace treaty which is still valid today. In 1994, Israel signed a peace treaty with the Hashemite Kingdom of Jordan and paid the price of returning some land it had poached along their common border in the south. This treaty, too, is still effective today. If Israel wanted to have a peace agreement with Syria, it would be within its reach through negotiations. But there is a price tag: complete Israeli withdrawal from the Golan Heights. The problem is that on the northern front, as on the eastern front, Israel prefers land to peace.

Quite soon after the ending of hostilities in June 1967, Israel started building civilian settlements in the Occupied Territories. These settlements are illegal, all of them, without a single exception, and they are the main obstacle to peace. Thus, as a result of its refusal to relinquish the fruits of its military victory, little Israel became a colonial power, oppressing millions of civilians in the Occupied Territories. It is largely for this reason that in the aftermath of its victory in the June 1967 war, Israel began to lose its international legitimacy while the PLO began to gain it.

The Oslo Accords

Like all other significant landmarks in the history of the Israeli-Palestinian conflict, the Oslo Accords has generated a great deal of controversy. It was signed on the lawn of the White House on 13 September 1993 and it represented a historic compromise between the two warring peoples. The historic compromise was clinched by a hesitant handshake between Yitzhak Rabin and Yasser Arafat. Despite all its shortcomings, the Oslo Accords constituted a historic breakthrough in the struggle for Palestine. It fully deserved the over-worked epithet 'historic' because it was the first agreement between the two principal parties to the conflict.

The Oslo Accords did not promise or even mention the brave phrase 'an independent Palestinian State'. Its more modest aim was to empower the Palestinians to run their own affairs, starting with the Gaza Strip and the West Bank town of Jericho. The Accord is completely silent about all the key issues in this dispute. It says nothing about the future of Jerusalem, it says nothing about the right of return of the 1948 Palestinian refugees, it says nothing about the status of Israeli settlements in the Occupied Territories, and it does not indicate the borders of the Palestinian entity. All these key issues were left for negotiations towards the end of the transition period of five years. So Oslo was basically an experiment in Palestinian self-government.

For Yitzhak Rabin, Israel's security was the paramount consideration. Provided Israel's security was safeguarded, he was prepared to move forward and he did take another significant step forward by signing, on 28 September 1995, the Interim Agreement on the West Bank and the Gaza Strip, commonly known as Oslo II. Rabin's murder, two months later, dealt a body-blow to the fledgling peace process. We do not know what might have happened had Yitzhak Rabin not been assassinated. What we do know is that after his murder the peace process began to break down.

Why did the Oslo peace process break down? There are two conflicting answers. One answer is that the original Oslo Accords was a bad deal for Israel and that it was doomed to failure from the start. My answer is that Oslo was not a bad agreement, but rather a modest step in the right direction equipped with a sound gradualist strategy. The peace process broke down because Rabin's Likud successors, led by Binyamin Netanyahu from 1996 to 1999, reneged on Israel's side of the deal. There were other reasons for the breakdown of the peace process, notably the resort to terror by Palestinian extremists. But the single most fundamental reason was the continuing colonisation of the West Bank. This happened under both Labour and Likud governments after the signature of the Oslo Accords. It was a violation of the spirit, if not of the letter of the Oslo Accords.

The building of Jewish settlements on occupied land is not just a blatant violation of the Fourth Geneva Convention but an in-your-face aggression against the Arabs who live there. So is the so-called 'security barrier' that Israel is building on the West Bank. Settlement expansion on the West Bank can only proceed by confiscating more Palestinian land. It amounts to ruthless land-grabbing. And it is simply not possible to engage in land-grabbing and to pretend to be doing peace-making at the same time. Land-grabbing and peace-making are incompatible: they do not go together. It is one or the other and Israel has made its choice. It prefers land to peace with the Palestinians and that is why the Oslo peace process broke down.

The Gaza War

The fourth and final watershed in the history of the Israeli-Palestinian conflict on which I would like to offer a few reflections is the Gaza war unleashed by Israel on 27 December 2008. This was the climax of the strategy of the iron wall, of shunning diplomacy and relying on brute force to impose Israel's will on the Arabs. 'Operation Cast Lead', to give the war its bizarre official title, was not really a war but a one-sided massacre.

On 7 January 2009, while the operation was in progress, I published a long article in the G2 section of the *Guardian*. The title I gave the article was 'Israel's Insane Offensive' but the *Guardian*, typically, forgot to print the title. As will be clear from the title, I was extremely angry when I wrote this article. The article began by quoting a memo that Sir John Troutbeck, a senior official in the Foreign Office, wrote on 2 June 1948, to the Labour Foreign Secretary, Ernest Bevin. Troutbeck castigated the Americans for creating a gangster state headed by 'an utterly unscrupulous set of leaders'. I used to think that this judgement was too harsh, but Israel's vicious assault on the people of Gaza, and the complicity of George W. Bush in this assault, reopened the question.

Very briefly, my view of the Gaza War is that it was illegal, immoral, and completely unnecessary. The Israeli government claimed that the war in Gaza was a defensive operation. Hamas militants were firing Qassam rockets on towns in the south of the country and it was the duty of the Israeli government to take action to protect its citizens. This was the objective of Operation Cast Lead. The trouble with this official line is that there was an effective cease-fire in place in the months preceding the war. Egypt brokered the cease-fire between Israel and Hamas in June 2008. This cease-fire had a dramatic effect in de-escalating the conflict. In the first six months of that year, the average monthly number of rockets launched from Gaza on southern Israel was 179. After the cease-fire came into effect, the monthly average dropped to three rockets between July and October. It was Israel that violated the cease-fire. On 4 November 2008, the Israel Defence Forces (IDF) launched a raid into Gaza that killed six Hamas fighters, thus bringing the cease-fire to an abrupt end. If all that Israel really wanted was to protect its citizens in the south, then all it had to do was to follow the good example set by Hamas in respecting the cease-fire.

The Egyptian-brokered cease-fire agreement also stipulated that Israel would lift the blockade of Gaza. After Hamas seized power in Gaza in June 2007, Israel started restricting the flow of food, fuel, and medical supplies to the strip. A blockade is a form of collective punishment that is contrary to international law. But even during the four months of the cease-fire, Israel failed to lift the blockade. Despite all the international protests, and despite all the boats organised by peace activists to carry humanitarian aid to Gaza, the savage blockade is still in force today.

During the war, the IDF used its superior power without any restraint. The casualties of the Gaza war were around 1400 Palestinians, most of them innocent civilians, and 13 Israelis. In the course of this war, the

IDF deliberately inflicted a great deal of damage on the infrastructure of the Gaza Strip. It destroyed thousands of private houses, government buildings, police stations, mosques, schools, and medical facilities. The scale of the damage suggests that the real purpose of the war was offensive, not defensive.

It seems to me that the undeclared aims of the war were twofold. One aim was politicide, to deny the Palestinians any independent political existence in Palestine. The second aim of the war was regime change in Gaza, to drive Hamas out of power there. In the course of the war, war crimes were committed by both sides. These war crimes were investigated by an independent fact-finding mission appointed by the UN Human Rights Council and headed by Richard Goldstone, the distinguished South African judge. Goldstone found that Hamas and the IDF had both committed violations of the laws of war. The IDF, however, received more severe strictures on account of the scale and the seriousness of its violations.

My conclusion may come to you as a shock but it is not a conclusion I have reached lightly: Israel has become a rogue state. My academic discipline is International Relations. In the academic literature in this field, three criteria for a rogue state are usually put forward: one, a state that habitually violates international law; two, a state that either possesses or seeks to develop weapons of mass destruction; and three, a state which resorts to terror. Terror is the use of force against civilians for political purposes. Israel meets all three criteria and therefore, in my judgement, it is now a rogue state. It is because Israel behaves like a rogue state that it is well on the way to becoming a pariah state.

Dr Chaim Weizmann, Israel's first president, wrote in his autobiography that it is by its treatment of the Palestinians that Israel will be judged. It is accordingly by this yardstick that I judge Israel — and I find it sadly wanting. This is a melancholy conclusion to a rather depressing set of reflections. Let me therefore end on a more hopeful note. The hopeful note comes from a letter written in September 2010 by Eyad Sarraj, a psychiatrist from Gaza, to Lynne Segal, one of the sponsors of the Jewish aid boat to Gaza:

Dear Lynne,

You write to me, and I must tell you that I am very inspired by the coming voyage of a Jewish boat to break the siege on Gaza. I have helped and worked with and received other boats, but this is the most significant one for me, because it carries such an important message. It brings to us and tells the world that those we Palestinians thought we should hate as our enemies can instead arrive as our friends, our brothers and sisters, sharing a love for humanity and for our struggle for justice and peace. I will wait with anticipation to shake hands with them and hold them dear in close embrace. They are my heroes.

Please, never despair that you cannot bring peace, and never give up work for a just world. When I see, read, and relate to Jews who believe in me as an equal human being, and who tell me that their definition of humanity is not complete without me, I become stronger in my quest for justice and peace. I learnt long ago that there are Jews in and outside Israel who belong with me in the camp of friends of justice and peace. I have always strongly believed that we can live together, that we must live together. We have no other choice except to live together. It is because of people like you, and events like this, that I will never give up on the hope.

With my best and warmest

Eyad Sarraj

Fig. 8   Tom Hurndall, Palestinian children playing in the street in Jerusalem,
April 2003. All rights reserved.

6. Being Palestinian[1]

Karma Nabulsi

Palestinians possess more than enough culture, language, history, and ethnicity to fall within the traditional claims of a nation, and therefore to base identity upon a combination of these categories. But a people is more than a nation, as both our existential predicament and unceasing struggle over generations demonstrate. How does one define the nature of this extra feature that identifies us as a people?

In this chapter I will illustrate and explain how my own identity is not based on a combination of the national particularisms that gave rise to the Palestinian people, but rather, upon the glue which keeps us together. My identity is based exclusively on the general will. What exactly is the general will of a people? The general will of a people is what makes it cohere, gives it sense and purpose and expression. It is the basis for the creation of the social contract, it is the foundation for the theory of democracy itself. Yet it is commonly said that it is more or less undiscussable since it is totally unmeasurable. That it is purely metaphysical, and that it is therefore — and also — undefinable. Because the general will is not empirical, and because there is no clear way of analysing it, surveying it, or of classifying it. Nor is there any single or combined methodology that can capture either its performance or its essence. It is emphatically not ethnic, nor is it based on language, custom, religion, race, nor on the nation. And more than that it is never ever static: it moves, it grows, and it changes: it is both relational and unquantifiable. In his wonderful introduction to his translation of Rousseau's Social Contract, GDH Cole explains the operation of the

---

1   The author is grateful to Sudhir Hazareesingh of Balliol College, Oxford and to Marc Stears of University College London for their helpful comments.

      https://doi.org/10.11647/OBP.XXX.07

general will in two parts: 'The General Will is realized not whenever that is done which is best for the community, but when, in addition, the community as a whole has willed the doing of it'.[2]

In order to set out how and why it has happened that I rely upon the general will rather than traditional nationalist claims for identity, it is necessary to first present the particularism and history of the Palestinian people who are largely a refugee population. Next it will explain how the general will functions within Palestinian society, which crosses borders and host countries to express itself. It will conclude with examples of why Palestinian identity is so caught up in an essential struggle to create just institutions, especially for the protection of the rights of refugees, and why this latter issue is cast within the dual quest for liberty and democracy which — in our case as in most people's — are intertwined.

The Palestinian People

There is a fashionable, and somewhat sympathetic way of seeing the modern Palestinian predicament: as a Diaspora, as an international business community: highly educated, rootless, existential, cosmopolitan. A mirror image of the Jewish Diaspora on the European continent. Such exiles will find their way easily after the final settlement in a globalised world, connecting to their community by internet, perhaps adding a Palestinian passport to that of the US, of Britain, or of Jordan. But this is largely a false image, merely that of an elite, those who managed to get passports or savings out, or went to the Gulf or to America in the 1950s and '60s. Although it is true Palestinians possess an enormous flourishing of talent and skill — doctors, engineers, scientists, artists, architects, teachers — and are from the coastal towns and cities as well as from the countryside; still the overwhelming character of the Palestinian people remains that of a landed people with a close bond to their homeland. Farmers and peasants, intimately connected to the land, although for three generations now born in camps, often only a few kilometres from their destroyed villages, empty fields. Hundreds of thousands of whom are officially excluded from certain professions in

---

2   J. J. Rousseau, Introduction, *The Social Contract and the Discourses*, London, Everyman Dent, 1913, p. xxxvi.

some of the countries that host them, who have no hope of any future. Refugees, with no travel documents of any kind, who dream only of return.

The Palestinian refugee camps were created during and just after the establishment of Israel. These camps remain the most enigmatic facet of Palestinian life and society to those outside it: how many Palestinians are refugees? Where are they scattered? A survey recently undertaken at a Scottish university discovered that only 9% of the British public were aware that the West Bank and Gaza is currently under a military occupation. Yet the refugees are more central to Palestinian identity than the military occupation of the West Bank and Gaza by Israel since 1967, where the locus of the Palestinian state is to be. Indeed, the original dispossession and continued displacement from their homes in 1948, the unhappy fate of the majority of Palestinians is (as it has always been) the core of the conflict, and still remains almost entirely unknown.

Palestinian refugees make up over one third of the world's refugee population, and they are also one of the oldest of refugee groups. Currently there are around five million refugees, and they consist of the majority of the Palestinian people, just over two thirds, and include refugees from the 1948 war as well as the Six-Day War of 1967, which created another half million Palestinian refugees. So there are several different generations and different types of refugees, some living scattered in the fifty-nine UN-registered refugee camps throughout the West Bank and Gaza, Jordan, Syria, Lebanon. However, most of the refugees whose families registered with the UN after 1948 (now 3.8 million) don't even live in the camps, and what is more, many refugees never registered with the UN at all. Others live in the rest of the Arab world, from Baghdad to Cairo; some, more recently, in Europe and in America, many are even Israeli citizens, and are living in unrecognised villages close to their razed homes inside Israel.

The creation of the refugee crisis can largely be attributed to the dramatic events which live on in the Palestinian memory as the Nakbah (Catastrophe); the fragmentation, devastation, and total rupture of Palestinian society in 1948. The Palestinian villages in Galilee and elsewhere were demolished by the authorities of the new state of Israel once the original inhabitants were driven out or fled during the fighting. This largely peasant society found themselves confined to refugee camps not far from their original homes, some only a few kilometres away, where they are to this day.

The international community at that time believed that the United Nations had a special responsibility to Palestinian refugees, given that their terrible predicament was created as a direct result of the UN decision to partition Palestine. Indeed, the UN resolution that dealt with the urgent refugee crisis, General Assembly Resolution 194 of 1948, is yet to be implemented, because Israel refuses to do so. Every Palestinian refugee today knows the meaning of this UN resolution which deals with their fate and their rights, calling for the return of those refugees who wish it to their homes, as well as compensation.

The United Nations was more successful in establishing an institution to care for the ongoing humanitarian crisis of the refugees, the United Nations Relief and Works Agency (UNRWA), which began its operations in 1950, which it still carries out to this day. But its mandate is limited — it does not provide anything other than minimal relief, it cannot provide representation for the refugees, and it cannot offer the vital legal protections that the UN's High Commission for Refugees offers to all other refugee populations. The political organisation of the camps by the popular resistance movements in the mid-1960s — Fatah, the Popular Front, the Democratic Front etc. — emerged as a result of the despair engendered by these failings, although Palestinians every year heard the international community and the Arab states insisting on the right of return of refugees, nothing was done. Through the 1960s, '70s and '80s, the Palestinian movement actually operated through a variety of means in the camps: organising unions, hospitals, creating factories and employment in them, and co-ordinating and collaborating with the other national liberation movements, such as SWAPO and the ANC, and international institutions and agencies.

The refugee camps in Gaza, Jordan and Lebanon were where the guerrilla groups were established and from where they drew their membership. By 1970 these various groups had merged into the Palestine Liberation Organisation, forming a government in exile, and establishing embassies and diplomatic relations across the world. It was comprised of a National Council made up of representation from the parties, the unions, and the differing exile constituencies. Much of the regional conflict that emerged in the 1970s and 1980s was a result not just of Israel's attempt to crush the political infrastructure, such as the 1982 invasion, but of the Arab state's continual attempt to control the Palestinians' political independence, and the destabilisation it created throughout the Arab world. This erupted into battles such as that in Jordan in 1970, and in Lebanon in 1985 and 1986 during the so-called War of the Camps.

How does the will of a people, scattered over several countries, regions and continents, express itself with any assurance under these extreme conditions? Fourteen years ago, the Palestinian leadership sought to capture in words enough of what we were as a people that it might hold us all together: the Palestinian Declaration of Independence, proclaimed on 15 November 1988 in Algiers by the Palestine National Council, our parliament in exile. Somehow it succeeded: it articulated and managed to reflect enough of the things that we were, as well as an inclusive enough notion that we could all adhere to, whoever we were or wherever we were. Communist anti-nationalists or the faithful; marxists or conservative nationalists; refugees living in the camps of Lebanon and Jordan or as exiles living in Knightsbridge and Rotterdam and Dubai; under occupation or in prison; in a foreign country with false papers and no work permit or second generation holding the passport of a foreign land but forever Palestinian. The millions under occupation or the millions more living in refugee camps or outside of them since 1948, since 1967; since, for many of us, we were born. This declaration manages this not by claiming to be the expression of the birth of a nation, but as something much more profound; it does so as an expression of the general will of the Palestinian people. The proclamation also managed to evoke many notions of the homeland that Palestinians themselves could adhere to. By 1988 the notions of Palestine that we had acquired in the years of following the violent expulsions, the dispossession, and exile of 1948 created such a multiplicity of meanings and attachments, of sentiments and descriptions, that we had become 'a country of words'.[3]

---

3   Mahmoud Darwish, 'We Travel Like Other People', in *Victims of a Map*, trans. Adballah Udhari, London, El Saqi, 1984, p. 31.

'A Country of Words'

Before exploring the complexity of the 1998 declaration, it is interesting to look at the first proclamation of independence which was issued during the war for Palestine while the catastrophe was just unfolding, since it is its very opposite. Laconic and fairytale-like in its plainness, it was published on 10 January 1948 by members of the Palestinian National Council, meeting in the city of Gaza. Its telegraphic simplicity renders it almost heart-breaking in its brief, rushed, inarticulacy. There was no need to describe who we were, how we were, or how we got there. What the homeland was, much less what it meant to us, or even us to it. On that day, in the minds of the leaders of the Arab Higher Council, there was no prescience, no revelation, nor any hint of the destiny that Palestine and her people would endure over the next fifty-two years. The text is hasty, the predicament conceived as a mere temporary affair. This battle would be resolved and we would go on working the land and living in our cities. We would prevail. So Palestine is simply described as bounded by four other Arab states with the Mediterranean to her west, and her people described as 'citizens' who 'will enjoy their liberties and their rights', that they be inspired by Palestine's 'glorious history' and that they 'serve human civilisation'.[4] The difference in just forty years is extraordinary, our perpetual temporary crisis meant that language had become all-powerful in the construction of homeland. This condition was portrayed by the poet Mahmoud Darwish in *We Travel Like Other People*, which he wrote shortly after the siege of Beirut in 1982. The poem begins with: 'We travel like other people, but we return to nowhere', and it ends: 'We have a country of words. Speak, speak so that I can put my road on the stone of a stone./ We have a country of words. Speak speak so we may know the end of this travel.'

The words that needed to be used in 1988 to capture the essence of the state for all Palestinians had to evoke a place that was grown not from a nation, but rather from the sense of many; not from one people, but from many peoples, not drawn from one religion, but consciously aware of its existence as the source of many. The Declaration of the State of Palestine describes us thus: 'Nourished by an unfolding series of civilizations

---

4   *The Declaration of Independence 1988 issued by the Palestine National Council*, Jerusalem, PASSIA (Palestinian Academic Society for the Study of International Affairs), 1990.

and cultures, finding inspiration in its spiritual and historical heritage rich in variety and kind, the Palestinian Arab people has, throughout history, continued to develop its identity in an integral unity of land and people'. This connection to the land is fused to the notion of a homeland of peoples, and is an expression of their attachment to it. But the sentimental attachment is not the source of Palestine's sovereignty. Nor does the source of the sovereignty reside in the struggle for it. Indeed it is not through fighting for it or sacrificing oneself to it that one 'earns' the homeland. Nor are the people created from the wound of the Nakbah. The homeland is there, already their antebellum, and the relationship is one of connection of the people that live on it with it. In a simple, tangible, non-abstract way. Not in an imagined, nostalgic way. It is in this manner that it is not a struggle to be a people. The state thus becomes a place of quiet and calm, of peace and compassion, which negates the need for a war to have an identity, or in order to create one: 'The call went out from Temple, Church, and Mosque that to praise the Creator, to celebrate compassion and peace, was indeed the message of Palestine'. The document expresses, time after time, a witnessing of the people's will constantly regenerated through the passage of time, protean: 'From generation unto generation, the Palestinian people gave of itself unsparingly in the valiant battle for liberation and homeland.' It then portrays the unmistakeable workings of the general will in its most visible manifestation: 'For what has been the unbroken chain of our peoples' rebellions except the heroic embodiment of our will for independence? And so the people was sustained in the struggle to stay, and to prevail'.[5] It is within this very will that the both the state and the people have their source and their identity.

Where precisely is the physical locus of this homeland for Palestinians? The proclamation's answer was to give a remarkably simple definition of the State of Palestine, which nonetheless adhered to an absolute logic then, and a concept that still holds equally true today: 'The State of Palestine is the state of Palestinians wherever they may be.' It is thus the expression of the general will of all Palestinians at that very moment of time. And the majority of us were not on the land our parents came from, or where we ourselves were born. Where

---

5   *The Declaration of Independence 1988.*

were we and what were we in 1988, that we could make our will known, to ourselves and to others? So scattered throughout time and space; some of us frozen inside these temporal and spatial spheres, but many more of us far too fluid, slipping through borders and out of our bodies like no other people I knew in recent history: dying in strange places violently, or alienated from ourselves, far away from our origins. In 1988 we said that we would recognise the State of Israel (which continued to deny us), and to give up the claim of a state in 78% of historic Palestine. So if we wanted to return to a Palestinian state, we would only go to one small part of it. If we wanted to return to our own actual homes — the towns, farms, and villages that we had been dispossessed of — it would be under Israel's sovereignty, which we then recognised, then accepted. The effect of a generation of Israelis who had built a new society on our lands, inside our houses. And by then we understood we could not impose our tolerant vision of inclusiveness: their exclusivity and their exclusion of us was all they wanted from us, after all. Yet how could we have decided such crucial things? And how did we make this will manifest so that we all recognised this vision of the homeland had been arrived at by all of us, wherever we were?

Representing the General Will of the Palestinian People

It was through representing all the things we were that I came to learn of these highly political notions of homeland, their complexity, and that they became my own. So my own rather odd notions of Palestine, which had developed whilst growing up in Beirut, Washington, and Rabat, were utterly altered and superseded by the years I lived and worked as a PLO official and representative in the 1970s and throughout the 1980s in Beirut, New York, Tunis, Cyprus, London and other places, and whilst travelling to the four corners of the world as a representative of a people in search of the homeland, in search of state, in search of return. I am not sure where academics are meant to draw their notions of identity from, but I know the ones I hold today did not emerge through an exploration of the huge wave of literature on nationalism, identity, multiculturalism, ethnic and minority rights, political philosophy, nor even of a modern cosmopolitanism.[6] Instead, it developed through a political education which I learnt from a practice: from a way of being, of thinking, of speaking, of doing. Not an inarticulate essentialism of innate culture but rather a conscious, inclusive, ceaseless political action.

One of the main ways was to seek to accurately reflect us as a people. Through this means one ended up, in effect, learning how many things a people could actually be, of the nature of the home inside all Palestinians that connects us, as well as the home we create when we are with each other. In order to represent a people who are persistently and violently denied sovereign identity, the craft, the political art, and the obligation is to portray the general will as fully as possible. To show the rich, strange and unique nature of a people, and in so doing to demonstrate equally, and without fail, the universal within this: that they are a people like any other, inasmuch as they are particular, from a certain time and place. Drawn from a myriad of traditions, ethnicities, religions, political ideologies and classes. And are complete and inalienable, not dissolved through their dispossession and denial. The other universal is that they come together to make decisions and to deliberate as one general will, as peoples seek to do. Some of whom have the fortune to possess the democratic institutions, the place, the structures, the space, and the laws to protect them in this deliberation.

Just one of my tasks those years was explaining the nature of our cause to those who either knew very little of us or what they did know was so wide of the mark as to be fantastical. I met with anyone: representatives of states and heads of them, with diplomats, trade unionists, NGOs, international institutions, artists, schoolchildren, constituencies, national parliaments, university unions, clubs, officials of political parties, workers, humanitarian organisations, civil servants,

---

6   See, for example, Isaiah Berlin's powerful but predisposed view of nationalism (i.e., created from a national psychic wound) in 'The Bent Twig: On the Rise of Nationalism', in *The Crooked Timber of Humanity* (London, John Murray, 1990); and also his association of the general will with the most unpleasant sort of positive freedom in 'Two Concepts of Liberty', in *Four Essays on Liberty* (Oxford, Oxford University Press, 1969), p. 34. Hannah Arendt is another example of this. In *On Revolution*, she pairs Rousseau's name constantly with that of Robespierre, in an understanding of the general will that is bound intimately with the work of the Committee of Public Safety of France in 1793; she uses the concepts of the nation, the national interest and the general will interchangeably throughout as if they were the same thing. See *On Revolution* (London, Penguin, 1990), esp. pp. 76–79.

journalists, writers. With some of them, my task was to persuade them
to help, to be virtuous, to act. With all of them, it was to see us, really see
us. In this endeavour my practice was always twofold: illustrating this
plurality of notions of homelands that exist amongst Palestinians with
how they also come together as one. How there is the collective and
the individual dream, and also that there is the present reality which
we face united. Rather than simply present my own definition, my own
notion. Indeed, my definition of Palestinian identity is the general will.
Whenever I am amongst it, I am home.

The people to whom I spoke about our cause came from all walks
of life, and I saw them in the different capacities my work demanded:
officially, secretly, publicly, informally, accidentally, but the people of
whom I spoke were all the same. They were the same because they
were in exactly the same predicament by virtue of being Palestinian.
Palestinians, no matter where they were, no matter what they were
doing, found themselves (and find themselves still) living in the same
mysterious and acute situation, and they also saw themselves in this
manner quite clearly. And more: they all saw the same answer to
their predicament, without question, when the homeland's absence
would make itself apparent. So I could see the corporeal contours and
the tangible character of the general will, the will that is said to be so
invisible. It manifested itself to me through various manners and means,
constant in its presence; the familiar; home. As Nicias told his fellow
Athenians on Syracuse during the Peloponnesian war, the city is inside
the people: 'it is men who make the city, and not walls nor ships, empty
of men'.[7]

In the years of 1987 and 1988 there was the Intifada, as palpable an
expression of the general will of a people as one could find in modern
times.[8] The daily uprising against military occupation which lasted for
over two years, where hundreds of thousands of civilians were beaten,
imprisoned, and thousands shot for throwing stones at the occupying
army, for working under siege and curfews and through the popular

---

7   Thucydides, *The History of the Peloponnesian War*, trans. Blanco and Roberts (London,
    W. W. Norton, 1998), Book 7, ch. 77, s. 7.
8   There was a series of popular general strikes and insurrections and rebellions by
    Palestinians throughout the twentieth century, especially in the 1920s and 1930s
    when under British rule.

committees, the unions, the underground leadership and political parties to express the will to be independent, self-governing, sovereign. But as Rousseau noted in *The Social Contract*, this will cannot be partial. In a chapter entitled "That Sovereignty is Indivisible", he writes: 'Sovereignty, for the same reason that makes its inalienable, is indivisible; for the will is either general[9] or it is not; it is the will either of the body of the people, or only of a part of it.'[10] Palestinians of the West Bank and Gaza, whilst having refugee camps from 1948 within that part of the land, were not the majority of the people, they were only a part of it. The majority of the people had been dispossessed and were living outside of Palestine in refugee camps and exile. So how did they make their will manifest? Throughout the 1970s and 1980s I saw manifestations of the general will through a variety of roles and means, constant, manifold, present. The normal democratic structures that pertain to a landed people were not there, but we knew, if we were faithful in our jobs, what the will of the people was to the most precise and detailed degree, and on every issue of substance that had to do with our way forward, a future settlement, a minimal justice. There were hundreds of popular committees, unions, the political parties, associations, newspaper editors, journals, charities, schools, camp leaders, university teachers, trade union members and associations. There was our parliament in exile, there was other exiled associations and communities. Each weighed in to take their part of the whole, part of the living creature that was the general will. The close links between Palestinians inside and those outside the homeland in fact created a homeland itself, this bond which held us together as a people was lucent, so easy for someone like me to see, witness as I was to the crescendo of constant traffic: the phone calls and faxes, the underground networks, the private and public meetings, the political platforms that united all the parties, of children's letters, the appeals, the multiple travel documents, the petitions, the armed resistance in the camps and throughout invasions and sieges, the thousand inventive and creative ways that a people asserts itself, expresses itself, and binds

9   Rousseau adds in a note here 'To be general, a will need not always be unanimous; but every vote must be counted: any formal exclusion destroys generality'. J. J. Rousseau, *Le Contrat Social, Oeuvres Complètes*, Gagnebin and Raymond (eds) (Paris, Pléiade, 1959–1995), vol. iii, p. 369.
10   Ibid.

itself to each other, even whilst floating above the ground full of the intolerable weight of landlessness.

So in order to represent this sovereign will with fairness, and as we were obligated to do, from 1991 to 1993 at the talks in Washington our delegation tried to negotiate for a democratic structure that would represent us — elections for Palestinians outside as well as inside at the same time, offering the Israelis and Americans several models of precedence: Western Sahara, or Namibia, countless examples of how the will of a people that was spread across borders could be united in an even momentary infrastructure, in order that Palestinians could participate in the creation of their own governance, and build basic laws that would be fair. As is known, the implementation of these principles were denied to us. One could even say that the obvious aim was to sever this link between the people, between those inside and those outside, the link which holds us all together. In 1995, elections were held in the West Bank and Gaza only, the European Union pouring millions into democratisation processes, election campaigning, transparency, and all the other means traditionally used in order to try to capture and reflect the general will of a people. Yet all the while leaving out the majority. The majority were silent in the suspension of their sovereignty, although it was understood, witnessed. Also, 'this is not to say that the commands of leaders may not be taken for general wills as long as the sovereign is free to oppose them and does not do so. In such a case the people's consent has to be presumed from universal silence'.[11] They had been informed it was merely a temporary affair, it would become a final status issue, it would be addressed soon.

What happens when a people place their sovereignty in the hands of their leadership, and their leaders' own hands are then tied, and they are lost in a terrible prison, as if trapped in a dark enchantment? When their leaders are to all intents and purposes removed from the body of the majority of their people, and no longer can find themselves virtuously embedded deep within the body politic? The people eventually take their force back, for it is sovereign. Whilst honouring the predicament of their leaders, respecting them and understanding their plight, and their good intentions, their sincere attempts, the relentless forces facing them. For authority is only lent, and only for as long as the leadership can find a

---

11   Ibid., p. 369.

way to represent it: 'sovereignty, since it is nothing less than the exercise of the general will, can never be alienated, and that the Sovereign, who is nothing but a collective being, can only be represented by himself: the power indeed may be transmitted, but not the will'.[12]

Rediscovering the General Will

In the first half of 2000, some few months before the Second Intifada began, a British Commission of Enquiry was established by a group of cross-party members of Parliament, representing the parliamentary Middle East Councils. The aim was to enquire into the situation of the Palestinian refugees. To those initiating the enquiry, the portrayal of the nature of the refugee's predicament had been warped through the long evolution of the Oslo peace process. They had become a 'final status issue', a mere variable amongst the many other intractable issues such as water, or conflated into a line on a map, such as the topic of 'borders'. It appeared their political agency was being removed from them, robbed of them, and they had been reduced in perception to the category of a desperate and unfortunate humanitarian plight, turned into numbers, into statistics. They were no longer a people, with the rights of belonging that accrues to all peoples. They had become, quite simply, a massive problem for the negotiators then attempting to resolve the conflict between the Palestinians and Israel.

The aim of the Commission was to ask them how they saw their legal right to return being implemented, and their views of the homeland. The Commission travelled to Syria, Jordan, Lebanon, the West Bank and Gaza, wherever Palestinian refugees were, and talked to hundreds and hundreds of individuals, representatives of popular committees of the refugee camps and from as wide a spectrum as they could manage. The beauty of the report was in that the bulk of it was oral evidence, verbatim testimony, by those who have been excluded from the majority of narratives of exile of the Palestinians,[13] and these have now been faithfully

---

12 Ibid., p. 368.
13 As Salim Tamari points out in 'Bourgeois Nostalgia and Exilic Narratives', in Robin and Strath (eds), *Homelands: Poetic Power and the Politics of Space* (Brussels: P. I. E., 2003), p. 76: '[n]evertheless the absence of the voice of average people from these private histories and biographies is indeed an astonishing void. It is the task of new

transcribed into both English and Arabic versions of the report.[14] The Commission promised to translate and keep their evidence intact, and not truncate these narratives or take them out of context.[15] These pieces of evidence are not the histories of the dispossession itself (which are often referred to by those who participated in the Commission's work), but more simply the political will of ordinary refugees today who have been excluded from the decision-making process of recent years.

Inside of these oral accounts, these testimonies surrounding their understanding of the right of return, all of the Palestinian identity is there, as well as Palestine itself, encapsulated in the will to simply remain a people. So when I hear or read these aspirations of belonging, I too am at home. When they speak of how they see our will lasting forever, like Muhammad Nusayrat:

> We believe in a comprehensive and just solution which will enable the Palestinian people to regain their stolen rights, so we can contribute to human civilisation as we used to do. I disagree with my colleagues that old Palestinians love and remember Palestine the most. The truth is that the new generation of Palestinians are not weaker but rather stronger than the older generation in their love and desire for Palestine.[16]

When Adnan Shahada speaks today of the manner in which Palestinian fellaheen who are now refugees feel a direct tangible attachment to the land, it is the very same that I heard every day in the camps of Tal al Za'ater, Sabra, Shatila, Rachidiyeh in the Lebanon in the 1970s and 1980s.

---

researchers to provide this voice with the forum and appropriate tools (such as oral histories) so that it can be restored and articulate its own experience'.

14   The Commission's Report contains a preface by Professor Richard Falk, who was part of the three-person United Nations Commission on Human Rights sent to the region during the Intifada in the spring of 2001 (see the UN's human rights report at https://www.un.org/unispal), and was also part of the international legal team in the summer of 1982 (Sean MacBride International Commission of Inquiry into the Israeli Invasion of 1982). Although the report has sections which provide analysis, historical and legal contexts, general themes, experts' evidence, and several key recommendations by the British Commission of Parliamentarians, the bulk of the report (some 250 of its 315 pages) is the submitted oral and written evidence by refugees themselves. *Right to Return: Joint Parliamentary Commission of Inquiry on Palestinian Refugees*, 2nd edn, London, Labour, Conservative, Liberal Democrat, Middle East Councils, March 2001.

15   During the Commission's trip to the region, many refugees and members of NGOs representing refugees' welfare mentioned, in particular, the recent Atkinson Report, which they all felt misrepresented their views.

16   Muhammad Nusayrat, from Nusayrat, Jericho, *Right to Return*, p. 112.

For some of you, or for European logic in general, it is difficult to understand why some people have this strong attachment to a certain place. In Western culture, people move from one country to another, where they settle down and live their life. However, the homeland has a great significance for us. It means belonging, self-esteem and history for the generations who live in that part of the earth... I would like to remind you that the right of return is an essential human value and not only a Palestinian political issue. It is also the issue of belonging. Thank you.[17]

When I hear Amal Jado say that the refugee camp will never be tolerable, that it is unbearable, this is also my feeling. I do not live in a camp, but whilst other Palestinians still live in them, it is exactly as if I do as well. She said:

I am a refugee from Aida refugee camp, a member of the local committee there. I just want to reinforce the right of return for women.... I was raised in the refugee camp. The camp has never been my home and it never will be. I will never accept it as my home. It is a fact that I want to reinforce here. My home is the homeland that I have never seen...[18]

Ziyad Sarafandi sees the will of the Palestinian struggle for a state as what sustains him in his life, as do I:

There was an international plan to transform the Palestinian people into a nation of refugees... we resisted the powers that sought to destroy our identity. This was done with a great deal of sacrifice, whether through the fierce fighting in Jordan and Lebanon, or in Palestine through the Intifada. It was all done to confirm that we are a people who have rights that we adhere to. We resist.[19]

I see the general will as a living body, and as such, Palestine means something to us, just as we mean something to it. Palestine itself has created something inside of me, exactly as Amni Jibril could see its creation inside her students in the refugee camps of Lebanon: 'I am also a teacher. I hear from my children how Palestine is in their hearts and they ask many questions about their villages. It is something Palestine has created in them.'[20]

---

17   Adnan Shahada, from Yasur, *Right to Return*, p. 34.
18   Amal Jado, originally from Al-Maliha (Jerusalem), *Right to Return*, p. 84.
19   Ziyad Sarafandi, originally from Yibna, *Right to Return*, p. 112.
20   Amnah Jibril, originally from Haifa, *Right to Return*, p. 276.

My idea of return to Palestine is not one of violence and destruction, or exclusion of the other in order to be myself. My vision is just exactly like the one Haifa Jamal spoke of when she said: 'We will not repeat the mistake of the Israelis and make our existence in our land dependent upon the non-existence of the people who are already living here. Israelis thought that their existence on the soil of Palestine meant the non-existence of the other. We do not consider this so. We do not wish to tell them to leave'.[21] I see the possibilities just exactly as someone who has been living every day of his life in a shelter in a camp for years, as Ibrahim Abu Hashash does, 'we do not mind to live with our Jewish neighbours, side by side. We were asked: if there was a settlement which was built on a Palestinian village, what would you like to do with it? The answer is simple, we will live side by side with the Israelis'.[22] Like Ahmad Salah in Lebanon, it gives me such a strange feeling not to be able to get close to it still, after all this time, and yet it is now so near. He explained:

> An older person came from Palestine to the border and said to me, 'I am your uncle'. We signalled to each other across the border. But I had a very strange feeling because I couldn't get close to him, to embrace him. We couldn't get close, there was wire and soldiers between us. It is also the same when you see your homeland and you can't reach it, because they put barbed wire in front of you.[23]

My identity is drawn from all these notions, and through the Commission's report one can see they exist as unambiguously today as they did in 1988. But more importantly, the right of return represents a collective will, the force and power of a people, even more the heart of my identity and home, its constant presence since the filaments that attach it through time and space are larger and more intimate still than the sense of a particular place. As Rousseau declared in his opening of the *Discourse on Origins of Inequality*, the homeland he prefers is the one where 'love of one's country meant a love of its fellow-citizens rather than a love for the land'.[24]

---

21   Haifa Jamal, originally from Shafa Amr (Haifa) *Right to Return*, p. 21.
22   Ismail Abu Hashash, originally from Iraq el-Manshiya, *Right to Return*, p. 44.
23   Ahmad Salah, originally from Nahaf (Acre), *Right to Return*, p. 267.
24   J. J. Rousseau, *Oeuvres Complètes*, p. 112.

Conclusion

In one of the recommendations of the Commission of Enquiry's report, it notes that the European Union has spent a good deal of time, energy, and money on mechanisms of the general will (elections and so forth) in the West Bank and Gaza in the mid-1990s as part of the Oslo peace process. It therefore recommends that they should now go on to help recreate various mechanisms of the general will for all the Palestinians who are outside, in exile, in refugee camps, from Latin America to Amman, so they can restore the associational life that has been destroyed by generations of war.[25] These structures would not be in order to show who represents them — everyone knows their representative is the PLO, all refugees and exiles say it without question or hesitation. The mechanisms are, rather, to help the PLO to represent them properly, to give them the same ability that all other governments have, which is to feel the people's will around them, so that they can understand it, and so that they can serve it. Nor do the refugees want surveys or opinion polls concerning these rights.[26] The only way democracy works is through embodying the living relationship between a people and their government, and making sure that the organic and associational structures that let people participate, make their will known. When these links are severed, as has happened through war, it becomes much more difficult and dangerous for the political will of a people to be seen. But the will itself has not disappeared, as this recent British Parliamentary Report, for example, has shown. And Palestinians have always found a way to make their will known, generation after generation, constant, manifold, ever present. I have used Rousseau's Social Contract throughout this essay in order to illustrate a reading of the general will that seems to me illustrated in the endeavours of the Palestinian people for a state and for the right to return, and because it captures the understanding I have of my own identity, my own sense

---

25 *Right to Return*, pp. 49–57.

26 As Amna Ghanayam, of the Shu'fat Women's Centre said 'Holding a referendum about this right [of return] is an insult to the Palestinian people because it questions their loyalty to their homeland. Every Palestinian dreams of return. I have been asked "Return or Jerusalem?" This question, as far as I am concerned is the same as "which one of your eyes do you want to knock out, the left or the right?"' Amnah Ghanayem, originally from Tal al Rish (Jaffa), *Right to Return*, p. 83.

of homeland. Indeed I use it because of Rousseau's sensitive and (it seems to me) perfect understanding of the general will, as well as for his elegant portrayal of its workings and mechanisms. I conclude this essay on my understanding of identity, however, with another author's definition, that of the philosopher Denis Diderot, who was Rousseau's contemporary. It captures the way of the homeland that I have had the good fortune to grow up in.

> The general will is, in each individual, a pure act of the understanding, which reasons in the silence of the passions about what a man can demand of his fellow-man and about what his fellow-man has the right to demand of him.[27]

---

27 Denis Diderot, 'Le Droit Naturel', in *Encyclopédie ou Dictionnaire Raisonné des Sciences, des Arts et des Metiers* (Paris: Imprimerie Nationale, 1950), vol. i, p. 58. See also, in English, John Mason and Robert Wokler (eds), Denis Diderot, *Political Writings* (Cambridge: Cambridge University Press, 1992), pp. 20–21. This same formulation was actually used by Rousseau to describe the General Will in the first draft of the *Social Contract*, known as the Geneva Manuscript.

Fig. 9 Tom Hurndall, Palestinian children in shelled house in Rafah, April 2003.

7. Dismantling the Image of the Palestinian Homosexual: Exploring the Role of Alqaws[1]

Wala AlQaisiya, Ghaith Hilal and Haneen Maikey

The Zionist colonisation of Palestine holds at its premise racial, sexual, and gendered discourses through which colonial power is exercised. It is through the production and creation of certain types of knowledge and specific domains of truth that the colonial regime perpetuates and reinforces its mechanisms and modes of governments on the colonisers, making them internalise a certain conduct. This chapter seeks to understand the means through which the Zionist colonial regime influences the production of specific objects of knowledge: sexuality and the image of the homosexual in Palestine. It wants to pinpoint the ways through which its power hinges on the bodies and desires of the colonised and, specifically, how the image of homosexuals came to be perceived and understood in determined ways within the Palestinian context and throughout its recent history.

It is from the unfolding presentation of the points of intersection between a determined structure of colonial power and its knowledges of sexuality that the role of indigenous feminist/queer organising becomes fundamental. As Palestinian activists and academics that are

---

1   A version of this chapter first appeared in Bakshi, S., Jivraj, S. and Posocco, S. (eds), *Decolonizing Sexualities: Transnational Perspectives, Critical Interventions* (Oxford: Counterpress, 2016), pp. 125–40.

    https://doi.org/10.11647/OBP.XXX.08

committed to engaged analyses and praxis towards decolonising gender and sexuality in our communities, we see that highlighting the work of *alQaws for Gender and Sexual Diversity* and its relevance to the Palestinian context and struggle is a necessary task, being an open feminist queer space that aspires to 'disrupt sexual and gender based oppression and challenge regulation, whether patriarchal, capitalist or colonial of our sexualities and bodies'.[2] AlQaws unveils how the decolonisation of a certain type of knowledge on sexuality and its deriving modes of conduct is what can lay the foundation for a radical disruption of the colonial Zionist structure.

The first part of this chapter investigates the recent historical determination of power and knowledge that shaped the image of the Palestinian homosexual, enabling the formulation of two specific portraits of the Palestinian queer: the collaborator and the *Israelised*, leading to the image of the Westernised agent. In a constant effort to interrogate and challenge those structures of power that allowed their promulgation, the second part draws on how Pinkwashing was specifically adopted as a Zionist colonial tactic through which the image of the Palestinian victim queer with its racial and normalising logic around meanings of sexuality and homosexuality came to be enabled and constructed. This is followed with an analysis of alQaws's work and the relevance of their local strategies to challenge such narratives and essentially dismantle the image that has been ascribed to the Palestinian homosexual.

The Image of the Homosexual: Major Historical Events

From our own personal experiences and from working in the field, we know that the image of the homosexual in the Palestinian context can be summed up by the 'Other'. As people living under a settler-colonial regime, this Other came to be constructed in relation to the coloniser and the Western values it bears and represents. Thus the image of the Palestinian homosexual at its worst links to that of the collaborator, a person who is involved in directly giving out information to the coloniser and, at its best, relates to an *Israelised* person who has adopted Israeli ways of living. This also relates to the image people have of the

---

2   http://www.alQaws.org/about-us.

Westernised agent, or those infamously described as complicit in the project of 'transforming their cultures into copies of Euro-America'.[3] In order to understand the means by which this image came to the fore in Palestinian society, one has to trace discourses and events in search of what Foucault identifies as 'instances of discursive production ... of the production of power [and] the propagation of knowledge, which makes possible 'a history of the present'. (quoted in Sullivan, 2003, 1). The following focuses on events starting from the First Intifada, through Oslo, continuing to the current political situation where intersections between politics and sexuality come to the fore in the Palestinian context. This, in turn, explains the consolidation of the current image of the Palestinian homosexual as rooted in the collaborator and/or Israeli and Westernised agent image that alQaws works on dismantling.

As the eruption of the Palestinian First Intifada (1987–1993) came to signify the epitome of a national struggle against the fist of the Zionist colonial regime, it also marked a historical moment for the consolidation of Palestinian nationalist agency, with its gendered and ultimately heterosexual implications. Joseph Massad (1995) traces the 'conceiving of the masculine' in Palestinian nationalist discourses which come to echo the masculinist heteronormative seeds found earlier in European and even Zionist national projects. Thus, the Intifada rose to depict the long awaited 'Palestinian wedding' as the *communiqués* of the Unified National Leadership of the Uprising (UNLU) came to describe it; manifesting the 'apogee of heterosexual love' where 'the heterosexual reproduction of the family is at the centre of the nationalist project' (Massad, 1995, 477). Whilst the Intifada was at the peak of a national project which also sought to define Palestinianness against any colonial contamination, as Massad (1995) describes it, Israel was doing its best to intensify tactics aiming to foster its ideological foundation that renders natives' bodies and land 'inherently rapable and invadable' (Smith, 2008, 312).

---

3   With reference to Joseph Massad's critique of those identified as 'the complicit' gay internationalist Arabs, who are normalising and imposing Western gay identities that are not relevant to the Arab context, see F. Ewanje Epee and S. Maqliani-Belkacem (2013), 'The Empire of Sexuality: An Interview with Joseph Massad', *Jadaliyya*, http://www.jadaliyya.com/pages/index/10461/the-empire-of-sexuality_an-interview-with-joseph-m.

For Israel, the Intifada was an underground movement, with elements of unpredictability and spontaneity, which made it very difficult to contain by Israeli intelligence services. This is where Israel used tactics of infiltrating Palestinian factions in order to break their work through coercing Palestinian individuals into collaboration. This tactic was implemented through the usage of threats and blackmail against the *docile* bodies it targeted, through control and observation, and produced as mediums for the inscription of its power. Homosexuality, pre-marital sex as well as drugs and/or alcohol use, amongst other activities that were socially frowned upon in Palestinian society, were utilised to coerce Palestinians into working with Israeli authority if they did not wish to face the consequences of being publicly exposed. This took place at the time when the image of the homosexual as a collaborator as well as *Israelised* came to be enforced. The reaction of Palestinian factions, which defined these immoral behaviours as a threat that needed to be uprooted from political activism, was short-sighted and legitimised further the blackmail of Palestinians by the Israeli intelligence forces. Moreover, these same tactics were later used by different Palestinian factions and armed groups to discipline non-conforming behaviours, gender expressions, and those who were suspected to be homosexual during the anarchy of the late 1990s to early 2000s.

Such strategies of "cleansing" society, echoing the Foucauldian understanding of power in its *sanitising* form, were part of the bigger power paradigm that the signing of the Oslo Accords, the new era of so-called economic peace, between Israel and the PLO brought to the fore. The establishment of the Palestinian Authority (PA) as a governing body, which came as a means of 'resecuring the authoritative leadership of the Diaspora-based elite' (Parsons, 2005), helped to consolidate long-enshrined ideals of the nationalist agent that was not only masculine but also 'bourgeois in-the-making' (Massad, 1995, 479). The creation of a Palestinian bureaucratic elite within a PA's authoritarian and neo-patrimonial regime was being encouraged and sustained — this time — by the international community (Le More, 2008, 6). Their funding for the new entity continued so long as it inflicted on the Palestinians the penalties required for noncompliance with the new sphere of securitisation and diplomacy through which Israel continued to retain its control (Le More, 2008, 6). As internal volatility grew in the late 1990s due to Israel's expansionist regime and intensified closure policies, the same donor community that used to 'turn a blind eye to reports of mismanagement corruption and human rights abuses' started proposing changes in the PA institutions (Le More, 2008, 6). Two years after the eruption of the Second Intifada in 2000, a marker of PA's inability to guarantee Israel's security, proposals to reform PA institutions solidified and became more attuned towards a new leadership that could 'deter terror' following the agenda of good governance and human rights. Such ideals came forth within a project of modernity whose ontological foundations continue to rely on the construction of its oriental Other who is always *failing*. One could here be reminded of Žižek's useful understanding of ideology through Lacan that 'every perception of a lack or a surplus' always involves a disavowed relation of domination (Žižek, 1995, 11). In this case, the 'not enough of this too much of that' is simply another colonial tool under the disguise of 'not enough of democracy, too much of religion', 'not enough of modernity, too much homophobia', etc.

From here, one comes to understand the setting of the criteria for LGBT rights in accordance with the *frame* of 'sexually progressive' countries that define a universal model to follow (Butler, 2010, 110). Massad (2007, 161) draws on US discourse on human rights which engendered the proliferation of the Gay International agenda and framework where 'western male white-dominated organizations' advocate for rights of 'gays and lesbians all over the world'. Such universalisation of LGBT rights which binds LGBT movements elsewhere to forms of organising and gains made in the Stonewall era is what Jasbir Puar draws on in her definition of homonationalism, where LGBTQ people all over the world 'experience, practice and are motivated by the same desires and their politics are grounded in an understanding that ties the directionality of their love and desire to stable identity from which to make political claims' (Mikdashi, 2011). With Israeli LGBT people following the same trajectory, Israel's 'gay decade' came forth following the decriminalisation of sodomy in 1988 (Gross, 2001). This in turn triggered an interest in the LGBT legal status under the PA whereby the 'colonizer's standards and achievements became the yardstick by which the colonized were measured and to which they had to conform' (Maikey, 2012), ignoring the fact that the same 'anti-sodomy' laws were removed from the Jordanian penal code, which the PA inherited in 1957. Such Western interests and findings towards the status of gay rights in Palestine after Oslo enforced the image of the Palestinian homosexual as a Western agent.

Besides the imperial and coloniser standards that were shaping the discourse around nation building and gay rights, another, no less worrying discourse began to arise among Palestine solidarity activists who took the South African model of endorsement of constitutional protection in 1996, following the dismantlement of the apartheid regime, as the bar by which other nationals were to be judged. These examples and dynamics of the International and its homogenising force towards the same trajectory of development within the *reductive frame* of liberal discourses of rights ignores and glosses over native experiences of sexual politics. This includes the dynamics that shaped Palestinian LGBT and other feminist groups before and after the Second Intifada who started to formulate a separate agenda from their Israeli partners. Palestinian queer activists, who later established alQaws, stopped going to the Israeli Jewish organization *Jerusalem Open House* as their identification with the Palestinian liberation struggle was reinforced during the Second Intifada and the brutal killings of Palestinian demonstrators inside Israel. These events came to confirm once again the genocidal premise of the settler-colonial regime which traps the natives within the realm of the *homo sacer*;[4] one that leaves us with the critical question regarding the relevance of human rights for those who are already ceaselessly and systematically reduced by the settler-colonial regime to the realm and reality of no rights.

Gaza came to represent such a reality following the Palestinian political disintegration after the 2006 elections leading to donors' imposed sanctions in disapproval of Hamas and finally Israel's imposed siege on the strip since 2007. That was also the year when alQaws officially separated from the *Jerusalem Open House* as Palestinian queer consciousness was emerging in relation to the political reality in which it was embedded. The Israeli aggression on Gaza in 2009 further solidified a more radical political discourse amongst Palestinian queers in alQaws. It also mapped a further separation from Israeli LGBT

---

4   In reference to those excluded from the political community and reduced to 'bare life', see Žižek (2005).

politics, which were committed to emblems of Israeliness, including service in the army, through which their entry into Israeli consensus was guaranteed (Walzer, 2000, 235). Following the shootings at Bar-Noar in 2009 (the attack in a gay bar in Tel Aviv which led to the killings of two people), some Palestinian queers were banned from expressing their solidarity in fear of them 'talking politics'. Israeli right-wing politicians, who had praised the killings of Gazans a few months earlier, proclaimed a 'Do Not Kill' message to the rhythm of the Israeli national anthem at the vigil; a song celebrating the exclusively Jewish nature of the 'land of Zion'. This dynamic further exposed Israeli LGBT politics as an expression of queer modernity — progressive and gay-loving — that relies at its essence on and works to perpetuate and *naturalise* the settler-colonial regime and its logic of native exclusion and elimination (Morgenson, 2011, 16).

The exclusionary essence of the settler-colonial regime comes within a global power dynamic and the violence enshrined in neoliberalism and its ideological cognates, securitisation, the necessity to protect from the terrorist Muslim Other, and hetero-/homo-normativisation. Such was the need in 2005, following the Second Intifada and the donors' need to 'reform' Palestinian security section (Dana, 2014), to propagate 'the new Palestinian man' with millions of US dollars which, according to its pundits, enabled the structural analytic of a 'gender blurring' agenda in the West Bank where women, too, can join the mission of fighting 'terrorism'. (Daraghmeh and Laub, 2014). This is the terrorism that Gaza has now come to represent due to its containment of the Muslim/monster Other whose elimination is encouraged and called upon in Israeli public discourse. Thus, the construction of Gaza comes as the homophobic space whilst the West Bank or Ramallah in particular, with its US-trained security guards, is becoming perceived as the more open, 'gay friendly' space (Chang, 2016). This issue was raised in alQaws's recent interactions with some international donors, who expressed interest in knowing more about what they called it 'the new scene of gay friendly cafés in Ramallah', and hinting that they had heard Ramallah was becoming similar to the gay haven of Tel Aviv. In doing so, the colonial regime comes to sustain itself through a logic of *divide et impera* (divide and rule) by creating more categories, divisions, and barriers that ought to be *internalised* in order to act as if the colonial regime is non-existent. Hence, what remains is the acting out of these fantasies (i.e., liberal Ramallah/ Backward Gaza) where an image of Europe could be conceived whilst disavowing the failure to which these fantasies are bound. In fact, these fantasies are part and parcel of a larger hierarchising structure that is embedded in the image of the Palestinian homosexual and the extent of homophobia/backward space to which it is relegated. Thus, those coming from the 1948 territories (Palestinians living in Israel) come first, followed by those in liberal Ramallah, who are then followed by the rest of the West Bank, and finally, at the bottom of the ladder, comes Gaza. Pinkwashing as a colonial tactic contributed to the consolidation of such an image and its hierarchising effect.

The Pinkwashing Logic

When one approaches the dynamics inherent to the image of the homosexual in Palestine, it is impossible to ignore the link between Zionism and Pinkwashing. It is necessary to shed light on how Zionist politics influence both the analysis and the campaign of Pinkwashing. This campaign is one that uses ostensibly 'progressive' policies around gay tolerance to hide and distract from practices of colonialism. In this framing, we understand Pinkwashing as 'a tactic of Zionism and an influential discourse of sexuality that has emerged within it' (Schotten and Maikey, 2012). Therefore, anti-Pinkwashing works as an analysis and practice that 'continues to uncover and makes visible the racial, ethnic, and sexual violence that informs Zionist ideology' (Schotten and Maikey, 2012). In order to further expose the connection between Pinkwashing and Zionism, it is crucial to deconstruct the main logics and notions behind this campaign that was relentlessly marketed as a 'Gay Rights Campaign'. To phrase it slightly differently, alQaws is interested in exploring what makes this Pinkwashing project a successful campaign that is appealing to queer people around the world, or what makes Zionism appealing to queers around the world.

Firstly, Pinkwashing is an ontologically racist and colonial project that does not simply emphasise how Israel is a fun, fabulous, open, modern — thus democratic and liberal — state, but is mainly based on dehumanising Palestinians, Arabs and Muslims by presenting them as homophobic, backward, and barbaric. In the Pinkwashing narrative, homophobia and intolerance toward non-conforming sexual and gender expressions, identities, and behaviours, is a disease rooted in society while tolerance is inherent to Israel as a liberal modern project. Such is the orientalist logic where the other is reduced to a set of realities and values that fit the opposite side of the binary (progressive/backward). It is a familiar Zionist tactic that reframes the relationship between Israel and Palestine from "coloniser-colonised" to one that distinguishes between those who are "modern and open", and those who are presented as "backward and homophobic". Thus, it simplifies and anaesthetises the fundamental violence on the basis of which colonialism thrives.

Secondly, Pinkwashing's promotion of a modern/backward binary shows how it is premised on a notion of progress where the other is always-already dehumanised in the definition of the "modern and progressive" self. But, Pinkwashing is also framed in a way that speaks to those who have assimilated and internalised Islamophobic, racist, and anti-Arab messages into their vision of "progressiveness" and "modernity" as it is reflected in the liberal white gay project in the last two decades. In this sense, engaging with Pinkwashing is not only promoting a racist narrative about Palestinians, but more disturbingly its popularity of Pinkwashing among gay groups may lead us to assume that these notions (i.e., racism and Islamophobia) exist in our own communities. In our opinion, this says more about the political choices of queer communities around the globe, than about the clear colonial interest reflected in Pinkwashing, and maybe suggests an intersectional understanding of countering this in our communities.

Thirdly, Pinkwashing follows a gay rights approach which isolates some queer identities from others and conceals the structural inequalities that make certain (Jewish, Israeli) bodies and identities "acceptable" and others (Palestinian, Arab) not. In other words, Pinkwashing is based on Western gay organising frameworks and notions and in this sense, it is creating a common language and a common cause with other gay (middle-class, white) individuals and communities. Pinkwashing relies heavily on the logic of "gay rights" as it is commonly understood and practiced by these communities — a single-issue politics based on one's sexual identity to the exclusion of other interconnected injustices based on race, ethnicity, class, gender, and other difference. The reliance on the gay rights frame of analysis allows Israel to promote and publicise itself as gay-friendly, concealing its settler-colonial premise which is based on intense forms of sexual regulation that are both gendered and racialised.[5]

Israeli LGBT Groups "Saving" Palestinian Queers

Since its inception in 2005, the "Re-branding Israel" campaign — with its focus on gay rights — included partnerships with LGBT Israeli groups, who were and still are directly complicit with this new state-funded project.[29] Together with government-led bodies, Israeli LGBT groups promote gay tourism to Tel Aviv, advocate for Israel as the world LGBT ambassador, and present the IDF as a tolerant army for gay Israelis ('serving with pride'). Thus, the Pinkwashing campaign is seen and considered by Israeli LGBT leaders and groups as the ultimate sign of state recognition, and we, in alQaws, continue to argue that Pinkwashing could not thrive without this unconditional support, and crucial role of the Israeli LGBT community.

Besides their direct involvement in promoting Pinkwashing, both globally and locally, LGBT Israeli leaders and groups are actively part of the production of the racist discourse about Palestinians in general, and LGBT Palestinians in particular. The main aspects of this discourse are: 1) the need to save Palestinian LGBTQs from their own homophobic families and society; 2) the exclusion of the broader context of settler colonialism vis-à-vis LGBT issues; 3) the denial of agency: erasure of the Palestinian queer movement (IGY, https://igy.org.il/en/).

Once again, it is possible to trace how Israeli Pinkwashing ideology functions through the presentation of Palestinian society as either "too homophobic" or "not active enough", echoing Žižek's (1995, 11) famous understanding of 'too much of this', 'not enough of that'. Pinkwashing also takes the form of the Israeli government's initiatives to promote gay tourism. This programme stems directly from Israeli homonationalism

---

5   This manifests in a few emblematic examples, such as the 2003 Citizenship and Entry Emergency Law that bars Palestinians married to Israelis from becoming citizens, ultra-Orthodox Jewish campaigns for gender segregation in public spaces, and the denial of Jewish-Jewish marriages inside Israel unless the couple is "converted" according to Orthodox principles.

and LGBT Israelis' commitment to define and promote Israel in relation to its gay parties and beaches and its locals who are welcoming foreigners in (e.g., *GAY TLV Guide*, http://www.gaytlvguide.com/). Such acts of welcoming others in are another means of naturalising the settler-colonial regime through Israeli queer desires and bodies expressing *ownership* of and locality to indigenous land and hence entitlement to *invite* tourists in. These ideals of queer tourism are also a significant source of income for Israel. In this case, Pinkwashing represents the underlying logic of neoliberalism in the guise of "democracy" and "gay rights".[6] It allows the generation of economic profit through such universal ideals of "gay tourism", thus reproducing the colonial system in its abuse of indigenous resources.

The Impact of Pinkwashing on Palestinian Queers: Internalising the Image

Challenging the premise of Pinkwashing entails an exploration of its impact on and implications for LGBT Palestinians. AlQaws identifies two main notions that are assimilated by Palestinian LGBT individuals and communities due to the Pinkwashing campaign.

Firstly, *the coloniser standards and fantasies* about gay rights, homophobia, and racism are internalised in Palestinian LGBTQ communities. As a form of colonisation, Pinkwashing promotes the false idea that the Palestinian LGBTQ individuals and communities have no agency or place inside their own societies. This creates a detrimental and toxic colonial relationship where the colonised comes to perceive the colonisers' presence as necessary for providing that which fulfils our fantasies.

Secondly, the main notions that describe the personal lives and experiences of LGBT Palestinians are *victimhood and pain*. In the attempt to strengthen Pinkwashing and dehumanise Palestinians, Palestinian

6   The Palestinian Campaign for the Academic and Cultural Boycott of Israel (PACBI) has defined normalisation specifically in a Palestinian and Arab context 'as the participation in any project, initiative or activity, in Palestine or internationally, that aims (implicitly or explicitly) to bring together Palestinians (and/or Arabs) and Israelis (people or institutions) without placing as its goal resistance to and exposure of the Israeli occupation and all forms of discrimination and oppression against the Palestinian people.' See *PACBI*, https://bdsmovement.net/pacbi.

queer bodies, personal stories, challenges, and pain have been used constantly as "proof" of our society's "not enough progress". In this regard, the main accomplishment is to make queer Palestinians victims of their own families and communities, triggering in them a desire or a dream to flee homophobic Palestine and reach the coloniser's sandy beaches. According to this logic, the society and families of Palestinian queers are the main cause of their problems, and their existences as queers relies on their ability to hate their own support system. This is yet another way of isolating sexual and gender violence from the broader context of colonised Palestine. As their problems are reduced to sexual orientations, LGBT Palestinians are left with the option of being victims and/or hating their families; hence, their only solution is to look towards the colonisers for safety. This in turn creates the victim-saviour dynamic which in recent years has been at the centre of representations of the relationship between Palestinians and Israeli queers. This saviour/victim dynamic glosses over the fact that Palestinians, whether queer or not, cannot cross over to reach what is presumed to be their "safe-haven Israel". This is not only due to the concrete presence of the barriers, including the apartheid wall, that Israel installs to hinder Palestinian daily mobility but also effectively due to the Israeli legal system which is, designed to deny Palestinians' sheer existence. Furthermore, it is fundamental to stress that fetishising Palestinian queer bodies and pain means creating this hierarchy between different bodies in Palestine.

On the one hand, there are the bodies that Israelis do not care to kill and erase — as it happens in Gaza — and there are those bodies, the queer bodies, which should be saved. The only Palestinian who is worth saving, therefore, is the one that falls within exotic Israeli fantasies about who the Palestinian queer is.

Dismantling the Image

The dominant social and political construction of the image of the Palestinian homosexual is directly impacted by the continuous exploitation of Palestinian queers' bodies and sexualities, to fulfil the goals of the coloniser (i.e. blackmailing queers to become collaborators, the suggestion that queer Palestinians are victims waiting for an Israeli saviour, promoting a false narrative about Palestinian society's homophobia, etc.). Furthermore, in recent years, foreign governments and some gay international organisations have started to express clear interest in meetings or encounters with alQaws activists as a way to challenge the PA and/or civil society organisations to "respect" gay rights. This new dynamic, which is affected by the growing role of foreign governments and funding in Palestine, is further enforcing the notion of homosexuality as a Western issue in the eyes of Palestinian society. Furthermore, this dynamic entails a disturbing subtext that any "progress" in making Palestine more "tolerant" to gay rights and especially amongst authorities, is a sign that the project of building the Palestinian state fits the ultimate modernity standards of "gay tolerance". More concretely, by moving forward with this project, foreign governments will not only gain greater legitimacy through their intervention in the state-building process in Palestine, but will also frame the PA and Palestine as a new player in the modern world. It goes without saying that this dynamic is taking place in a vacuum, as if Palestine is not colonised. AlQaws saw a crucial challenge to address and disrupt this discourse, by developing a locally informed and holistic analysis regarding sexuality and homosexuality in Palestine. Sexual and bodily freedom cannot be separated from the fight against Israeli colonialism. Thus comes the need for a movement that understands and engages with its political reality.

However, there is a strong tendency within Palestinian society to prioritise struggles and a hierarchy of liberation; putting the Palestinian national struggle at the top of the list while other struggles (e.g. women's rights, gender and sexuality rights, and minority rights) come last. Hence, besides being seen as Israelising collaborators or Westernising intruders, the mere fact of talking of the intersectionality or hierarchy of struggles is seen as a diversion from the main cause, or as another force to fragment an already fragmented society. Therefore, the goal of dismantling this image, within Palestinian society and more importantly within LGBTQ communities, will remain a complex political project. AlQaws's leadership has integrated this project and analysis in their work by addressing four different layers: we explore these four layers in the following sections of the chapter.

Decolonising Palestinian Identity within the Palestinian Queer Community

AlQaws works with a large group of Palestinian queers across historical Palestine to enlarge our base of grassroots political activists through different platforms and groups. In these groups, civil society organisations, student groups, and LGBTQ groups, alQaws works on building (from our own experiences) intersectional analyses of the powers of oppression at hand, from colonialism to patriarchy and capitalism. AlQaws concentrates on challenging the Pinkwashing discourse that many Palestinian queers have internalised, by transforming our image of ourselves from one of victimhood in our homophobic societies, and distance from our families and communities, to one of an active battle for justice aimed at rebuilding these burnt bridges, and shaping the society in which we desire to live. For instance, in alQaws youth groups, we work collectively on understanding the links between sexual oppression and colonialism, and how our bodies, desires and sexualities have been used by Israel. Furthermore, in these groups we are committed to exploring both how homophobia and sexual oppression are constructed in Palestinian society, as well as to relating to the strategies of resilience used by individuals and groups to express their sexualities in such a complex context.

Imagining a Decolonised Palestine

Decolonising our sexualities means directly resisting the policies of fragmentation and division of Palestinians, as the main colonial/Zionist strategies used systematically since 1948. The main goal of this strategy is to continue to divide and rule Palestinians into sub-social religious groups: Christians, Druze, Muslims, Bedouin, Palestinians of Jerusalem, Arab Israelis, West Bankers, Gazans, etc. Through this, Israel aims to prove that Palestinians did not exist before 1948, and reifies the old Zionist logic of "a land without a people for a people without a land", for if there are people on this land, they are nothing but "grazing nomads" who will always fail to have a sense of collective identity and history.

Being one of the few groups working on both sides of the 'Green Line' that divides Israel from the 'OPTs',[7] alQaws was always aware of how much these divisions were reproduced in LGBTQ spaces, too often creating a specific hierarchy of power relations that is familiar to wider society. Commitment to building LGBTQ communities across Palestine means that a crucial aspect of queer organising should be tackling this issue in a deep and constant way. In alQaws's spaces, activists from different parts of Palestine, who never met before, were meeting and working together for the first time. National meetings of alQaws, which take place in the West Bank, are sometimes the first opportunity for queers from Ramallah and Haifa to meet, offering a space in which their internalised attitudes about each other may be challenged and deconstructed. It is not a one-off task, but an ongoing process that we address and challenge through our national strategies and local leadership initiatives. While we address these differences in our local work, this approach offers a glimpse to the undivided and decolonised Palestinian society that our work contributes to achieving. Holding this approach and implementing it through various levels of our organisation challenges the very existence of Zionism.

Refusal to Normalise with Israeli LGBTQ Groups

Based on alQaws's experience, which started as part of an Israeli Zionist organisation and the understanding of it as part of a broader colonial experience, alQaws refuses, as a principle, to work with any group, including Israeli LGBT groups and other civil society organisations and groups, that do not have a clear political stance that confronts and challenges Israeli settler colonialism, Zionism, and Jewish supremacy. AlQaws's community will not engage in any action, project, or partnership that normalises the Zionist colonial entity and the

---

7   Besides the fragmentation policies, it is important to mention how the separation of Palestinians is also achieved through ninety-nine fixed checkpoints (fifty-nine internal checkpoints and forty inspection points before entering Israel); more than 500 physical obstructions (iron gates, concrete blocks, and more) blocking access roads to main traffic arteries in the West Bank; sixty-five kilometres of closed roads inside the West Bank open to Israelis only; and the 430 miles of apartheid wall.

colonised-coloniser relationship as disguised by an agenda for "social justice" and "gay rights".[8]

Challenging the Hegemony of Western LGBT Organising

The decolonisation of sexualities within alQaws and the queer Palestinian movement cannot happen without addressing the global politics related to gay rights. AlQaws works on building alliances with activists, groups and civil society organisations who are committed to sexual and gender diversity. In doing so, it shifts the attention from the negative image associated with homosexuality and focuses instead on a wider understanding of sexuality and gender. This creates a movement open to all, and not only LGBTQ-identifying people, focusing on feminist/queer analysis as a lens through which to understand the links between the different oppressions we face rather than trapping ourselves in single-identity, a-political activism that fails to confront the root causes of oppression.

Despite its structural limitations, alQaws's work resists the hegemony of LGBTQ Western organising approaches and frameworks, and questions its relevance to different Global South-based queer groups. During the last decade, alQaws published different articles and texts deconstructing the four notions of coming out, homophobia, pride, and visibility (Maikey and Shamali, 2016). It showed how locally-informed strategies are possible, more inspiring and, most importantly, more relevant to our context. Some of the questions that helped alQaws activists in this process were: how can we frame our struggle as against homophobia when we do not publicly discuss sexuality? Are pride parades the ultimate celebration of freedom and visibility in a context where millions of Palestinians have no access to water, health care,

---

8   The Palestinian Campaign for the Academic and Cultural Boycott of Israel (PACBI) has defined normalisation specifically in a Palestinian and Arab context "as the participation in any project, initiative or activity, in Palestine or internationally, that aims (implicitly or explicitly) to bring together Palestinians (and/or Arabs) and Israelis (people or institutions) without placing as its goal resistance to and exposure of the Israeli occupation and all forms of discrimination and oppression against the Palestinian people". See *PACBI*, https://bdsmovement.net/pacbi.

mobility, work, etc.? How can individual visibility be understood in a family-based society? Is coming out, as understood and practiced in the West, a crucial step for healthy and open life? What are the means of a healthy and open life for LGBTQ people whose bodies, minds and reality is colonised?

Conclusion

Once sexuality and the image of the Palestinian queer are contextualised properly, unfolding the connections and intersections with the Zionist colonial regime, contrary to what most Western LGTBQ groups propose, sexuality comes to be understood not as an isolated component, or a single issue, of society. Rather, this manoeuvre of unveiling the fantasies that are projected on to the other, which combines academic and activist work in a constant dialogical relationship, shows how discourses of sexuality are deeply embedded in a structure of power whose ultimate goal is the oppression, if not the total elimination, of the other. Therefore, starting from this premise, alQaws tries to face and dismantle those racial sexual and gendered discourses that the Zionist colonial regime generates in order to enforce a process of subjugation of Palestinians. It is for this reason that alQaws believes in the need to engage in an open and honest discussion around the domains of *truths* that sexuality in general, and the image of the Palestinian homosexual in particular, are invested in and aim to propagate. If oppression is to be fought and a more just order of society is to emerge, the relationship with our bodies and how power hinges on them needs to be challenged in a radical, fundamental manner.

Bibliography

Butler, J., *Frames of War* (New York: Verso, 2010).

Chang, A., 'Exploring Gay Palestine', *Passport*, 2016, http://www.passportmagazine.com/exploring-gay-palestine/.

Dana, T., 'The Beginning of the End of Palestinian Security Coordination with Israel?' *Jadaliyaa*, 2014, http://www.jadaliyya.com/pages/index/18379/the-beginning-of-the-end-of-palestinian-security-council.

Daraghmeh, M. and Laub, K., 'Palestinian Presidential Guard Unveils its First Female Fighters — Headscarved Commandos Taking New Ground', *The Independent*, 2014, https://www.independent.co.uk/news/world/middle-east/palestinian-presidential-guard-unveils-its-first-female-fighters-headscarved-commandos-taking-new-ground-9244604.html.

Gross, A. 'Challenges to Compulsory Heterosexuality: Recognition and Non-Recognition of Same-Sex Couples in Israeli Law', in Wintermute, R. and Andenaes, M. (eds), *Legal Recognition of Same-Sex Partnerships: A Study of National, European and International Law* (Oxford: Hart Publishing, 2001), pp. 391–414, https://doi.org/10.5040/9781472562425.ch-020.

Le More, A., *International Assistance to the Palestinians After Oslo: Political Guilt, Wasted Money* (New York: Routledge, 2008), https://doi.org/10.4324/9780203928332.

Maikey, H., 'The History and Contemporary State of Palestinian Sexual Liberation Struggle', in Lim, A. (ed.), *The Case for Sanctions Against Israel* (London and New York: Verso, 2012), pp. 121–30.

Maikey. H. and Shamali, S., 'International Day Against Homophobia: Between the Western Experience and the Reality of Gay Communities', 2016, http://www.alqaws.org/siteEn/print?id=26&type=1.

Massad, J., 'Conceiving the Masculine: Gender and Palestinian Nationalism', *Middle East Journal*, 49.3 (1995), 467–83.

Massad, J., *Desiring Arabs* (Chicago: University of Chicago Press, 2007).

Mikdashi, M., 'Gay Rights as Human Rights: Pinkwashing and Homonationalism', *Jadaliyya*, 2015, https://www.jadaliyya.com/Details/24855/Gay-Rights-as-Human-Rights-Pinkwashing-Homonationalism.

Morgensen, S. L., *Spaces Between Us: Queer Settler Colonialism and Indigenous Decolonisation* (Minneapolis: University of Minnesota Press, 2011), https://doi.org/10.5749/minnesota/9780816656325.001.0001.

Parsons, N., *The Politics of the Palestinian Authority: from Oslo to Alaqsa* (London: Routledge, 2005), https://doi.org/10.4324/9780203020951.

Schotten, H. and Maikey, H., 'Queers Resisting Zionism: On Authority and Accountability Beyond Homonationalism', *Jadaliyya*, 2012, https://www.jadaliyya.com/Details/27175/Queers-Resisting-Zionism-On-Authority-and-Accountability-Beyond-Homonationalism.

Smith, A., 'American Studies without America: Native Feminisms and the Nation-State', *American Quarterly*, 60.2 (2008), #312, https://doi.org/10.1353/aq.0.0014.

Sullivan, N. *A Critical Introduction to Queer Theory* (Edinburgh: Edinburgh University Press, 2003), https://doi.org/10.1515/9781474472944.

Walzer, L., *Between Sodom and Eden: A Gay Journey through Today's Changing Israel* (New York: Columbia University Press, 2000).

Žižek, S., *Mapping Ideology* (London: Verso, 1995).

Žižek, S., 'Against Human Rights', *New Left Review*, 34 (2005), 115–33.

Fig. 10 Tom Hurndall, Shelled buildings in Rafah, April 2003.

8. Archaeology, Architecture and the Politics of Verticality[1]

Eyal Weizman

Since the 1967 war, when Israel occupied the West Bank and the Gaza Strip, a colossal project of strategic, territorial and architectural planning has lain at the heart of the Israeli-Palestinian conflict.

The landscape and the built environment became the arena of conflict. Jewish settlements — state-sponsored islands of "territorial and personal democracy", manifestations of the Zionist pioneering ethos — were placed on hilltops overlooking the dense and rapidly changing fabric of the Palestinian cities and villages. "First" and "Third" Worlds spread out in a fragmented patchwork: a territorial ecosystem of externally alienated, internally homogenised enclaves located next to, within, above or below each other. The border ceased to be a single continuous line and broke up into a series of separate makeshift boundaries, internal checkpoints and security apparatuses. The total fragmentation of the terrain on plan demanded for the design of continuity across the territorial section. Israeli roads and infrastructure thereafter connected settlements while spanning over Palestinian lands or diving underneath them. Along these same lines, Ariel Sharon proposed a Palestinian State on a few estranged territorial enclaves 'connected by tunnels and bridges', while further insisting that Israel would retain sovereignty on the water aquifers underneath Palestinian areas and on the airspace and electromagnetic fields above them.

---

1   This lecture and chapter was extracted from Weizman, E., 'The Politics of Verticality: The West Bank as an Architectural Construction', *Mute Magazine*, 1 (2004), 27, https://www.metamute.org/editorial/articles/politics-verticality.

    https://doi.org/10.11647/OBP.0345.09

Indeed, a new way of imagining territory was developed for the West Bank. The region was no longer seen as a two-dimensional surface of a single territory, but as a large three-dimensional volume, containing a layered series of ethnic, political and strategic territories. Separate security corridors, infrastructure, and underground resources were thus woven into an Escher-like space that struggled to multiply a single territorial reality.

What was first described by Meron Benvenisti as crashing 'three-dimensional space into six dimensions — three Jewish and three Arab' became the complete physical partitioning of the West Bank into two separate but overlapping national geographies in volume across territorial cross sections, rather than on a planar surface.

The process that split a single territory into a series of territories is the "Politics of Verticality". Beginning as a set of ideas, policies, projects and regulations proposed by Israeli state-technocrats, generals, archaeologists, planners and road engineers since the beginning of the occupation of the West Bank, it has by now become the common practise of exercising territorial control as well as the dimension within which territorial solutions are sought.

Archaeology

When the Zionists first arrived in Palestine late in the nineteenth century, the land they found was strangely unfamiliar; different from the one they consumed in texts photographs and etchings. Reaching the map co-ordinates of the site did not bring them there. The search had to continue and thus split in opposite directions along the vertical axis: above, in a metaphysical sense, and below, as archaeological excavations.

That the ground was further inhabited by the Arabs and marked with the traces of their lives complicated things even further. The existing terrain started to be seen as in a protective wrap, under which the historical longed-for landscape was hidden. Archaeology attempted to peel this visible layer and expose the historical landscape concealed underneath. Only a few metres below the surface, a palimpsest made of five-thousand-year-old debris, traces of cultures and narratives of wars and destruction was arranged chronologically in layers compressed with stone and by soil.

Biblical Archaeology as a scientific discipline was initiated by William Foxwell Albright's excavation works in Palestine in the early 1920s. Archaeology was seen as a sub-discipline in biblical research, a tool for the provision of objective external evidence that will prove the originality of ancient traditions. Biblical Archaeology attempted to match traces of Bronze Age material ruins with biblical narratives.

This legacy suited modern Israel well. In its early days, the state attempted to fashion itself as the successor of ancient Israel, and to construct a new national identity rooted in the depths of the ground. Material traces took on immense importance, as an alibi for the Jewish return. But differing from the American branch of biblical archaeology, the Israeli one was secular, working to create a secular 'fundamentalism' that saw the Bible both as a document in need of verification and as a source that can be relied upon as evidence.

If the land to be "inherited" was indeed located under the surface, then the whole subterranean volume became a national monument, from which an ancient civilisation could be politically resurrected to testify for the right of present-day Israel.

At the centre of this activity, quickly its very symbol, was Yig'al Yadin, the former military chief of staff turned archaeologist. Seeking to supply Israeli society with historical parallels to the struggles of Zionism, he focused his digging on the periods of the biblical occupation and settlement of the Israelites in Canaan, on ancient wars and on monumental building and fortification works carried out by the kings of Israel. In his methodology, weapons were studied more than any other ingredients of life.

Even the excavation works were conceived as inherently military: sites were located after an observation from detailed maps and aerial photographs, excavation camps were regimented by military discipline, and transportation was relying on military vehicles and helicopters.

After the Six-Day War, archaeological sites and data became more easily available. The mountains of the West Bank are where most sites of biblical significance are located. Most organised archives of archaeology and antiquity: the East Jerusalem-based Rockefeller Museum, the American school for Oriental Research, the French École Biblique with their collections and libraries came under Israeli control.

The settlement project of the West Bank was based on an attempt to anchor new claims to ancient ones. Some settlements were constructed adjacent to or over sites suspected of having a Hebrew past. Making the historical context explicit allowed for the re-organisation of the surface, creating an apparent continuum of Jewish inhabitation. Settlements even recycled history by adopting the names of biblical sites, making public claim to genealogical roots. The visible landscape and the buried one were describing two different maps in slippage over each other.

Archaeological Architecture

The 1967 war marks a stylistic transition in Israeli architecture. The wave of nationalistic sentiment that followed the "liberation" and unification of Jerusalem, together with the surveying of abundant archaeological sites in the West Bank were incorporated overnight into a new mode of architectural production. The practice of archaeology was extruded into a new building style.

In the 1950s and 1960s state-sponsored housing developments reflected the socialist ethos in the austere, white-block model of European Modernism. But as Zvi Efrat claims, when the Six-Day War wound-up, national taste was radically transformed. The focus of architectural inspiration shifted from European Brutalism to Jerusalemite Orientalism. The "organic" structures of the oriental old city of Jerusalem were reproduced in endless light and material studies, in charcoal drawings and in archaeology albums.

Then, without the rhetorical manifestos that announce the immanent emergence of a new avant-garde, new neighbourhoods, especially in and around Jerusalem, started boasting arches and domes (most often reproduced in prefabricated concrete) colonnades and courtyards, within "old city-like" clusters of buildings clad with a veneer of slated Jerusalem stone.

Concrete skeletons were wrapped with layers embodying series of references varying from the biblical to the oriental, crusader Arab and even mandatory style, used separately or all together. It was this architectural postmodernism *"avant la lettre"*, that reflected the confusion of a newly inaugurated national-religious identity.

The Vertical Schizophrenia of the Temple Mount

Subterranean Jerusalem is at least as complex as its terrain. Nowhere is this truer than of the Temple Mount/Haram al-Sharif. The ascent of the then Prime Minister Ariel Sharon to the Temple Mount in 2000 and the bloodshed during the Intifada that followed were not unique. The Temple Mount/Haram al-Sharif has often been the focal point of the conflict.

The Haram al-Sharif compound is located over a filled-in, flattened-out summit on which the Al-Aqsa Mosque and the Dome of the Rock are located. The mount is supported by retaining walls, one of which is the Western Wall, whose southern edge is known as the Wailing Wall. The Western Wall is part of the outermost wall of what used to define the edge of the Second Temple compound.

Most archaeologists believe that the Wailing Wall was a retaining wall supporting the earth on which the Second Temple stood at roughly the same latitude as today's mosques. But the Israeli delegation at Camp David negotiations argued that the Wailing Wall was built originally as a free-standing wall, behind which (and not over which) stood the Second Temple. What follows is that the remains of the Temple are to be found *underneath* the mosques and that what separated the most holy Jewish site from the Muslim mosques is a vertical distance of a mere ten metres. That vertical separation into the above and below was the source of the debate that followed.

Since East Jerusalem was occupied in 1967, the Muslim religious authority (the Wakf) has charged that Israel is trying to undermine the compound foundations in order to topple the Al-Aqsa Mosque and the Dome of the Rock, and to clear the way for the establishment of the Third Jewish Temple. Jewish groups contend that the Wakf's extensive work in the subterranean chambers under the mosques is designed to rid the mountain of ancient Israelites remnants, and that the large-scale earth works conducted in the process destabilise the mountain and have generated cracks in the retaining wall of the mount.

On 24 September 1996, Prime Minister Binyamin Netanyahu, wanting to demonstrate his control of all layers of the city, ordered the opening of a subterranean archaeological tunnel running along the foundation of the Western Wall, alongside the Haram al-Sharif/Temple Mount compound.

The opening of the 'Western Wall Tunnel' was wrongly perceived as an attempt at subterranean sabotage. But Palestinian sentiments were fuelled by memories of a similar event that occurred in December 1991 which saw another excavated tunnel under the Harram collapsing and opening a big hole in the floor of the Mosque of Atman ben-Afan.

Israel's chief negotiator at Camp David, Gilead Sher, told how, during the failed summit on 17 July 2000 in the presence of the whole Israeli delegation, Barak declared: 'We shall stand united in front of the whole world, if it becomes apparent that an agreement wasn't reached over the issue of our sovereignty over the First and Second Temples. It is the Archemedic point of our universe, the anchor of the Zionist effort [...] we are at the moment of truth.'

The two delegations laid claim to the same plot of land. Neither side was willing to give it up. In attempts to reconcile the irreconcilable, intense spatial contortions were drawn on variously scaled plans and sections of the compound.

The most original bridging proposal at Camp David came from the then US President Bill Clinton. After the inevitable crisis, Clinton dictated his proposal to the negotiating parties. It was a daring and radical manifestation of the region's vertical schizophrenia, according to which the border between Arab East and Jewish West Jerusalem would, at the most contested point on earth, flip from the horizontal to the vertical — giving the Palestinians sovereignty on top of the Mount while maintaining Israeli sovereignty below the surface, over the Wailing Wall and the airspace above it. The horizontal border would have passed underneath the paving of the Haram al-Sharif, so that a few centimetres under the worshippers in the Mosque of al-Aqsa and the Dome of the Rock, the Israeli underground would be dug up for remnants of the ancient Temple, believed to be 'in the depth of the mount'.

In order to allow free access to the Muslim compound, now isolated in a three-dimensional sovereign wrap by Israel, Barak, embracing the proposal, suggested 'a bridge or a tunnel, through which whoever wants to pray in al-Aqsa could access the compound'.

But the Palestinians, long suspicious of Israel's presence under their mosques, have flatly rejected the plan. They claimed (partly bemused) that 'Haram al-Sharif [...] must be handed over to the Palestinians — over, under and to the sides, geographically and topographically.'

Regarding the truth about the remnants of the Temple 'in the depth of the mount', there are few and varied scholarly studies and opinions. But Charles Warren, a captain in the Royal Engineers. who was in 1876 one of the first archaeologists to excavate the tunnels and subterranean chambers under the Haram/Temple Mount, recorded no conclusive ruins of the Temple, but a substance of completely different nature:

> The passage is four feet wide, with smooth sides, and the sewage was from five to six feet deep, so that if we had fallen in there was no chance of our escaping with our lives. I, however, determined to trace out this passage, and for this purpose got a few old planks and made a perilous voyage on the sewage to a distance of 12 feet... The sewage was not water, and not mud; it was just in such a state that a door would not float, but yet if left for a minute or two would not sink very deep...

If that Indiana Jones-type description was correct, what Clinton and the negotiating teams hadn't realised was that the Temple Mount sat atop a network of ancient ducts and cisterns filled with generations of Jerusalem's sewage.

Storrs' Stare of Medusa

Perhaps Jerusalem's best-known by-law is the one enacted in 1918 by the first British military governor of the city, Sir Ronald Storrs, soon after he started his term in office. The first urban by-law of the British mandate in Palestine required square, dressed natural stone — Jerusalem stone — for the façades and visible external walls of all new buildings constructed in the city.

This historicist by-law, later confirmed by the Jerusalem District Building and Town Planning Commission in 1936, determined the image of Jerusalem more than any other law, by-law or programme devised by the authorities over the subsequent eighty years.

Storrs was the officer in commanded of the battle for Jerusalem in General Allenby's army. So deep was his admiration for Jerusalem, fuelled by romantic and religious zeal, that whilst fighting the Ottoman army, and subsequently taking Jerusalem off their hands, he issued an order according to which during the battle none of Jerusalem's buildings must be destroyed. Storrs' aim was to protect the holy city as he imagined it, and repel all threats to its 'hallowed and immemorial tradition'. During the time of his rather peaceful reign, the city's growing poverty on the one hand and its rapid expansion on the other threatened to overrun its image much more than the potential destruction of war.

Whilst enacting the by-law demanding the stone finish, Storrs sought to regulate the city's appearance, to resist time and change, and could not have realised that whilst dressing Jerusalem in a single architectural uniform, he in effect created the conditions for its excessive expansion, self-replication, and sprawl as a single entity.

In the context of contemporary Jerusalem, the stone does more than just fulfil an aesthetic agenda of preservation — it defines visually the geographic limits of Jerusalem and more importantly — since Jerusalem is a holy city — marks the extent of its holiness.

The idea of Jerusalem as the City of God, and thus as a holy place, is entrenched in Judeo-Christian belief. In their Diaspora, Jews started yearning for a city that became in their imagination increasingly disassociated from the reality of the physical site. Jerusalem itself became holy rather than a place containing holy sites.

If the city itself is holy, then, in the contemporary context, the totality of its buildings, roads, vegetation, infrastructure, neighbourhoods, parking garages, shops and workshops is holy. A special holy status is reserved for the ground. And if the ground is holy, its relocation as stones from the horizontal (earth) to the vertical (walls), from the quarries to the façades of buildings, transfers holiness further. As Jerusalem's ground paving of stone climbs up to wrap its façades, the new "ground topography" of holiness is extended.

When the city itself is holy, and when its boundaries are constantly being negotiated, redefined, and redrawn, holiness becomes a planning issue. Shortly after the occupation of the eastern Arab part of the city, the municipal boundaries of Israeli Jerusalem were expanded to include the Palestinian populated eastern parts as well as large empty areas around and far beyond them (and the municipal area of Jerusalem grew from 33.5 square kilometres in 1952 to 108 square kilometres in 1967). These "new territories" annexed to the city, designed as "reserves" for future Israeli expansions, were required to comply with Storrs' by-law — their buildings to be clad in stone, preserving the traditional and familiar Jerusalem look — turning suburban neighbourhoods, placed on remote and historically insignificant sites far from the historical centre, to

"Jerusalem", and participating thus in the city's sacredness. The holy status, felt psychologically and defined visually in the stone, places every remote and newly built suburb well within the boundaries of 'the eternally unified capital of the Jewish people'.

Like the Gaze of Medusa, Storrs' law petrified new constructions into stone in new neighbourhoods, suburbs and settlements: shopping malls, kindergartens, community centres, synagogues, office buildings, electrical relay station, sports halls and housing were covered in stone, and as far as the stone façades were extended, the holiness of Jerusalem sprawled.

Jerusalem did not grow and develop naturally. The expansions of Jewish neighbourhoods after the 1967 war, into Arab lands to the north and the east, were designed to ensure the impossibility of a geographical re-division of the city into two distinct parts, Arab-Palestinian and Jewish. The fact that the new hilltop neighbourhoods were located according to this political and strategic logic, rather than according to urban logic, has created a disaster on a colossal scale. The new neighbourhoods demanded an ever-increasing paving of roads and an expensive network of infrastructure while their placement in remote locations left large, empty areas between them and the historical city centre.

The new suburban hilltop neighbourhoods built beyond the 1967 lines, on areas annexed to the city, are located farthest away from the centre and describe the outermost circle. Nonetheless, the stone regulations that apply there are as strict as those demanded for in the city centre. The symbolic centre has relocated to the periphery, leaving vast gaps in the urban fabric in-between. The relocation of the centre to the periphery was not only a symbolic move — the city inhabitants themselves, wary of the congested, multicultural and disputed city centre, opted for the ethnic, cultural and social homogeneity of the periphery. Approximately 200,000 Jewish people migrated within Jerusalem between 1990 and 1997, more than a half of them from the centre of the western city to the new periphery. These in-town migrants, seeking the aura of Jerusalem in its suburbs, have transplanted its holiness along with its stone.

The 1955 masterplan grants an important concession and incentive. Unlike other claddings, the stone, sometimes as thick as twenty-five centimetres, is allowed to project outside of the building envelope, thus occupying, on occasions where the building line corresponds with that of the street, public ground. The law acknowledges the fact that this cladding performs an important public function, and since public signs are meant to occupy public ground, the stone was allowed "to invade" the street. (In that respect, it is worth noting that architects building in Jerusalem found creative variations for the use of stone cladding, most notably Ram Karmi, then the architect of the Ministry of Housing, advocated the use of stone cladding vertically rather than horizontally — exposing the fact that the building is clad in stone and not built in it.)

The extension of the city's "holiness" to the new suburbs was conceived as part of an Israeli attempt to generate widespread public acceptance of the newly annexed territories, otherwise viewed as a political and urban burden. Whatever is called Jerusalem, by name and by the use of stone, lies at the heart of the Israeli consensus that "Jerusalem shall not be re-divided". The cladding of buildings in stone is an architectural ritual whose repetition attempts to fabricate a collective memory serving a nationalistic agenda.

Jerusalem, as a name, as an idea and as a city, has strong grips over the mind of its inhabitants. A city that was always perceived as an idea rather than a concrete, earthly reality has no boundaries besides those in the mind. The stone cladding functions thus to connect the transformed geographical reality of Jerusalem with the ephemeral idea of the heavenly city. This politically conscious use of geographical identity relies heavily on stone as a signifier to call forth the image of a mystic past. The public acceptance of the expansion of Jerusalem is made possible by the replication of its "character" and "feel". The spectator is left incapable of drawing the boundary between the city and its idea, between its earthly geographical reality and a sense of sanctification and renewed holiness epitomised in the salvation of the ground.

Although originally conceived to protect and preserve an aesthetic status quo, Storrs' stone by-law was extended by Israeli policy makers beyond the performance of mere aesthetic purposes. By visually defining the geographic limits of the city and marking the extent of its holiness, it has been made into a politically manipulative and colonising architectural device.

Terrain

More, then, than anything else, the Israeli-Palestinian terrain is defined by where and how one builds. The terrain dictates the nature, intensity and focal points of confrontation. On the other hand, the conflict manifests itself most clearly in the adaptation, construction and obliteration of landscape and built environment. Planning decisions are often made not according to criteria of economical sustainability, ecology or efficiency of services, but to serve strategic and national agendas.

The West Bank is a landscape of extreme topographical variation, ranging from four hundred and forty metres below sea level at the shores of the Dead Sea, to about one thousand metres in the high summits of Samaria. Settlements occupy the high ground, while Palestinian villages occupy the fertile valley in between. This topographical difference defines the relationship between Jewish and Palestinian settlements in terms of strategy, economy and ecology.

The politics of verticality is exemplified across the folded surface of the terrain — in which the mountainous region has influenced the forms the territorial conflict has produced.

Vertical Planning

Matityahu Drobles was appointed head of the Jewish Agency's Land Settlement Division in 1978. Shortly after, he issued *The Master Plan for the Development of Settlements in Judea and Samaria*. In this master plan he urges the government to

> [...] Conduct a race against time [...] now [when peace with Egypt seemed imminent] is the most suitable time to start with wide and encompassing rush of settlements, mainly on the mountain ranges of Judea and Samaria... The thing must be done first and foremost by creating facts on the ground, therefore state land and uncultivated land must be taken immediately in order to settle the areas between the concentration of [Palestinian] population and around it... being cut apart by Jewish settlements, the minority [sic] population will find it hard to create unification and territorial continuity.

The Drobles master plan outlined possible locations for scores of new settlements. It aimed to achieve its political objectives through the re-organisation of space. Relying heavily on the topography, Drobles proposed new high-volume traffic arteries to connect the Israeli heartland to the West Bank and beyond. These roads would be stretched along the large west-draining valleys; for their security, new settlement blocks should be placed on the hilltops along the route. He also proposed settlements on the summits surrounding the large Palestinian cities, and around the roads connecting them to each other.

This strategic territorial arrangement has been brought into use during the Israeli Army's invasion of Palestinian cities and villages. Some of the settlements assisted the IDF in different tasks, mainly as places for the army to organise, re-fuel and re-deploy.

The hilltops lent themselves easily to state seizure. In the absence of an ordered land registry in time of Jordanian rule, Israel was able to legally capture whatever land was not cultivated. Palestinian cultivated lands are found mainly in the valleys, where the agriculturally suitable alluvial soil erodes down from the limestone slopes of the West Bank highlands. The barren summits were left empty.

The Israeli government launched a large-scale project of topographical and land-use mapping. The terrain was charted and mathematised, slope gradients were calculated, the extent of un-cultivated land marked. The result, summed up in dry numbers, left about thirty-eight per cent of the West Bank under Israeli control, isolated in discontinuous islands around summits. That land was then made available for settlement.

Community Settlements

The "Community Settlement" is a new type of settlement developed in the early 1980s for the West Bank. It is in effect a closed members' club, with a long admission process and a monitoring mechanism that regulates everything from religious observance to ideological rigour, even the form and outdoor use of homes. Settlements function as dormitory suburbs for small groups of Israelis who travel to work in the large Israeli cities. The hilltop environment, isolated, with wide views, and hard to reach, lent itself to the development of this newly conceived utopia.

In the formal processes, which base mountain settlements on topographical conditions, the laws of erosion had been absorbed into the practice of urban design. The mountain settlement is typified by a principle of concentric arrangement, with roads laid out in rings following the topographical lines around the summit.

The "ideal" arrangement for a small settlement is a circle. But in reality the particular layout of each depends on site morphology and the extent of available state land. Each is divided into equal, repetitive lots for small, private, red-roofed homes. The public functions are generally located within the innermost ring, on the higher ground.

The community settlements create cul-de-sac envelopes, closed off to their surroundings, promoting a mythic, communal coherence in a shared formal identity. It is a claustrophobic layout, expressing a social vision that facilitates the intimate management of the lives of the inhabitants.

Optical Urbanism

High ground offers three strategic assets: greater tactical strength, self-protection, and a wider view. This principle is as long as military history itself. The Crusaders' castles, some built not far from the location of today's settlements, operated through the reinforcement of strength already provided by nature. These series of mountaintop fortresses were military instruments for the territorial domination of the Latin kingdom.

The Jewish settlements in the West Bank are not very different. Not only places of residence, they create a large-scale network of "civilian fortification" which is part of the army's regional plan of defence, generating tactical territorial surveillance. A simple act of domesticity, a single-family home shrouded in the cosmetic façade of red tiles and green lawns, conforms to the aims of territorial control.

But unlike the fortresses and military camps of previous periods, the settlements are sometimes without fortifications. Up until recently, only a few settlements agreed to be surrounded by walls or fences. They argued that they must form continuity with the holy landscape; that it is the Palestinians who need to be fenced in.

During the First Intifada many settlements were attacked, and debate returned over the effect of fences. Extremist settlers claimed that protection could be exercised solely through the power of vision, rendering the material protection of a fortified wall redundant and even obstructive.

Indeed, the form of the mountain settlements is constructed according to a geometric system that unites the effectiveness of sight with spatial order, producing "panoptic fortresses", generating gazes to many different ends. Control — in the overlooking of Arab town and villages; strategy — in the overlooking of main traffic arteries; self-defence — in the overlooking of the immediate surroundings and approach roads. Settlements could be seen as urban optical devices for surveillance and the exercise of power.

In 1984 the Ministry of Housing published guidance for new construction in the mountain region, advising: 'Turning openings in the direction of the view is usually identical with turning them in the direction of the slope ... [the optimal view depends on] the positioning of the buildings and on the distances between them, on the density, the gradient of the slope and the vegetation'.

That principle applies most easily to the outer ring of homes. The inner rings are positioned in front of the gaps between the homes of the first ring. This arrangement of the homes around summits, outward looking, imposes on the dwellers axial visibility (and lateral invisibility), oriented in two directions: inward and outward.

Discussing the interior of each building, the guidance recommends the orientation of the sleeping rooms towards the inner public spaces and the living rooms towards the distant view. The inward-oriented gaze protects the soft cores of the settlements, the outward-oriented one surveys the landscape below. Vision dictated the discipline and mode of design on every level, even down to the precise positioning of windows: as if, following Paul Virilio, 'the function of arms and the function of the eye were indefinitely identified as one and the same'.

Seeking safety in vision, Jewish settlements are intensely illuminated. At night, from a distance they are visible as brilliant white streaks of light. From within them, the artificial light shines so brightly as to confuse diurnal rhythms. This is in stark contrast to Palestinian cities: seeking their safety in invisibility, they employ blackouts as a routine of protection from aerial attacks.

In his verdict in support of the "legality" of settlement, Israeli High Court Justice Vitkon argued,

> One does not have to be an expert in military and security affairs to understand that terrorist elements operate more easily in an area populated only by an indifferent population or one that supports the enemy, as opposed to an area in which there are *persons who are likely to observe them* and inform the authorities about any suspicious movement. Among them no refuge, assistance, or equipment will be provided to terrorists. The matter is simple, and details are unnecessary.

The settlers come to the high places for the "regeneration of the soul". But in placing them across the landscape, the Israeli government is drafting its civilian population alongside the agencies of state power, to inspect and control the Palestinians. Knowingly or not, settlers' eyes, seeking a completely different view, are being "hijacked" for strategic and geopolitical aims.

The Paradox of Double Vision

The journey into the mountains, seeking to re-establish the relation between terrain and sacred text, was a work of tracing the location of "biblical" sites, and constructing settlements adjacent to them. Settlers turned "topography" into "scenography", forming an exegetical landscape with a mesh of scriptural signification that must be "read", not just "viewed".

For example, a settlement located near the Palestinian city of Nablus advertises itself thus:

> Shilo spreads up the hills overlooking Tel Shilo, where over three thousand years ago the children of Israel gathered to erect the Tabernacle and to divide by lot the Land of Israel into tribal portions... this ancient spiritual centre has retained its power as the focus of modern day Shilo.

Rather than being a resource for agricultural or industrial cultivation, the landscape establishes the link with religious-national myths. The view of the landscape does not evoke solemn contemplation, but becomes an active staring, part of an ecstatic ritual: 'it causes me excitement that I cannot even talk about in modesty', says Menora Katzover, wife of a prominent settlers' leader, about the view of the Shomron mountains.

Another sales brochure, published for member recruitment in Brooklyn and advertising the ultra-orthodox settlement of Emanuel, evokes the pastoral: 'The city of Emanuel, situated 440 metres above sea level, has a magnificent view of the coastal plain and the Judean Mountains. The hilly landscape is dotted by green olive orchards and enjoys a pastoral calm.'

There is a paradox in this description. The very thing that renders the landscape "biblical" — traditional inhabitation, cultivation in terraces, olive orchards and stone buildings — is made by the Arabs whom the settlers come to replace. The people who cultivate the 'green olive orchards' and render the landscape biblical are themselves excluded from the panorama.

It is only when it comes to the roads that the brochure mentions Arabs, and that only by way of exclusion. 'A motored system is being developed that will make it possible to travel quickly and safely to the Tel Aviv area and to Jerusalem on modern throughways, *bypassing Arab towns*' (emphasis in the original). The gaze that can see a "pastoral, biblical landscape" will not register what it doesn't want to see — the Palestinians.

State strategy established vision as a means of control, and uses the eyes of settlers for this purpose. The settlers celebrate the panorama as a sublime resource, but one that can be edited. The sight-lines from the settlements serve two contradictory agendas simultaneously.

The Emanuel brochure continues, 'Indeed new Jewish life flourishes in these hills of the Shomron, and the nights are illuminated by lights of Jewish settlements on all sides. In the centre of all this wonderful bustling activity, Emanuel, a Torah city, is coming into existence.'

From a hilltop at night, a settler can lift his eyes to see only the blaze of other settlements, perched at a similar height atop the summits around. At night, settlers could avoid the sight of Arab towns and villages, and feel that they have truly arrived 'as the people without land — to the land without people'. (This famous slogan is attributed to Israel Zangwill, one of the early Zionists who arrived to Palestine before the British mandate, and described the land to which Eastern European Zionism was headed as desolate and forsaken.)

Latitude thus becomes more than merely relative position on the folded surface of the terrain. It functions to establish literally parallel geographies of "First" and "Third" Worlds, inhabiting two distinct planes, in the startling and unprecedented proximity that only the vertical dimension of the mountains could provide.

Rather than the conclusive division between two nations across a boundary line, the organisation of the West Bank's particular terrain has created multiple separations, provisional boundaries, which relate to each other through surveillance and control. This intensification of power could be achieved in this form only because of the particularity of the terrain.

The mountain settlements are the last gesture in the urbanisation of enclaves. They perfect the politics of separation, seclusion and control, placing them as the end-condition of contemporary urban and architectural formations such as "New Urbanism", suburban enclave neighbourhoods or gated communities. The most ubiquitous of architectural typologies is exposed as terrifying within the topography of the West Bank.

The assassination of Palestinian militants within their cities was made possible by technological advances and the ability to achieve rapidly integrative systems. Beyond the hardware of the aerial platforms, it is the soft technological application of information and communications technology that allows for the synergetic integration of military equipment. This integration relies on the control of the airways and the electromagnetic spectrums, thus making essential the possession of total control of the airspace. With the presence and availability of this technology, acts of personal liquidation became subjected only to will.

If the potential of iron bombing to horrify the imagination has already been exhausted, this next step of warfare, in which armies could target individuals within a battlefield or civilians in precise urban warfare, when summary executions are carried out after short meetings between army generals and politicians working their way down "wanted" men lists, makes warfare an almost personal matter, and sets with it a new horizon of horror.

Bibliography

Boeri, S. 'Border Syndrome', in Franke, A., Weizman, E., Boeri, S. and Segal, R. (eds), *Territories* (Berlin: KW and Walther Keoing, 2003).

Etkes, D., 'Settlement Watch', *Peace Now*, 2003, https://peacenow.org.il/en//category/settlements

Graham, S., *Urbicide*, in Jenin, 2002, www.opendemocracy.net.

Halper, J., *The Matrix of Control*, https://icahd.org/get-the-facts/matrix-control.

Kemp, A., 'Border space and national identity in Israel', in: Yehuda Shenhav (ed.), *Theory and Criticism, Space, Land, Home, Jerusalem and Tel Aviv* (Jerusalem: The Van Leer Jerusalem Institute and Hakibbutz Hameuchad Publishing House, 2000), pp. 13–43

Lein, Y., 'Behind the Barrier', Jerusalem: B'Tselem, 2003, http://www.btselem.org/Download/2003_Behind_The_Barrier_Eng.doc.

Lein, Y. and Weizman, E., 'Land Grab', Jerusalem: B'Tselem, 2002, https://www.btselem.org/download/200205_land_grab_eng.pdf.

Ministry of Agriculture and the Settlement Division of the World Zionist Organization, *Masterplan for Jewish Settlements in the West Bank Through the Year 2010 and Masterplan for Settlement for Judea and Samaria, Development Plan for the Region for 1983–1986*. Jerusalem: Ministry of Agriculture and the Settlement Division of the World Zionist Organization, 1983.

Rotbard, S., 'Tower and stockade', in Segal, R. and Weizman, E. (eds), *A Civilian Occupation, Tel Aviv and London* (Tel Aviv and London: Babel Press and Verso Press, 2003), pp. 59–67.

Segal, R. and Weizman, E., 'The Mountain', in: Segal, R. and Weizman, E. (eds), *A Civilian Occupation* (Tel Aviv and London: Babel Press and Verso Press, 2003), pp. 39–58.

Sharon, A. with Chanoff, D., *Warrior: The Autobiography of Ariel Sharon* (New York: Simon & Schuster, 2001).

Weizman, E., *The Politics of Verticality*, 2002, www.opendemocracy.net.

Fig. 11 Tom Hurndall, Tank in Rafah, April 2003.

9. Israeli Apartheid: A Matter of Law

Daniel Machover

Israel's rule over the Palestinian people may be characterised as a regime of apartheid, with its individual actions constituting crimes of apartheid. I was one of the legal advisers to the Russell Tribunal On Palestine (RTOP or 'Russell Tribunal') which convened on six occasions, not all of which I was able to assist with (from March 2010 to September 2014) (http://www.russelltribunalonpalestine.com/en/index.html).

The third session was held in Cape Town in November 2011 and what I will set out below is an updated summary of the RTOP's findings — available in full but not updated via this link: http://www.russelltribunalonpalestine.com/en/sessions/south-africa/south-africa-session-%E2%80%94-full-findings. The Tribunal made findings with regard to Israel's policies and practices vis-à-vis the Palestinian people with reference to the international legal prohibition of apartheid under the following headings: The definition and status of apartheid under international law; Application of the definition of apartheid to Israeli policies; and practices vis-à-vis the Palestinian people.

Definition and Status of Apartheid under International Law

Apartheid is the Afrikaans word for 'separateness' or 'separate development' that was used to designate the official state policy of racial discrimination implemented in South Africa between 1948 and 1994. Indeed, 'apartheid' came to be prohibited by international law because

 https://doi.org/10.11647/OBP.0345.10

of the experience of apartheid in southern Africa, which had its own unique attributes.

However, the legal definition of apartheid applies to any situation anywhere in the world where the following three core elements exist: (i) that two distinct racial groups can be identified; (ii) that 'inhuman acts' are committed against the subordinate group; and (iii) that such acts are committed systematically in the context of an institutionalised regime of domination by one group over the other. Apartheid acquired that specific legal meaning in international law by virtue of treaties enacted from the 1960s onwards. The crime of apartheid involves individual inhuman acts committed in the context of the abovementioned institutionalised regime.

The legal definition of apartheid is based primarily on the 1973 Convention on the Suppression and Punishment of the Crime of Apartheid (the 'Apartheid Convention') as the most comprehensive articulation of the meaning of apartheid under international law, but also draws on the International Convention for the Elimination of all forms of Racial Discrimination (ICERD) and the Rome Statute of the International Criminal Court (ICC).

Adopted in 1965, ICERD was the first international legal instrument that expressly prohibited apartheid, with Article 3 specifying the obligation of States parties to the Convention to oppose such a regime: 'States Parties particularly condemn racial segregation and apartheid and undertake to prevent, prohibit and eradicate all practices of this nature in territories under their jurisdiction'. However, ICERD did not provide a precise definition of apartheid. The Apartheid Convention was adopted in 1973 in order to make it possible to take more effective measures at the international and national levels with a view to the suppression and punishment of the crime of apartheid. The Apartheid Convention refers directly to Article 3 of ICERD in its preamble and is intended to complement the requirements of Article 3 of ICERD. Article 1 of the Apartheid Convention builds on earlier resolutions of the UN General Assembly by declaring apartheid to be a crime against humanity. Notably, Israel voted with the majority in favour of that resolution. As a result, the Convention obliges States parties to adopt legislative measures to suppress, discourage and punish the crime of apartheid and makes the offence an international crime which is subject to universal jurisdiction.

Article 2 of the Apartheid Convention provides a clear definition of what constitutes apartheid for the purposes of international law. It defines apartheid as *'inhuman acts committed for the purpose of establishing and maintaining domination by one racial group of persons over any other racial group of persons and systematically oppressing them'*, and goes on to enumerate a list of such inhuman acts. The formulation used in Article 7(2)(h) of the Rome Statute of the International Criminal Court, adopted in 1998, is very similar, defining apartheid as inhumane acts 'committed in the context of an institutionalised regime of systematic oppression and domination by one racial group over any other racial group and committed with the intention of maintaining that regime'.

The three core elements of the definition of apartheid are addressed below: i.e. the requirement of two distinct racial groups; the commission of acts listed as 'inhuman acts' of apartheid; and the institutionalised nature of the domination.

The definition of apartheid requires domination by one racial group over another, thus requiring two distinct racial groups. The Apartheid Convention itself does not define a racial group. ICERD, however, gives a broad construction to the meaning of the term 'racial', with racial discrimination including discrimination based on race, colour, descent, or national or ethnic origin. The meaning of a racial group for the purposes of ICERD is therefore established as a broad and practical one. In essence, it means an identifiable group. If a group identifies itself as such, and is identified as such by others, for example through discriminatory practices, then it comes under the protection of the Convention.

The concept of 'race' has long been shown as a social construct, not a biological category. International human rights law recognises a wider scope for the meaning of race than traditional 'black vs. white' parameters, and the UN Committee on the Elimination of all forms of Racial Discrimination has included groups that would not be considered 'races' in that traditional sense, including caste groups in South Asia, non-citizen groups such as migrant workers, and nomadic peoples. As testimony to the Russell Tribunal by experts on the question of race in international law has shown, the determination of a racial group under international law is ultimately not a scientific question, but a practical one.

Article 2 of the Apartheid Convention and Article 7(2)(j) of the Rome Statute both refer to inhuman acts that may constitute apartheid when committed in a context of racial domination, while Article 5 of ICERD enumerates a list of rights which must be guaranteed to all humans free from racial discrimination. The Russell Tribunal drew principally on Article 2 of the Apartheid Convention as the primary guiding framework regarding the definition of apartheid.

The following 'inhuman acts' are established in Article 2 as constitutive of apartheid:

> For the purpose of the present Convention, the term 'the crime of apartheid', which shall include similar policies and practices of racial segregation and discrimination as practised in southern Africa, shall apply to the following inhuman acts committed for the purpose of establishing and maintaining domination by one racial group of persons over any other racial group of persons and systematically oppressing them:
>
> (a) Denial to a member or members of a racial group or groups of the right to life and liberty of person:
>   (i) By murder of members of a racial group or groups;
>   (ii) By the infliction upon the members of a racial group or groups of serious bodily or mental harm, by the infringement of their freedom or dignity, or by subjecting them to torture or to cruel, inhuman or degrading treatment or punishment;
>   (iii) By arbitrary arrest and illegal imprisonment of the members of a racial group or groups;
>
> (b) Deliberate imposition on a racial group or groups of living conditions calculated to cause its or their physical destruction in whole or in part;
>
> (c) Any legislative measures and other measures calculated to prevent a racial group or groups from participation in the political, social, economic and cultural life of the country and the deliberate creation of conditions preventing the full development of such a group or groups, in particular by denying to members of a racial group or groups basic human rights and freedoms, including the right to work, the right to form recognized trade unions, the right to education, the right to leave and to return to their country, the right to a nationality, the right to freedom of movement and residence, the

right to freedom of opinion and expression, and the right to freedom of peaceful assembly and association;

(d) Any measures including legislative measures, designed to divide the population along racial lines by the creation of separate reserves and ghettos for the members of a racial group or groups, the prohibition of mixed marriages among members of various racial groups, the expropriation of landed property belonging to a racial group or groups or to members thereof;

(e) Exploitation of the labour of the members of a racial group or groups, in particular by submitting them to forced labour;

(f) Persecution of organizations and persons, by depriving them of fundamental rights and freedoms, because they oppose apartheid.

The language of the Apartheid Convention indicates that this list is *illustrative rather than exhaustive*, and that not each and every inhuman act described is necessary for a regime of apartheid to exist. A broader potential range of policies is implied by the qualifier of *similar policies and practices ... as practiced in southern Africa* (emphasis added). The 'shall include...' wording suggests that not all practices cited in Article 2 are required for a positive finding of apartheid. That a narrower range of policies could constitute a case of apartheid is demonstrated by the history of apartheid South Africa, where, for example, Article 2(b) regarding the intended *physical destruction* of a group was not applicable. South Africa's Truth and Reconciliation Commission concluded in this regard that the apartheid regime did not sustain an intentional policy to physically destroy the black population. Such conclusions on individual practices do not preclude an overall finding of a comprehensive system that has not only the effect but the purpose of maintaining racial domination by one racial group over the other.

From both the Apartheid Convention and Rome Statute formulations, it is clear that the essence of the definition of apartheid is the systematic and institutionalised character of the discrimination involved. This systematic element distinguishes the practice of apartheid from other forms of prohibited discrimination. Thus, for the inhuman acts listed above to constitute a regime of apartheid, it is not enough that they occur in random or isolated instances. They must be sufficiently widespread, integrated and complementary to be described as systematic. Such acts must also be sufficiently rooted in law, public policy and formal institutions to be described as institutionalised.

The prohibition of apartheid is established as part of customary international law (meaning that even states that are not party to the conventions prohibiting apartheid are still bound to uphold the prohibition) and as a norm of *jus cogens* (the most fundamental category of international legal rules, from which no derogation is ever permitted). It is also a universal prohibition, which although formulated in response to the situation in southern Africa was always intended to apply beyond southern Africa.

Application of the definition of Apartheid to Israeli Policies and Practices vis-à-vis the Palestinian People

It is now possible to consider whether Israeli policies and practices affecting the Palestinian population may be characterised as apartheid within the meaning of international law, with reference to the core elements of the definition of apartheid as outlined above.

Palestinians identify themselves as a group of people who share a common origin, history and culture, as well as social and political structures and networks that have ensured a continuing bond despite forced displacement and fragmentation. The entire Palestinian people is a single group, regardless of current geographic location or constructed legal status. All Palestinians — refugees in exile; those under military occupation in the West Bank (including Jerusalem) and Gaza Strip; those who have remained in the territory that is now Israel identify themselves as indigenous to Palestine, where they lived and held citizenship until the end of the British Mandate in 1948. They are considered a single people entitled to collective self-determination.

Under Israeli law and policy, group membership is an official category imposed and monitored by the state, not simply a voluntary identity. Israeli Jews are a group unified by law, sharing the same legal status wherever they reside, while Palestinian Arabs are a separate group, sub-divided into citizens, occupied residents (whose residence rights may be lost if they leave the territory in which they live), and refugees who do not have the right to return to any part of historic Palestine.

No such restrictions apply to Jews: in fact, those who are not citizens already can acquire Israeli citizenship automatically by relocating to Israel or the Occupied Palestinian Territory. The law that enables this, Israel's 1950 Law of Return, codifies the descent-based aspect of Jewish identity. Palestinians who hold Israeli citizenship are not defined in the same legal category as Jewish citizens, who enjoy the further privileges of 'Jewish nationality'. The Jewish nation considers itself a distinct group with a unique claim as the historical indigenous people of Palestine. (N.B. This has been highlighted and embedded in law with the passage in July 2018 of the Nation State Law.)

The existence of 'racial groups' is fundamental to the question of apartheid. The situation in Israel/Palestine is not defined in terms of traditional conceptions of 'race' as it was in apartheid South Africa. On the basis of expert evidence heard during the Cape Town session, the Tribunal concluded that international law gives a broad meaning to the term 'racial' as including elements of ethnic and national origin, and therefore that the definition of 'racial group' is a sociological question, not a biological one. Perceptions (including self-perceptions and external perceptions) of Israeli Jewish identity and Palestinian identity illustrate that Israeli Jews and Palestinian Arabs can readily be defined as distinct racial groups for the purposes of international law. From the evidence received, it was clear to the RTOP jury that two distinct, identifiable groups exist in a very practical sense and that the legal definition of 'racial group' applies to all circumstances in which the Israeli authorities have jurisdiction over Palestinians.

The Russell Tribunal's application of the constitutive acts of apartheid to Israel's practices followed the headings and structure of Article 2 of the Apartheid Convention as detailed above. Individual inhuman acts committed in the context of such a system are defined by international law as crimes of apartheid. The RTOP heard abundant evidence in its Cape Town session of practices that constitute the 'inhuman acts' set out below perpetrated against the Palestinian people by the Israeli authorities.

> Denial to a member or members of a racial group or groups the right to life and liberty of person: By murder of members of a racial group or groups

The RTOP received evidence of widespread deprivation of Palestinian life through military operations and incursions, a formal policy of 'targeted killings', and the use of lethal force against demonstrations.

Examples of large-scale Israeli military operations in which Palestinian civilians have been targeted and disproportionately killed include Operation 'Defensive Shield' (2002), Operation 'Determined Path' (2002), Operation 'Rainbow' (2004), Operation 'Summer Rains' (2006), Operation 'Autumn Clouds' (2006), Operation 'Hot Winter' (2008), and Operation 'Cast Lead' (2008–2009).

The use of lethal force against Palestinian demonstrations is a frequent factor of life in villages such as Bil'in and Ni'lin.

Ongoing daily military incursions that involve low but consistent Palestinian casualty figures. The Israeli human rights group B'Tselem keeps a tally of fatalities from 29 September 2000 in three periods: before Operation Cast Lead; during Operation Cast Lead; and since Operation Case Lead, which indicates that Israeli security forces have killed close to 10,000 Palestinians living in Gaza and the West Bank.[1]

Palestinians living within Israel have also been a target of lethal force as when 13 peaceful protestors were killed by Israeli police in October 2000.

Through an official state policy of *targeted killings* — which constitute extrajudicial executions — the Israeli military targets Palestinian activists and members of armed groups, with the aim of suffocating any possible resistance to Israel's rule. These killings affect not only the *targets*, but large numbers of civilians including family members and civilians. Hundreds of Palestinian civilian fatalities have resulted from air strikes and targeted killing operations by Israeli commandos.

> By the infliction upon the members of a racial group or groups of serious bodily or mental harm, by the infringement of their freedom or dignity, or by subjecting them to torture or to cruel, inhuman or degrading treatment or punishment

The Russell Tribunal heard evidence of the substantial history and continuing practices of torture and ill-treatment of Palestinian prisoners

---

1   This total is at October 2021, see https://www.btselem.org/statistics/fatalities/before-cast-lead/by-date-of-event   and   https://www.btselem.org/statistics/fatalities/during-cast-lead/by-date-of-event.

in Israeli prisons. Incarcerated Palestinians are categorised as *security prisoners* and subject to a specific regime of interrogation by the Israeli Security Agency, which often uses methods that amount to ill-treatment and torture.

Jewish-Israeli prisoners, regardless of their crimes, are generally not categorised as security prisoners and are not subject to analogous interrogation or ill-treatment.

The Russell Tribunal also noted forms of cruel, inhuman and degrading treatment through: movement restrictions that subject Palestinians to humiliation by Israeli soldiers and Palestinian women being forced to give birth at checkpoints; house demolitions as a form of inhuman and degrading treatment with severe psychological consequences for men, women and children.

The RTOP therefore found that Palestinians are subjected to torture and ill-treatment in the context of widespread deprivation of liberty through policies of arbitrary arrest and administrative detention without charge. The Russell Tribunal found that such measures frequently go beyond what is reasonably justified by security concerns and amount to a form of domination over the Palestinians as a group.

Palestinians in the occupied territories are routinely subject to arbitrary arrest and detention (including lengthy periods of pre-trial detention without access to legal assistance) and fall under the jurisdiction of a military court system that falls far short of international standards for fair trial. An entirely different legal system applies to Israeli Jews, who are subject to Israeli civil law and civil courts, with significantly enhanced procedural and substantive rights from arrest through to sentencing.

Israel's widespread practice of administrative detention without charge or trial, involves detention periods of up to six months at a time which can be, and often are, renewed and prolonged indefinitely, affecting Palestinian adults and minors, whereas not applied to Israeli Jews.

The Russell Tribunal considered that, although Israeli policies of blockade and collective punishment in the Gaza Strip in particular and consequent restrictions on vital supplies of food and medicine entail grave consequences for Palestinian life and health, they do not meet the threshold required by this provision of intent to cause the physical destruction of the Palestinian people.

Instead, living conditions imposed are calculated to cause the displacement of the Palestinian in whole or in part from Israeli jurisdiction.

The entire Israeli legal system establishes an enormous gap between Israeli Jews and Palestinian Arabs, with legislation typically designed to favour Israeli Jews and keep Palestinian Arabs in a situation of inferiority. This can be clearly seen through certain illustrative examples.

Several Israeli laws prevent Palestinian refugees from returning and recovering their land, thus violating their right to enter and leave the country, freedom of movement and residency and the right to a nationality. In Israel, the unequal distribution of resources for education and cultural activities for Palestinians, restrictions on family reunification for spouses with residence permits on different sides of the Green Line and the lack of representation in the civil service are violations of rights that feed in to Israel's prevention of Palestinian development and participation in political and social life.

Palestinians who work in Israel have enormous difficulties in joining Israeli trade unions or forming their own trade unions in Israel. Further rights violations preventing Palestinian development and political participation include privileges afforded to Jews in the sphere of land ownership, house demolitions and building restrictions; as well as pervasive restrictions on the freedom of opinion and expression through the closure of organisations, prohibition on public gatherings and demonstrations and media censorship by the Israeli authorities.

In summary, Palestinians are subjected to systematic human rights violations that preclude their development and prevent the Palestinians as a group from participating in political, economic, social and cultural life.

Palestinian refugees who remain displaced are also victims of apartheid by virtue of the ongoing denial of their right to return to their homes, as well as by laws that remove their property and citizenship rights. Policies of forced population transfer remain widespread, particularly in the Occupied Palestinian Territory. Civil and political rights of Palestinians including rights to movement, residence, freedom of expression and association are severely curtailed. Palestinian socio-economic rights are also adversely affected by discriminatory Israeli policies in the spheres of education, health and housing.

The Israeli Jewish and Palestinian populations are separated and allocated different physical spaces, with varying levels and quality of infrastructure, services and access to resources.

In Israel, Palestinians live in crowded spaces, often unable and unauthorised to refurbish or construct houses, living in villages that are sometimes not even officially recognised. Israeli Jews occupy larger expanses of land, guaranteed by Jewish national or government-managed agencies (Jewish National Fund, Israel Land Administration), which ensure that 93% of the land is reserved for exclusive Jewish use.

The landscape of the West Bank is dominated by exclusively Israeli-Jewish settlements and their associated regime of separate roads, security buffer zones, checkpoints and the Wall which interrupt the contiguity of the territory, and ensure that Palestinian communities are confined to isolated enclaves. Israeli settlers enjoy the protection of the authorities and military, with their own laws and preferential access to scarce resources such as water, to the detriment of the Palestinian population. Palestinians are prohibited from entering settlements (unless with special permission, such as for workers), military zones and 'natural reserves', meaning that almost half of the West Bank territory is closed to its Palestinian population. These settlements are linked by roads for the exclusive use of Israeli Jews. Palestinian movement restricted and access to farmland is restricted by a pervasive permit system. Regarding access to beaches, for example, in Israel's defence it is commonly stated that Israel does not segregate such access, in the way that South Africa designated certain beaches for whites and certain beaches for blacks or non-Europeans. Significantly, the Russell Tribunal heard evidence describing how Palestinian access even to beaches along the Palestinian shore of the Dead Sea is prohibited by Israeli regulations.

The expropriation of Palestinian property in general has continued since the creation of the State of Israel, and is underpinned by a series of laws and Military Orders that have stripped Palestinians of much of their land.

Accordingly, the evidence has made it plain to the RTOP that since 1948 the Israeli authorities have pursued concerted policies of colonisation and appropriation of Palestinian land. Israel has through its laws and practices divided the Israeli Jewish and Palestinian populations and allocated them different physical spaces, with varying levels and quality of infrastructure, services and access to resources. The end result is wholesale territorial fragmentation and a series of separate reserves and enclaves, with the two groups largely segregated. The Russell Tribunal heard evidence to the effect that such a policy is formally described in Israel as *hafrada*, Hebrew for 'separation'.

Although Israel has no exploitation system of labour of the Palestinian population, its policies have restructured the Palestinian workforce by suppressing Palestinian industry, establishing restrictions on exports and other measures that have increased the Occupied Palestinian Territory's dependence on Israel and — now more than ever before — on international aid. Until the mid-1980s, Israel intensively used Palestinian labour for work connected to agriculture and construction, with appalling employment conditions and without any of the benefits enjoyed by Israeli Jewish workers. But since 1993, the number of Palestinian workers in Israel has plummeted from over 100,000 to just a few hundred. And since the construction of the Wall, there are hardly any Palestinian workers employed in Israel. Since Hamas won the January 2006 elections in the Gaza Strip, no workers from this area whatsoever have access to Israel.

Israel persecutes and imposes restrictions on those who oppose the regime of segregation, who condemn human rights violations or who criticise the actions of the Israeli military. It also suppresses demonstrations in the Occupied Palestinian Territory, both by organisations and individuals, against the Wall or the discriminatory administration of land, water and infrastructure. Such persecution (and it must be noted here that persecution of dissent in this context of the victimisation of those opposing discriminatory practices is different from 'the crime of persecution') manifests itself through the closure of organisations, travel bans and arbitrary detention of political and human rights activists and related restrictions on freedom of expression and thought.

A Systematic and Institutionalised Regime of Racial Domination

The inhuman acts listed above do not occur in random or isolated instances. They are sufficiently widespread, integrated and complementary to be described as systematic. They are also sufficiently rooted in law, public policy and formal institutions to be described as institutionalised.

In the Israeli legal system, preferential status is afforded to Jews over non-Jews through its laws on citizenship and Jewish nationality, the latter of which has created a group privileged in most spheres of public life, including residency rights, land ownership, urban planning, access to services and social, economic and cultural rights (see list of legislation and proposed legislation in the annex to these findings). The Russell Tribunal heard expert evidence detailing the relationship between the State of Israel and the quasi-state Jewish national institutions (the Jewish Agency, World Zionist Organisation, and Jewish National Fund) that embed and formalise many of the material privileges granted exclusively to Israeli Jews. Regarding the West Bank, the Tribunal highlighted the institutionalised separation and discrimination revealed by the existence of two entirely separate legal systems: Palestinians are subject to military law enforced by military courts that fall far short of international fair trial standards; Israeli Jews living in illegal settlements are subject to Israeli civil law and a civil court system. The result is a vastly different procedure and sentence for the same crime, committed in the same jurisdiction, by members of a different group. An apparatus of administrative control implemented through pervasive permit systems and bureaucratic restrictions adversely affects Palestinians throughout the territories under Israeli control. In contrast to the explicit and readily available South African apartheid legislation, the Russell Tribunal drew attention to the obscurity and inaccessibility of many laws, military orders and regulations that underpin Israel's institutionalised regime of domination.

Conclusions

Israel subjects the Palestinian people to an institutionalised regime of domination amounting to apartheid as defined under international law. This discriminatory regime manifests in varying intensity and forms against different categories of Palestinians depending on their location.

The Palestinians living under colonial military rule in the Occupied Palestinian Territory are subject to a particularly aggravated form of apartheid. Palestinian citizens of Israel, while entitled to vote, are not part of the Jewish nation as defined by Israeli law and are therefore excluded from the benefits of Jewish nationality and subject to systematic discrimination across the broad spectrum of recognised human rights. Irrespective of such differences, the Russell Tribunal therefore concluded that Israel's rule over the Palestinian people, wherever they reside, collectively amounts to a single integrated regime of apartheid.[2]

Fig. 12 Tom Hurndall, A hand gesture from an Israeli APC at the Rafah border, April 2003.

---

2   In the ten years since the November 2011 Cape Town session of the RTOP, the analysis presented here has been widely accepted by leading human rights groups in the region and internationally — by way of example see: https://www.hrw.org/report/2021/04/27/threshold-crossed/israeli-authorities-and-crimes-apartheid-and-persecution   and   http://www.btselem.org/publications/fulltext/202101_this_is_apartheid.

10. Dismantling Racism and Settler Colonialism: Challenges for the BDS Movement

Rania Masri

Where to begin, when one talks about Palestine? What can represent what Palestinians have been going through since at least the early 1940s?

I recently came across a story that may be representative. It is the story of Abdul Fatah Abed Rabbo, known as Abed Qotqot by his friends. Abed Qotqot had lived his entire life in the Dheisheh refugee camp in the occupied West Bank. He decided to leave the refugee camp and settle on a piece of land inherited from his family, from where he could see the original village that he was exiled from in 1948. This piece of land, which the Israelis acknowledge is his, falls under the Israeli-Jerusalem municipality, an occupied entity. Even though the occupying authority recognised his ownership of the land, they declared that he could not alter any aspect of that land. So he decided to live in a cave. He set up lights and an outdoor toilet. He couldn't bring in a water-well, so he transported water in gallons. And he fought the Israeli courts for his right to build something of a home in this cave. After more than ten years in court, and after the Jerusalem political municipality (an occupier force) began 'developing' the area (illegally) by establishing a park, and after the Israeli government announced another Jewish-only settlement expansion (also illegal), the verdict came out. The verdict was that Abed could stay in his cave, but that he could not alter the land. In other words, he could not get water, or electricity, or safe passage. They destroyed everything that he had built. He built it again. They

    https://doi.org/10.11647/OBP.0345.11

destroyed it again. He died at the age of fifty-four, still clinging to his dream of liberation and return (Jaber, 2015).

In 2015, Israeli Prime Minister Netanyahu announced the destruction of more than 400 Palestinian homes in the Israeli-controlled part of the occupied West Bank known as Area C. Area C encompasses sixty percent of the occupied West Bank, and it is fully under the control of the Israeli occupying army. The remaining Area A and Area B of the West Bank are also under control of the Israeli army, but they are presented as under the façade of the control of the Palestinian Authority (which continues to coordinate 'security operations' with the occupation and thus behaves worse than the Vichy government). Netanyahu thus ordered the destruction of 400 homes, in addition to the 20,000 homes in Jerusalem set to be demolished.

Since 1967, according to Israeli records, at least 27,000 Palestinian 'homes' in the occupied West Bank alone have been demolished. Israel defines 'a home' as any structure, so even if that structure is an apartment building housing numerous 'homes' and families, Israel defines it as one home.

And we know what happened in Gaza in 2014, after more than eight years of an illegal, criminal blockade, and after several Israeli military wars on the Palestinians in Gaza. Fifty-one days of Israeli assault resulted in the demolition of more than 100,000 homes. Since then, barely anything has been rebuilt. Six months after the last bomb on Gaza, there has not been one single big project built since 2014. No homes or schools or hospitals rebuilt. The reconstruction has effectively been non-existent. Gaza is in need of 1.5 million tons of cement and so far only 27,000 tonnes have been allowed in, because of both the Israeli criminal blockade and the Egyptian criminal blockade.

Also in 2015, eighty homes in Gaza were flooded. The water reached three metres in height. Not only was there significant rain, but the Israelis took this opportunity to open several dams and cause additional flooding. So eighty additional homes were left uninhabitable.

As with Abed Qotqot in the West Bank, Palestinians in Gaza have been forced to live in cave-like conditions: deprived of regular electricity and clean water. Electricity shortages are so severe that there is a regular supply of only four to six hours of daily electricity, and the vast majority of water in Gaza is not fit for human consumption. All within a prison-like enclosure.

Banksy found a way into Gaza. He said 'Gaza is often described as "the world's largest open air prison" because no-one is allowed to enter or leave. But that seems a bit unfair to prisons — they don't have their electricity and drinking water cut off randomly almost every day' (Vartanian, 2015).

These home demolitions, these deliberate, continuous home demolitions, are not limited to the occupied territories; they are not limited to the West Bank, Jerusalem, and Gaza. They have been ongoing against Palestinians with Israeli citizenship since 1948. More than 80,000 Palestinians with Israeli citizenship in the Negev live in villages that the Israeli government does not recognise. 'We recognise you and we recognise that we do not recognise you and thereby we deprive you of electricity and water and sufficient schooling.' There are eighty thousand Palestinians, and the Israeli government takes it to another level. When they do demolish Palestinian homes, of those holding Israeli citizenships and of those under occupation, they have the *chutzpah* to actually demand that inhabitants pay for the demolition of their own home.

In addition, the demolition is not limited to homes. Anything that stands in the way of the Jewish-only expansion of territory in historic Palestine gets destroyed. So, again in 2015, the Israelis issued demolition orders for a school near al-Khalil (Hebron); a school demolished for the expansion of yet another 50 km2 of a Jewish-only settlement.

For many of us, not just those of us who are Palestinian, but for those of us who have been following this struggle, we are not surprised. We have yet to be surprised by anything that the Israeli government or the Israeli military does, but still it *is* a bit surprising to know that the vast majority of Jewish-Israeli society openly supports discriminatory policies.

A poll from October 2012 reveals that a clear majority of Jewish Israelis (74%) support separate road systems for Israelis and Palestinians in the Occupied Territories. Sixty-nine percent openly support not just the annexation of the West Bank, but the denial of rights to Palestinians; they support annexation of the land while denying Palestinians the right to vote on whether the land ought to be annexed. And almost half of the Jewish Israelis polled openly supported the expulsion of Palestinians with Israeli citizenship. They openly support ethnic cleansing.

What does it mean when racism becomes so normalised? What does it mean for the actions of the military, academics, politicians, and Israeli society in general when racism becomes so normalised?

The crimes of settler colonialism become acceptable, even encouraged.

Constant closure of Palestinian villages and towns. Detention of men, women, and children for six months without charge, and the six months can be renewed indefinitely. Constant expansion of settlements for members of only one religion. Constant thefts of people's lands, of people's homes, amidst home demolitions, and amidst increasing military and settler violence. This is worse than apartheid.

What does it mean to the children, Palestinian and Israelis, when such racism become normalised, when such attacks become acceptable daily practice?

Maryam, an eleven-year-old Palestinian girl whose home, in Silwan (on the edge of occupied Jerusalem) was demolished, was interviewed in 2005. 'Hundreds of police and military officers attacked my home in Silwan', she said. She described how big dogs were primed to attack her mother who was holding her younger brother as she tried desperately to protect her home. She was terrorised by the loud noise of the bulldozers to such an extent that now the colour yellow frightens her. She lost the ability to speak and now has child-onset diabetes. 'The bulldozers have become something normal for Jews', she said. 'They have demolished too many homes in Silwan that the demolition of my home is normal. Home demolitions have become normal. The demolition of my home is normal, which makes me so upset at the world. I feel sick, very sick. I feel exhausted.'

An eleven-year-old child feeling exhausted by the normalcy of barbarism. Since 2005, the rate of home demolitions has only increased. Such 'normalcy' has only become 'more normalized'.

When I first read those words, I stopped and asked myself: has it become normal for me, to read of another home being demolished? Has it become normal for all of us to read of these continual attacks, since they have become quite continuous?

Maryam isn't from this small town east of Jerusalem. Maryam's family is from Haifa. Maryam's family's home was taken from them in Haifa in 1948. So this spiral of dispossession, of theft of land, theft of homes, it has been ongoing since 1948. And whenever anyone, and most particularly a child, loses their home, they lose their personal belongings, their memories, and their connections to the individuals and the family members who also lived with them. They also lose a place of sanctuary and a place of safety.

Meanwhile, the criminal is consistent, and the increasing detention of children is ongoing. According to Defense for Children International, 2014 was the 'most difficult year for Palestinian children' (DCI, 2015). 'Military detention is a reality for hundreds of Palestinian children each year, exposing them to physical and psychological violence, interrupting education, contributing to mental health issues, and placing large numbers of families under stress' (DCI, 2014). Twenty percent of all children detained by Israeli military and Israeli police were placed in solitary confinement; international law defines solitary confinement as torture. Seventy-five percent of children faced physical abuse. And to add to the horror: these children were not picked up from their homes in the afternoon with a knock on the door and a policeman placing them in a jeep with a lawyer. No, the Israeli government recently stated very clearly that it would continue its night-time raids of children's detention. Night-time raids: between midnight and five o'clock in the morning. Israeli military and Israeli police break down doors, drag the child out of bed, blindfold them, handcuff them, thrown them into the back of the jeep, and the vast majority are physically assaulted. Children.

Before the bombing of Gaza in 2014, the story of three missing Israeli teenage settlers gained notoriety, although the Israeli government knew their location. The story inflamed hatred against Palestinians to such an extent that Professor Mordechai Kedar, Israeli Professor of the Begin-Sadat Center for Strategic Studies, stated publicly that 'the only deterrent for those who kidnap the children and kill them is their knowledge that either their sister or their mother will be raped' (Shelhoub-Kevorkian et al., 2014). An open justification for the rape of women, and the response to this statement was not a call for him to apologise; rather, he was promoted academically, and promoted by the Israeli government via his placement on the list of official spokespersons for journalists.

His comments were not an aberration, but were supported by common Jewish-Israelis slogans during the war on Gaza in 2014, such as 'Go pound their mothers and come back to your mother', and images of a veiled woman, naked from the waist down, with a message saying, 'Bibi finished inside this time. Signed citizens in favor of the ground assault.'

Open, clear calls for rape of women.

Also popularised were shirts encouraging the killing of children. One image is of a pregnant, veiled woman with a sniper-cross hair on her belly, with the statement, '1 shot, 2 kills.' Another image shows a child in a cross-hair with a caption, 'every Arab mother should know that her son's fate is in my hands.'

Open, clear calls for the targeting and killing of children.

What these images reflect is how Palestinian women and Palestinian children have become literal and figurative targets for killing, and the ease with which their killing can be dismissed and justified, the ease with which certain lives can be set aside, without any shame.

How many other crimes, brutalities and murders are rendered invisible because their lives are rendered inconsequential and invisible? How many times does the Western media ignore such crimes, making them invisible? Note every time that the media refers to 'calm', every time *CNN* or the *New York Times* or the *Independent* or the *Guardian* speak of calm, they only mean calm for Israelis and not Palestinians, because Palestinians have received no calm since 1948. Palestinian fishermen off the coast of Gaza continue to be attacked. Palestinian farmers throughout the occupied territories continue to be attacked. Palestinians with Israeli citizenship within 1948 Palestine continue to be attacked and harassed. And almost weekly, Palestinian children are run down by settlers, deliberately. All of this is perceived as calm because Palestinians are rendered invisible, not just to the Jewish-Israeli society, but to others around the world who hold Israel up as a 'beacon of liberal democracy'.

When images dehumanise people, those images get connected to real-world violence, not just in Palestine but around the world, particularly in societies built on structural, institutional racism. In the US, innocent African American men's mugshots were used as target practice by the US police department in Florida (Izadi, 2015). What does it mean when your picture gets used as target practice? How does it contribute to the fact that a 'white police officer killed a black person nearly two times a week during a seven-year period ending in 2012, according to a 2014 USA Today review of the most recent accounts of justifiable homicide reported to the FBI' (Johnson et al., 2014)?

And what about when blockbuster movies dehumanise the occupied and elevate the occupier, as with the 2014 blockbuster movie *American Sniper*? US soldiers in the movie had names, love lives, children, hopes and dreams, while the Iraqis, and even the children in the film, were consistently represented as nameless, evil savages. Chris Kyle, the American sniper, actually said in his book, 'we are fighting savage despicable evil. [...] I only wish I had killed more. I loved what I did. It was fun. I had the time of my life.' This man, a sociopath, is now regarded as a hero in popular US culture.

We have all seen images that not only normalise racism, but celebrate it, pictures of US soldiers posing with glee after they torture Iraqi men in Guantanamo, and pictures of Israeli men posing as they kill Palestinian children. These pictures are reminiscent of the postcard images taken of the public lynching of African Americans in the United States. A continuation of the same kind of racism, used to justify settler colonialism or occupation.

2015 marked the fiftieth anniversary of the assassination of a great leader, Malcolm X. Malcolm (1965) called upon his comrades to 'make our grievances international and make the world see our problem was no longer a Negro problem or an American problem but a human problem. This is a problem for humanity, and a problem which should be attacked by all elements of humanity'.

The problem that we are facing in Palestine is not a Palestinian problem; it is not an Arab-Israeli 'conflict'. It is a problem for humanity, and it should be attacked by all elements of humanity.

Tom Hurndall and Rachel Corrie knew that. They knew when they put their bodies on the line and stood in solidarity that they were not standing out of love for Palestinians. They were standing out of love for humanity.

Tom Hurndall chose solidarity. He chose to put his body on the line. Those years ago, twenty-one-year-old Tom Hurndall was shot in the head by an Israeli sniper in Gaza while he was trying to defend children. Tom bravely put himself in the way of Israeli troops who were firing at Palestinian children, and an Israeli sniper, trying to kill children, chose to shoot him in the head, even after seeing that he was unarmed.

A week before Tom was shot, Rachel Corrie, an American Peace activist, was run over — twice — and killed by a custom-made

Caterpillar Israeli bulldozer as she tried to protect a Palestinian family home from being demolished yet again.

Tom Hurndall wrote about her death, 'I wonder how few or many people heard it on the news and just counted it as another death, just another number.'

The Israeli Supreme Court ruled in 2015 that the Israeli military could not be held responsible for damages in a war zone. The Israeli Supreme Court ruled in the same month that the Israeli military could not be held responsible for the death of Rachel Corrie. Rachel Corrie's family responded in a statement.

> We have come to see through this experience how deeply all of Israel's institutions are implicated in the impunity enjoyed by the Israeli military. Nevertheless, it is clear that this decision, affirming the August 2012 lower court finding, amounts to judicial sanction of immunity for Israeli military forces when they commit injustices and human rights violations. Rachel's case provides yet another example of how the Israeli justice system is failing to provide accountability. (Lazare, 2015)

I don't believe anyone was surprised by the Israeli court ruling. Just as, to be frank, I'm not surprised when another US police officer is acquitted for the shooting of an unarmed African American.

We — those of us fighting for justice and liberation and those of us recognising the liberation of Palestine as a fight for our own humanity — understand that the occupier, the oppressor, the one supporting a racist structure, always dismisses the lives of others to maintain his own standing.

Peter Beinart, a self-proclaimed Liberal Zionist and author of *The Crisis of Zionism*, writes:

> If we accept, for the sake of argument, that the creation of a Palestinian state roughly among the 1967 lines remains realistic and achievable, then there would still be 1.5 million Palestinian citizens of Israel within Israel, a prospect that causes Zionists considerable anxiety. I'm not asking Israel to be Utopian. I'm not asking it to allow Palestinians who were forced out (or fled) in 1948 to return to their homes. I'm not even asking it to allow full, equal citizenship to Arab Israelis, since that would require Israel no longer being a Jewish state. I'm actually pretty willing to compromise my liberalism for Israel's security and for its status as a Jewish state. (Goldberg, 2010)

He is willing to compromise his liberalism to take away other people's rights. I don't think that is his prerogative. Martin Luther King, Jr. said, 'they love the separate, the equal not so much.' Beinart, and other Zionists, support the separate to maintain the inequality.

Palestinian refugees, who are the vast majority of Palestinians, are denied their right of return to their homes and villages in 1948 Palestine, not because there is no room for them — since the majority of Palestinian villages have been converted into so-called green spaces. Rather, they are not allowed to go home because they are not Jewish, as Beinart and other Zionists clearly state. There is a word for such policy: 'ethnocracy', a system of government that elevates one community above another, and 'a political regime that facilitates expansion and control by a dominant ethnicity in contested lands' (Yiftachel, 2006). There is another, more mainstream, word for the Israeli state policy: the crime of Apartheid, according to the Rome Statute of the International Criminal Court, is defined as: 'inhumane acts [...] committed in the context of an institutionalized regime of systematic oppression and domination by one racial group over any other racial group or groups and committed with the intention of maintaining that regime' (Rome Statute of the International Criminal Court). The Convention on the Suppression and Punishment of the Crime of Apartheid (1973) further lists

> acts that fall within the ambit of the crime. These include murder, torture, inhuman treatment and arbitrary arrest of members of a racial group; deliberate imposition on a racial group of living conditions calculated to cause its physical destruction; legislative measures that discriminate in the political, social, economic and cultural fields; measures that divide the population along racial lines by the creation of separate residential areas for racial groups; the prohibition of interracial marriages; and the persecution of persons opposed to apartheid.

We recognise that, because we live in such insane, hypocritical times, where war is peace, and violence is calm, and apartheid is freedom and democracy, that merely telling the truth becomes revolutionary. In a time of universal deceit, telling the truth becomes a revolutionary act. And, today, it becomes our responsibility to critically speak the truth — clearly and powerfully. Israel is, according to international law, an apartheid state. It is clearly a settler-colonialist, apartheid state.

Reverend Desmond Tutu said, 'I am not interested in picking up crumbs of compassion thrown from the table of someone who considers himself my master. I want the full menu of rights' (Voices for Human Rights). Palestinians deserve the full menu of rights. These rights include the right of return to their homes and villages, the right to live free of military occupation and institutionalised apartheid, and, of course, the right to resist those crimes of settler colonialism and apartheid by any means necessary until the liberation of all of Palestine.

Our role, to assist in that struggle, is to resist as well. We begin by resisting the normalisation of surrender, cloaked as appeals for Palestinians to compromise on their rights.

We also resist the use of inaccurate language. For example, during the summer 2014 assault on Gaza, many continued to refer to 'Gazans', yet eighty percent of the people in Gaza are refugees, exiled from their villages in 1948. Thus, when they are referred to as Gazans, it implies Gaza is separate from Palestine. Rather, they are Palestinians in Gaza, as there are Palestinians in Ramallah, Haifa, Yaffa, and Al-Nasra.

And what about the language in our reference to those Palestinians killed by Israeli soldiers or settlers? Do we refer separately to the deaths of 'women and children', as was commonly done during the war? A child is an individual who lacks agency, sovereignty, and who lacks the ability to protect himself or herself. Some patriarchal communities may want to impose a lack of agency on women, but women still have agency, so they don't belong in the same category as children.

What is the consequence of including women and children in the same category, and separating them from men? By simply saying 'women and children', the implicit assumption is that men can be justifiably killed — because all Palestinians males are terrorist or may become terrorists — or that the murder of men should render less anger than the murder of women, because women cannot carry weapons and fight. Naturally, both of these assumptions are wrong.

Palestinian men and women do have the legal and moral right to carry weapons; they do have the right to defend themselves. Any occupied population, any oppressed population, has the right to defend itself and the right to determine its own means of liberation. Whether or not we agree with them is secondary to their right to determine their struggle for liberation.

So when we separate the women from the men, not only are we saying you can kill the men, but we are also saying that we don't salute the fighters, that we will only mourn the civilians. I mourn the children. I mourn the civilians. And I mourn every single Palestinian fighter who defended Gaza and they defended it heroically.

Using clear and powerful language also includes rejecting the 'legitimacy of a Jewish Israeli state'.

In 2007 (and this was not the first declaration!), a group of Palestinians and (a small group of) Israelis publicly declared their support for a 'One State Declaration' (2017).

> The historic land of Palestine belongs to all who live in it and to those who were expelled or exiled from it since 1948, regardless of religion, ethnicity, national origin or current citizenship status; Any system of government must be founded on the principle of equality in civil, political, social and cultural rights for all citizens. Power must be exercised with rigorous impartiality on behalf of all people in the diversity of their identities.

In 2015, the University of Southampton planned to have an academic conference entitled 'International Law and the State of Israel: Legitimacy, Responsibility and Exceptionalism' (Ben-Dor, 2014):

> The conference would have been the first of its kind and constitutes a ground-breaking historical event on the road towards justice and enduring peace in historic Palestine. It would have been unique because, while most attention today is directed at Israel's actions in the 1967 Occupied Territories, the conference seeks to expand the debate surrounding the nature of the State of Israel and the legal and political reality within it.[1]

An academic conference in a Western country openly questioning the legitimacy of the State of Israel means we are beginning to powerfully change the tide of the narrative, and changing the narrative is critical in the struggle against the legitimacy of apartheid.

We oppose the legitimacy of apartheid, and thus the State of Israel. We oppose settler-state colonialism, and thus the State of Israel. We oppose racism, discrimination, injustice, crimes against humanity, and

---

1   The conference was cancelled by the university. It was later organised by the University College Cork in 2017. See https://criticallegalthinking.com/2016/12/12/announcement-international-law-state-israel-legitimacy-responsibility-exceptionalism/.

constant theft, and thus we oppose the State of Israel. We declare it openly.

States, *per se*, don't have a right to exist. People do.

Does Israel does have the right to exist as a Jewish state? No. There is no right to be racist. There is, rather, a right for equality and liberation.

One critical tool for the struggle for equality and liberation is the Boycott, Divestment, and Sanctions Movement (BDS), a vibrant, global movement, launched in 2005, to end 'international support for Israel's oppression of Palestinians and pressure Israel to comply with international law' (https://bdsmovement.net/). BDS is a movement that rejects both occupation and apartheid. The movement is growing, internationally, and winning. There are multinational corporations, such as Veolia and G4S, that have lost their contracts because of their dealings with Israel.

And in just the one month of February 2015, there were numerous victories.

- More than 400 UK artists have taken a public pledge to 'support the Palestinian struggle for freedom, justice and equality.' 'In response to the call from Palestinian artists and cultural workers for a cultural boycott of Israel, we pledge to accept neither professional invitations to Israel, nor funding, from any institutions linked to its government until it complies with international law and universal principles of human rights (https://artistsforpalestine.org.uk/a-pledge/).' These artists have said no to financial incentives; they have said no to crossing the picket line. They have taken a stand for solidarity and conscience.

- Also that month, the largest student association in the US, the University of California Student Association, which represents more than 238,000 students in California covering ten campuses, passed a divestment against Israel resolution by a 9 to 1 vote.

- 73% of the SOAS community (faculty staff and students) voted for an academic boycott of Israel.

- The student government at the University of Toledo in Ohio passed a resolution to divest from Israel: 21 to 4.

Divestment. Academic Boycott. Cultural Boycott. Not only have there been more divestment resolutions passed in the UK and the US, but they have passed with an overwhelming majority.

Because we are getting stronger, we are being challenged. And it is another example of how our struggles are connected. Two members of the US Congress introduced a bill that would turn a very destructive trade deal — the TransAtlantic Trade and Investment Partnership (TTIP) under negotiation in 2015, which violates national sovereignty, violates European sovereignty, violates environmental laws and ethics, and labor unions — into a devastating weapon against the people of Palestine and all those seeking justice alongside them. This bill would have forced 'all 28 EU member states to crack down on European groups participating in BDS movement. The bill would have prohibited BDS campaigns and will add to the conviction that the US wants to use TTIP to undermine European democracy for its own geo-strategic and economic purposes.' The bill called for surveillance and information-gathering on 'politically motivated acts of boycott, divestment from, and sanctions against Israel'. If passed, and if TTIP got through, the bill would demand that European nations return to the US Congress every six months with surveillance information on all individuals, organisations and entities that participate in any way in BDS (Barnard and Hilary, 2015).

Our struggle is not only against institutionalised racism; it is a struggle against encroaching and increasing surveillance. So, in addition to supporting BDS, we need to be vehemently outraged at the concept of this extreme surveillance, in violation of democracy and sovereignty. We need to recognise that TTIP was more of the same Israeli policies; Israeli policies are basically: 'I like what you have; I'm going to take it, and for me to take it, I have to dismiss your life as less.' Isn't that what neoliberal economic policies are all about? Isn't that what so-called free trade economic policies are all about? 'I will work you to the bone, dismiss your life as irrelevant, impose modern-day slavery on you, barely give you any wages, try as much as I can to oppose your right to organize, and then have you produce something from a country that needs it more.' The economic structure needs to be altered, and this economic structure relies on racism, because if we didn't so easily dismiss the lives of workers around us, this economic structure would falter.

We understand that there are structures of violence we have to dismantle. As we dismantle those structures of violence, we build other structures of connectivity to other struggles because we understand the core of our struggle.

There is strength from looking at the connection of the struggle, from recognising that when folks in Ferguson, Missouri were facing tear gas made by the company in Pennsylvania that sends the same tear gas to the Israelis (and the Bahrainis and numerous other governments around the world), Palestinians in Gaza during the bombing and onslaught tweeted to people in Ferguson and told them how to respond to tear gas. A connection was made. Then, the first delegation from Ferguson went to Palestine. These African-American youth went from Missouri to Palestine; they felt the connection of the struggle. They both understood the horror of structural racism.

From Ferguson to Palestine, resistance is not a crime. From Ferguson to Palestine, racism is a crime.

We acknowledge what Audre Lorde (1984) said: 'without community, there is no liberation, only the most vulnerable and temporary armistice between an individual and her oppression.'

Lorde (1980) also said, 'There is no such thing as a single-issue struggle because we do not live single-issue lives. Malcolm knew this. Martin Luther King, Jr. knew this. Our struggles are particular, but we are not alone.'

We are not alone. Together, we stand in solidarity resisting occupation, settler colonialism, and racism. We connect our struggles. We create an honest narrative of unity and hope. And we oppose the normalisation of fear, hopelessness, and surrender. Rather, we organise in the belief, in the recognition, that liberation and equality are possible. And we remember the struggles that came before us, and learn from them.

I believe this, now more than ever, just like when comrades before us organised for the dismantling of political apartheid in South Africa and were told that they were imagining the impossible. They organised and they were victorious against political apartheid. The struggle continues. I do believe there will come a day when Zionism and racism will fall. The only question we are facing is how fast it will fall. BDS is one of the paths of resistance to make that collapse of apartheid faster. The question is not whether Zionism and apartheid in Palestine will be eliminated; the question is: how fast?

Let us work together to make the fall of apartheid faster, and the liberation of Palestine sooner.

Bibliography

Barnard, R., and Hilary, J., 'How EU-US trade deal could thwart 'boycott Israel' campaign', The Electronic Intifada, 2015, https://electronicintifada.net/content/how-eu-us-trade-deal-could-thwart-boycott-israel-campaign/14290.

Ben-Dor, O., 'CfP: International Law and the State of Israel: Legitimacy, Responsibility and Exceptionalism', 2014, https://criticallegalthinking.com/2014/04/10/cfp-international-law-state-israel-legitimacy-responsibility-exceptionalism/.

Convention on the Suppression and Punishment of the Crime of Apartheid, 1973, https://legal.un.org/avl/ha/cspca/cspca.html

DCI, 'How was 2014 for Palestinian children?', 2014, https://www.dci-palestine.org/how_was_2014_for_palestinian_children_1.

DCI, 'Most difficult year for Palestinian children', 2015, https://imemc.org/article/70290/.

Goldberg, J., 'Goldberg vs Peter Beinhart, Part II', *The Atlantic*, 2010, https://www.theatlantic.com/national/archive/2010/05/goldblog-vs-peter-beinart-part-ii/56934/.

Izadi, E., 'Florida police used mugshots of black men for target practice. Clergy responded: #UseMeInstead', *The Washington Post*, 2015, https://www.washingtonpost.com/news/morning-mix/wp/2015/01/25/florida-police-used-mugshots-of-black-men-for-target-practice-clergy-responded-usemeinstead/.

Jaber, S., 'The status quo that suffocates Palestinians', Mondoweiss, 2015, https://mondoweiss.net/2015/02/status-suffocates-palestinians/.

Johnson, K., M., Hoyer, and Heath, B. 'Local police involved in 400 killings per year', *USA Today*, 2014, https://www.usatoday.com/story/news/nation/2014/08/14/police-killings-data/14060357/.

Lazare, S., 'Rachel Corrie's family denied justice from Israel's highest court', Common Dreams, 2015, https://www.commondreams.org/news/2015/02/13/rachel-corries-family-denied-justice-israels-highest-court.

Lorde, A., 'Learning from the '60s', 1980, https://www.blackpast.org/african-american-history/1982-audre-lorde-learning-60s/.

Lorde, A., 'The Master's tools will never dismantle the master's house', 1984, https://collectiveliberation.org/wp-content/uploads/2013/01/Lorde_The_Masters_Tools.pdf.

Malcolm X., 'Address delivered in the Corn Hill Methodist Church, Rochester, New York. February 16, 1965', http://nationalhumanitiescenter.org/pds/maai3/community/text10/malcolmxworldproblem.pdf.

Rome Statute of the International Criminal Court, https://www.icc-cpi.int/resource-library/documents/rs-eng.pdf.

Shalhoub-Kevorkian, N., Ihmoud, S. and Dahir-Nashif, S., 'Sexual violence, women's bodies, and Israeli settler colonialism', Jadaliyya, 2014, https://www.jadaliyya.com/Details/31481.

The One State Declaration, 29 November 2017, https://electronicintifada.net/content/one-state-declaration/793.

Vartanian, H., 'New Banksys highlight plight of Palestinians in Gaza', HyperAllergic, 2015, https://hyperallergic.com/185876/new-banksys-highlight-plight-of-palestinians-in-gaza/.

Voices for Human Rights, 'Desmond Tutu, United for Human Rights', https://www.humanrights.com/voices-for-human-rights/desmond-tutu.html.

Yiftachel, O., *Ethnocracy Land and Identify Politics in Israel/Palestine* (Philadelphia: University of Pennsylvania, 2006).

Fig. 13 Tom Hurndall, ISM volunteers in action with IDF bulldozer at the Rafah
border, April 2003.

11. The Oslo Accords and Palestine's Political Economy in the Shadow of Regional Turmoil[1]

Adam Hanieh

Support for Palestine has long been a deeply held principle of political movements in the Middle East. Throughout much of the 1970s, Palestinian refugee camps in countries such as Jordan and Lebanon formed an important centre of revolutionary movements in the Arab world, providing fertile ground for political and military training for much of the region's Left (and, indeed, globally). These struggles of Palestinian refugees forced even the most pro-Western regimes in the region to pay lip service to the cause of Palestinian rights. In later decades, the successive uprisings of Palestinians living under Israeli military occupation provoked an outpouring of street demonstrations and other forms of protest across the Arab worlddemanding regimes sever political and economic ties with Israel and provide real support to the Palestinian struggle. The political networks that formed in these solidarity movements, often the most palpable expression of resistance to autocratic governments in the Middle East, would later play an important prefigurative role in the uprisings of 2011.

Given the preponderant weight of the question of Palestine to Middle East politics, it is striking how little substantive discussion there has been

---

1 The text of this chapter draws upon two previously published works by the author: 'The Oslo Illusion', *Jacobin Magazine*, 21 April 2013, https://www.jacobinmag.com/2013/04/the-oslo-illusion/ and *Lineages of Revolt: Issues of Contemporary Capitalism in the Middle East* (Chicago: Haymarket Books, 2013).

   https://doi.org/10.11647/OBP.03451.12

around issues of its political economy. In stark contrast to other parts of the region — where sharp analyses of capitalist development and the strategies adopted by states and ruling elites are regularly dissected and debated — Palestine remains largely viewed as a 'humanitarian issue'. Much solidarity work (both in the Arab world and further afield) typically emphasises the violation of Palestinian rights and the enormous suffering this entails, rather than Palestine's connection to the wider region and its articulation with forms of imperialist power. Placed in a category of its own, Palestine has become an exception that somehow defies the analytical tools used to unpack and comprehend neighbouring states.

In this chapter I aim to present a counter-narrative to this exceptionalism by examining some aspects of the political economy of Palestine, particularly through the period that has followed the 1993 Oslo Accords. Officially known as the Declaration of Principles on Interim Self-Government Arrangements, the Oslo Accords were signed between the Palestine Liberation Organisation (PLO) and the Israeli government on 13 September 1993. Firmly ensconced in the framework of a 'two-state solution', Oslo supposedly promised 'an end to decades of confrontation and conflict', the recognition of 'mutual legitimate and political rights', and the aim of achieving 'peaceful coexistence and mutual dignity and security and [...] a just, lasting and comprehensive peace settlement.' Its supporters claimed that Oslo would see Israel gradually relinquish control over territory in the West Bank and Gaza Strip, with the newly established Palestinian Authority (PA) eventually forming an independent state in these areas. The negotiations process and subsequent agreements between the PLO and Israel were to pave the way for the current situation in the West Bank and Gaza Strip. The Palestinian Authority, which now rules over an estimated 2.6 million Palestinians in the West Bank, has become the key architect of Palestinian political strategy. Its institutions draw international legitimacy from Oslo, and its avowed strategic goal of 'building an independent Palestinian state' remains grounded in the same framework. The incessant calls for a return to negotiations — echoed by US and European leaders on an almost daily basis — hark back to the principles laid down in September 1993.

Several decades on, it is now common to hear Oslo described as a 'failure' due to the ongoing reality of Israeli occupation. The problem with this assessment is that it mistakes the stated goals of Oslo for its real aims. From the perspective of the Israeli government, rather than ending the occupation of the West Bank and Gaza Strip — or addressing the substantive issues of Palestinian dispossession — Oslo's role was ultimately functional. By creating the *perception* that negotiations would lead towards some kind of 'peace', Israel was able to portray its intentions as those of a partner rather than as an antithesis of Palestinian sovereignty. Based upon this perception, the Israeli government used Oslo as a fig leaf to consolidate and deepen its control over Palestinian life, employing the same strategic mechanisms wielded since the onset of the occupation in 1967. Settlement construction, restrictions on Palestinian movement, the incarceration of thousands of Palestinians, and command over borders and economic life — all came together to form a complex system of control. A Palestinian face may preside over the day-to-day administration of Palestinian affairs, but ultimate power remains in the hands of Israel. This structure has reached its apex in the Gaza Strip — where over 1.7 million Palestinians are penned into a tiny enclave with entry and exit of goods and people largely determined by Israeli *dictat* (with part of the administration of this system subcontracted to regional neighbours such as Egypt). In this sense, there has been no contradiction between calls to support the 'peace process' and deepening colonisation — the former consistently worked to enable the latter.

No less importantly, Oslo had a pernicious political effect. By reducing the Palestinian struggle to a process of bartering around slithers of land in the West Bank and Gaza Strip, Oslo ideologically disarmed the not-insignificant parts of the Palestinian political movement that advocated continued resistance to Israeli colonialism and sought the genuine fulfilment of Palestinian aspirations. The most important of these aspirations was the demand that Palestinian refugees had the right to return to their homes and lands from which they had been expelled in 1947–1948. Oslo made talk of these goals appear fanciful and unrealistic, normalising a delusive pragmatism rather than tackling the foundational roots of Palestinian exile. Outside of Palestine, Oslo fatally undermined the widespread solidarity and sympathy with the Palestinian struggle built during the years of the First Intifada — displacing an orientation towards grassroots, collective support with a faith in negotiations steered by Western governments. It would take over a decade for solidarity movements to rebuild themselves.

It is worth remembering that amidst the clamour of international cheerleading for Oslo — capped by the Nobel Peace prize awarded jointly to Israeli Prime Minister Yitzhak Rabin, Foreign Minister Shimon Peres, and PLO leader Yasser Arafat in 1994 — a handful of perceptive voices forecast the situation we face today. Noteworthy amongst these opposition voices was Edward Said, who wrote powerfully against Oslo, commenting that its signing displayed 'the degrading spectacle of Yasser Arafat thanking everyone for the suspension of most of his people's rights, and the fatuous solemnity of Bill Clinton's performance, like a 20th-century Roman emperor shepherding two vassal kings through rituals of reconciliation and obeisance' (Said, 1993). Describing the agreement as 'an instrument of Palestinian surrender, a Palestinian Versailles', Said noted that the PLO would become 'Israel's enforcer', helping Israel deepen its economic and political domination of Palestinian areas and consolidating a 'state of permanent dependency'. Whilst analyses such as those of Said are important to recall simply for their remarkable prescience and as a counterpoint to the constant mythologising of the historical record, they are all the more significant today when virtually all world leaders continue to make the requisite genuflection at the altar of a chimerical 'peace process'.

Nonetheless, one question that often goes unaddressed in analyses of Oslo and the two-state strategy is *why* the Palestinian leadership headquartered in the West Bank has been so willingly complicit with this disastrous project. Too often the explanation for this reduces to essentially a tautology — something akin to 'the Palestinian leadership have made bad decisions because they are poor leaders.' The finger is often pointed at corruption, or the difficulties of the international context that limit the available political options. What is missing from this type of explanation is a blunt fact: *some* Palestinians have a great stake in seeing a continuation of the status quo. Over the last two decades, the evolution of Israeli rule has produced profound changes in the nature of Palestine's political economy. These changes have been concentrated in the West Bank, cultivating a social base that supports the political trajectory of the Palestinian leadership — one all too eager to relinquish Palestinian rights, while, in return, being incorporated into the structures of Israeli settler colonialism. It is this process of socio-economic transformation that explains the Palestinian leadership's submission to Oslo, and points to the need for a radical break from the current Palestinian political strategy.

The Social Base of Oslo

The 1993 signing of the Oslo Accords needs to be understood through the paramount importance of the US-Israel alliance to Middle East politics. As a settler-colonial state, Israel had come into being in 1948 through the expulsion of around three-quarters of the original Palestinian population from their homes and lands (Pappe, 2006). Precisely because of this initial act of dispossession and its overarching goal of preserving itself as a self-defined 'Jewish state', Israel quickly emerged as a key partner of foreign powers in the region (Honig-Parnass, 2011; Machover, 2012). Inextricably tied to external support for its continued viability in a hostile environment, Israel could be counted on as a much more reliable ally than any Arab state. During the 1950s, Israel's main external support had come from Britain and France. (In the region, Iran, up until its 1979 revolution, was the main ally of Israel.) But the June 1967 war saw the Israeli military destroy the Egyptian and Syrian air forces and occupy the West Bank, Gaza Strip, (Egyptian) Sinai Peninsula, and (Syrian) Golan Heights. Israel's defeat of the Arab states encouraged the United States to cement itself as the country's primary patron, supplying it annually with billions of dollars' worth of military hardware and financial support.

Following the collapse of the Soviet Union and its satellites from 1989–1992, US strategy in the Middle East continued to centre upon its alliance with Israel, alongside the oil-rich Gulf monarchies and other Arab client states such as Egypt and Jordan. However, the new international situation in the early 1990s saw a shift in how these various pillars of US power were articulated in the region. A key feature of this strategy was the goal of normalising economic and political relations between Israel and the Arab world. Precisely because of its long-privileged relationship with the United States — expressed most sharply in the massive receipts of aid without the conditionalities characteristic of loans to other states — Israel's economy had developed in a qualitatively different direction than those of its neighbours. Israel's capitalist class had emerged with the support of the state apparatus around activities such as construction, agriculture, and finance. But direct US financial support helped to enable the development of high value-added export industries connected to sectors such as information technology, pharmaceuticals, and security. In 2010, just under half of all Israeli exports (excluding diamonds) were considered 'high tech' (Brusilovsky and Gitelson, 2011, 5). Unlike with other states in the region, the United States had run a massive trade deficit with Israel since the signing of a US-Israel free trade agreement (FTA) in 1985. In this context, the push to normalisation would inevitably strengthen the position of Israel (and thus the United States) within regional hierarchies.

A precondition for this knitting together of various regional allies of the US was the dropping of Arab economic boycotts against the Israeli state. From the Israeli perspective, these boycotts were estimated to have cost a cumulative $40 billion from 1948–1994 (Retzky, 1995; Bouillon, 2006). But even more important for Israeli capital than the direct cost of being isolated from the Arab world were the barriers the boycott presented to the internationalisation of Israeli capital itself. In the mid-1980s, Israel had been hit by an economic crisis addressed in the neoliberal 1985 Economic Stabilisation Plan (ESP), which saw the privatisation of many state-owned companies and allowed the large conglomerates that dominated the Israeli economy to make the leap into international markets (Nitzan and Bichler, 2002). The ESP also opened the Israeli economy to foreign investment. Many international firms, however, were reluctant to do business with Israeli firms (or inside Israel itself) because of the secondary boycotts attached to the policies of Arab governments (Nitzan and Bichler, 2002, 337). In this sense, Oslo was very much an outcome suited to the capitalism of its time — the expansion of internationalisation that characterised the global economy of the 1990s.[2] In all these ways, Oslo presented itself as the ideal tool to

---

2   The other component to this was the transformation of the PLO into an apparatus dependent upon the support of other Arab governments and funding from the Gulf region. The PLO's isolation following its backing of Saddam Hussein in the 1990–1991 war also played a major role in its support for the Oslo process.

fortify Israel's control over Palestinians and simultaneously strengthen its position within the broader Middle East.

On the ground, the unfolding of the Oslo process was ultimately shaped by the structures of occupation laid down by Israel during the preceding decades. Through this earlier period, the Israeli government launched a systematic campaign to confiscate Palestinian land and construct settlements in the areas that Palestinians were driven out from during the 1967 war. The logic of this settlement construction was embodied in two major strategic plans, the Allon Plan (1967) and the Sharon Plan (1981). Both these plans envisaged Israeli settlements placed between major Palestinian population centres and on top of water aquifers and fertile agricultural land. An 'Israeli-only' road network would eventually connect these settlements to each other and also to Israeli cities outside of the West Bank. In this manner, Israel could seize the land and resources, divide Palestinian areas from each other, and avoid as much as possible direct responsibility for the Palestinian population. The asymmetry of Israeli and Palestinian control over land, resources and economy, meant that the contours of Palestinian state formation were completely dependent upon Israeli design.

Combined with military-enforced restrictions on the movement of Palestinian farmers and their access to water and other resources, the massive waves of land confiscation and settlement building during the first two decades of the occupation transformed Palestinian landownership and modes of social reproduction. From 1967 to 1974, the area of cultivated Palestinian land in the West Bank fell by around one-third (Samara, 1988). The expropriation of land in the Jordan Valley by Israeli settlers meant that 87% of all irrigated land in the West Bank was removed from Palestinian use (Samara, 1988, 91). Military orders forbade the drilling of new wells for agricultural purposes and restricted overall water use by Palestinians, while Israeli settlers were encouraged to use as much water as needed (Graham-Brown, 1990, 68). With this deliberate destruction of the agricultural sector, poorer Palestinians — particularly youth — were displaced from rural areas and gravitated towards working in the construction and agriculture sectors inside Israel. In 1970, the agricultural sector represented over 40% of the Palestinian labour force working in the West Bank. By 1987 this figure was down to only 26%. Agriculture's share in GDP fell from 35% to 16% between 1970 and 1991.[3]

Under the framework established by the Oslo Accords, Israel seamlessly incorporated these earlier changes to the West Bank into a comprehensive system of control. Palestinian life became progressively transformed into a patchwork of isolated enclaves — with the three main clusters in the north, centre and south of the West Bank divided from one another by settlement blocs. The Palestinian Authority was granted limited autonomy in areas where most Palestinians lived (so-called Areas A and B), but travel between these areas could be shut down at any time by the Israeli military. All entry to and from Areas A and B, as well as the determination of residency rights in these areas, was under Israeli authority. Israel also controlled the vast majority of water aquifers, all underground resources, and all air space in the West Bank, with Palestinians thus relying on Israeli discretion for their water and energy supplies. Israel's complete control over all external borders, codified in the 1994 Paris Protocol economic agreement between the PA and Israel, meant that it was impossible for the Palestinian economy to develop meaningful trade relations with a third country. The Paris Protocols gave Israel the final say on what the PA was allowed to import and export. The West Bank and Gaza Strip thus became highly dependent on imported goods, with total imports ranging between 70 and 80 percent of GDP (Palestinian Central Bureau of Statistics (PCBS), https://www.pcbs.gov.ps). By 2005, the Palestinian Central Bureau of Statistics estimated that 73.9 percent of all imports to the WB/GS originated in Israel while 87.9 percent of all WB/GS exports were destined for Israel.[4]

With no real economic base, the PA was completely reliant upon external capital flows of aid and loans, which were again under Israeli control. Between 1995 and 2000, 60 percent of the total PA revenue came from indirect taxes collected by the Israeli government on goods imported

---

3   For the Labour and GDP figures see Farsakh (2005, 41–42; 98). It should be emphasised that population figures in the West Bank and Gaza Strip are somewhat suspect given that, until 1997, the only census conducted in the area was one performed by the Israeli military in 1967 immediately after the occupation began.

4   PCBS—Total Value of Exports from Remaining West Bank and Gaza Strip by Country of Destination and SITC. Total Value of Imports for Remaining West Bank and Gaza Strip by Country of Origin and SITC, 2005. This dependency was only to increase with time.

from abroad and destined for the Occupied Territories. This tax was collected by the Israeli government and then transferred to the PA each month according to a process outlined in the Paris Protocol.[5] The other main source of PA income came from aid and foreign disbursements by the United States, Europe, and Arab governments. Indeed, figures for aid measured as a percentage of Gross National Income indicated that the West Bank and Gaza Strip was among the most 'aid dependent' of all regions in the world.

Changing Labour Structure

This system of control engendered two major changes to the political economy of Palestinian society. The first of these related to the nature of Palestinian labour, which increasingly became a 'tap' that could be turned on and off depending on the economic and political situation and the needs of Israeli capital. Beginning in 1993, Israel consciously moved to substitute the daily Palestinian labour force that commuted from the West Bank with foreign workers from Asia and Eastern Europe (Bartram, 1998). This substitution was partly enabled by the declining importance of construction and agriculture as Israel's economy shifted away from those sectors towards hi-tech industries and exports of finance capital in the 1990s. Between 1992 and 1996, Palestinian employment in Israel declined from 116,000 workers (33 percent of the Palestinian labour force) to 28,100 (6 percent of the Palestinian labour force). Earnings from work in Israel collapsed from 25 percent of Palestinian GNP in 1992 to 6 percent in 1996 (World Bank, 2001). Between 1997 and 1999, an upturn in the Israeli economy saw the absolute numbers of Palestinian workers increase to approximately pre-1993 levels, but the proportion of the Palestinian labour force working inside Israel had nonetheless almost halved compared with a decade earlier (Farsakh, 2005, 209–10).

Instead of working inside Israel, Palestinians became increasingly dependent upon public sector employment within the PA or on transfer payments made by the PA to families of prisoners, martyrs or the needy. Public sector employment made up nearly 25 percent of total

---

5   The Paris Protocol was signed in 1994 and gave precise expectations of which goods Palestinians were allowed to export and import, as well as tax regulations and other economic issues.

employment in the West Bank and Gaza Strip by mid-2000, a level that had almost doubled since mid-1996 (Palestinian Central Bureau of Statistics (PCBS), https://www.pcbs.gov.ps). More than half of the PA's expenditure was to go on wages for these public sector workers. The other major sector of employment was the private sector, particularly in the area of services. This was overwhelmingly dominated by very small family-owned businesses — over 90 percent of Palestinian private sector businesses employ less than ten people — as a result of decades of Israeli de-development policies (Palestinian Central Bureau of Statistics (PCBS), https://www.pcbs.gov.ps).

Capital and the Palestinian Authority

Alongside the increasing dependence of Palestinian families on either employment or payments from the Palestinian Authority, the second major feature of the socio-economic transformation of the West Bank was related to the nature of the Palestinian capitalist class. In a situation of weak local production and extremely high dependence on imports and flows of foreign capital, the economic power of the Palestinian capitalist class in the West Bank did not stem from local industry, but rather from proximity to the PA as the main conduit of external capital inflows. Through the Oslo years this class came together through the fusion of three distinct social groups: (1) 'Returnee' capital, mostly from a Palestinian bourgeoisie that had emerged in the Gulf Arab states and held strong ties to the nascent Palestinian Authority; (2) families and individuals that had traditionally dominated Palestinian society, often large landowners from the pre-1967 period (particularly in the northern areas of the West Bank); and (3) those who had managed to accumulate wealth through their position as interlocutors with the occupation since 1967. While the memberships of these three groups overlapped considerably, the first was particularly significant to the nature of state and class formation in the West Bank. Gulf-based financial flows had long played a major role in tempering the radical edge of Palestinian nationalism; but their conjoining with the Oslo state-building process radically deepened the tendencies of statisation and bureaucratisation within the Palestinian national project itself.

This new, three-sided configuration of the capitalist class tended to draw its wealth from a privileged relationship with the Palestinian Authority, which assisted its growth through means such as granting monopolies for goods such as cement, petrol, flour, steel and cigarettes, issuing exclusive import permits and customs exemptions, giving sole rights to distribute goods in the West Bank/Gaza Strip, and distributing government-owned land at below value. In addition to these state-assisted forms of accumulation, much of the investment that came into the West Bank from foreign donors through the Oslo years — e.g. road and infrastructure construction, new building projects, agricultural and tourist developments — were also typically connected to this new capitalist class in some form.

In the context of the PA's fully subordinated position, the ability to accumulate was always tied to Israeli consent and thus came with a political price — one designed to buy compliance with ongoing colonisation and enforced surrender. It also meant that the key components of the Palestinian elite — the wealthiest businessmen, the PA's state bureaucracy and the remnants of the PLO itself — came to share a common interest with Israel's political project. The rampant spread of patronage and corruption were the logical byproducts of this system, as individual survival depended upon personal relationships with the Palestinian Authority. The systemic corruption of the PA that Israel and Western governments regularly decried through the 1990s and the 2000s, was, in other words, a necessary and inevitable consequence of the very system that these powers had themselves established.

The Neoliberal Turn

These two major features of Palestinian class structure — a labour force dependent upon employment by the Palestinian Authority, and a capitalist class deeply imbricated with Israeli rule through the institutions of the PA itself — continued to characterise Palestinian society in the West Bank through the first decade of the 2000s. The division of the West Bank and Gaza Strip between Fatah and Hamas in 2007 deepened this transformation, with the West Bank subject to ever-more complex forms of movement restrictions and economic control. Simultaneously, Gaza has developed in a different trajectory, with Hamas rule reliant upon profits drawn from the tunnel trade and aid from states such as Qatar.

In recent years, however, there has been an important shift in the economic trajectory of the Palestinian Authority, encapsulated in a harsh neoliberal programme premised on public sector austerity and a development model aimed at further integrating Palestinian and Israeli capital in export-oriented industrial zones. This economic strategy only acts to further tie the interests of Palestinian capital with those of Israel, building culpability for Israeli colonialism into the very structures of the Palestinian economy. It has produced widening poverty levels alongside a growing polarisation of wealth. In the West Bank, real *per capita* GDP increased from just over $1400 in 2007 to around $1900 in 2010, the fastest growth in a decade (UNCTAD, 2011). At the same time, the unemployment rate remained essentially constant, at around 20%, among the highest in the world. One of its consequences was profound levels of poverty alongside the growing wealth of a tiny layer; indeed, the consumption of the richest 10% increased from 20.3% of total consumption in 2009 to 22.5% in 2010 (UNCTAD, 2011, 5).

In these circumstances, growth has been based on prodigious increases in debt-based spending on services and real estate. According to the United Nations Conference on Trade and Development (UNCTAD), the hotel and restaurant sector grew by 46% in 2010 while construction increased by 36% (UNCTAD, 2011, 2). At the same time, manufacturing decreased by 6% (UNCTAD, 2011, 2). The massive levels of consumer-based debt levels are indicated in figures from the Palestinian Monetary Authority (2011, 13), which show that the amount of bank credit almost doubled from 2008 to May 2010 — from $1.72 billion to $3.37 billion. Much of this involved consumer-based spending on residential real estate, automobile purchases or credit cards — the amount of credit extended for these three sectors increased by a remarkable 245% from 2008 to 2011 (Palestinian Monetary Authority, 2011, 13). These forms of individual consumer and household debt potentially carry deep implications for how people view their capacities for social struggle and their relation to wider society. Increasingly caught in the web of financial relationships, individuals seek to satisfy needs through the market, usually through borrowing money, rather than through collective struggle for social rights. The growth of these financial and debt-based relations thus acts to individualise Palestinian society. It had a conservatising influence over the latter half of the 2000s, with much of the population becoming more concerned with 'stability' and the ability to pay off debt rather than the possibility of popular resistance.

New Regional alliances: Israel and the Gulf States

As noted earlier, the impetus for the Oslo signing was strongly connected to the strategic attempt by the US to link its various regional allies into a single economic space, characterised by free trade and investment flows. This goal, however, was deeply shaken by the Arab uprisings that erupted across the Middle East throughout 2010 and 2011. Through their challenge to key regional allies — notably Egypt's Hosni Mubarak — these uprisings significantly destabilised the patterns of US regional hegemony that had been laid down since the Oslo Accords. In their initial phases, the uprisings represented an important moment of popular hope across the region, embodying a rejection of neoliberal authoritarianism and aspirations for a long sought-after transformation in socio-economic and political rights (Hanieh, 2013). In many ways, these uprisings represented the most significant upsurge of popular mobilisation since the post-war Arab nationalist struggles; the striking manner in which their political and social forms were generalised so rapidly across all states in the Middle East indicated a profound challenge to the regional order that had been extant in the region for the past five decades.

Since this initial phase, Western powers and their regional allies have moved decisively in an attempt to reconstitute state structures and the local bases of support on which their hegemony depends. Despite ongoing struggles, established elites have largely been able to win back political power. Military and state-supported repression was a critical element in this return to the status quo — seen, for example, in the assassinations of Tunisian opposition leaders Chokri Belaid and Mohammed Brahmi in 2013, and the May 2013 military coup in Egypt. Simultaneously, the devastating repression of the Assad regime in Syria and the ongoing disintegration of the Iraqi state helped to spur the growth of sectarian and Islamic fundamentalist movements across the region, further disrupting the social and political goals initially embodied in the uprisings.

Throughout these developments, the long-term aim of Israel's integration into the Arab world continues to be an important focus of Western policy, despite the popular Arab antipathy towards this goal. In particular, the close relationship between Israel and the Gulf monarchies — notably Saudi Arabia, and the UAE — has become an increasingly open feature of the new regional situation since 2011. This relationship is apparent in joint military exercises, as well as commercial and economic ties in the security, surveillance and high-tech sectors. There have also been public visits to Israel by high-ranking political figures in the Gulf, something that would have been unthinkable a few years ago.

For Palestine, these regional developments are closely interconnected to the processes described earlier. As noted, Palestinian political and economic elites are tightly linked to the Gulf states: the Gulf provides significant financial aid to the PA, and Palestinian capitalists are heavily involved in economic activities in the Gulf (and, in several cases, actually hold Gulf citizenships). There can be little doubt that the leading Gulf states are seeking to formalise their relationship with Israel under US auspices and, within this, the acquiescence of the Palestinian political leadership remains essential. The single major obstacle to this remains the aspirations of the wider Palestinian population — including the millions of Palestinian refugees scattered across the Middle East. Whether Palestinian rights are ultimately subordinated to the interests of this new pan-regional alliance remains an open question; but a political course increasingly directed by Washington, Tel Aviv, Riyadh, and Abu Dhabi will undoubtedly provoke major tensions within the Palestinian political project.

Beyond the impasse?

The current cul-de-sac of Palestinian political strategy is inseparable from these regional and domestic political economy dynamics. The two-state strategy embodied in Oslo has produced a Palestinian social class that draws significant benefits from its position atop these processes and its linkages with the structures of occupation. This is the ultimate reason for the PA's supine political vision, and it means that a central aspect of rebuilding Palestinian resistance must necessarily confront the position of these elites. Over the last few years there have been some encouraging signs on this front, with the emergence of new youth and other protest movements that have taken up the deteriorating economic conditions in the West Bank and explicitly targeted the PA's role in contributing to them. But as long as the major Palestinian political parties continue to subordinate questions of class to the supposed need for 'national unity' it will be difficult for these movements to find a deeper traction.

Moreover, the history of the last two decades shows that the 'hawks and doves' model of Israeli politics — so popular in the perfunctory coverage of the corporate media and wholeheartedly shared by the Palestinian leadership in the West Bank — is decidedly false. Force has been the essential mid-wife of 'peace negotiations'. Indeed, the expansion of settlements, movement restrictions and the permanence of military power have made possible the codification of Israeli control through the Oslo Accords. This is not to deny that real and substantive differences are present between various political forces within Israel; but rather to argue that these exist along a continuum rather than in sharp disjuncture to one another. Violence and negotiations are complementary and mutually-reinforcing aspects of a common political project, shared by all mainstream parties, and both act in tandem to deepen Israeli control over Palestinian life. The last two decades powerfully confirm this fact. The reality of Israeli control today is an outcome of a single process that has necessarily combined violence and the illusion of negotiations as a peaceful alternative. Indeed, the counterposing of a so-called Israeli peace camp and 'right wing extremists' acts to obfuscate the centrality of force and colonial control embodied in the political programme of the former.

The reality is that the overriding nature of the last six decades of colonisation in Palestine has been the attempt by successive Israeli governments to divide and fracture the Palestinian people, attempting to destroy a cohesive national identity by separating the Palestinian people from one another. This process is illustrated clearly by the different categories of the Palestinian people: Palestinian refugees, who remain scattered in refugee camps across the region; Palestinians who remained on their land in 1948 and later became citizens of the Israeli state; the fragmentation of the West Bank into isolated cantons; and now the separation of West Bank and Gaza Strip. All of these groups of people constitute the Palestinian nation, but the denial of this unity of the people has been the overriding logic of colonisation since before 1948. Both the Zionist left and right agree with this logic, and have acted in unison to narrow the Palestinian 'question' to isolated fragments of the nation as a whole.

Given this arrangement of social forces, any effective renewal of Palestinian political strategy is necessarily bound up with the dynamics of the regional scale as a whole. Those of us living in the UK have a crucial role to play in this process. This means not only supporting campaigns such as BDS but also confronting the complicity of the UK and other governments in sustaining *all* autocratic and repressive states across the region. As part of this, we must continue to show solidarity with the ongoing struggles for economic, political, and social rights in the Middle East — these have not been extinguished despite the repression of the last few years. Such a spirit of internationalism drove Tom Hurndall's selfless actions in Palestine, and he will long provide inspiration for all of us concerned with seeing real justice achieved.

Bibliography

Bartram, D. V., 'Foreign Workers in Israel: History and Theory', *International Migration Review* 32, 2 (1998), 303–25.

Bouillon, M. E., *The Peace Business: Money and Power in the Palestine-Israel Conflict* (London: I.B. Taurus, 2006).

Brusilovsky, H. and Gitelson, N., *Israel's Foreign Trade 2000–2010* (Jerusalem and Tel Aviv: Israel Central Bureau of Statistics, 2011).

Farsakh, L. *Palestinian Labour Migration to Israel* (New York: Routledge, 2005).

Graham-Brown, S., 'Agriculture and Labour Transformation in Palestine', in Glavanis, K. and Glavanis, P. (eds), *The Rural Middle East: Peasant Lives and Modes of Production* (London: Zed Books, 1990), pp. 53–69.

Hanieh, A., *Lineages of Revolt: Issues of Contemporary Capitalism in the Middle East* (Chicago: Haymarket, 2013).

Honig-Parnass, T., *The False Prophets of Peace: Liberal Zionism and the Struggle for Palestine* (Chicago: Haymarket Books, 2011).

Machover, M., *Israelis and Palestinians: Conflict and Resolution* (Chicago: Haymarket Books, 2012).

Nitzan, J. and Bichler, S., *The Global Political Economy of Israel* (London: Pluto Press, 2002).

Palestinian Monetary Authority, *Monthly Statistical Bulletin, May*. Ramallah, 2011.

Pappe, I., *The Ethnic Cleansing of Palestine* (London: Oneworld Publications, 2006).

Retzky, A., 'Peace in the Middle East: What Does It Really Mean for Israeli Business?', *Columbia Journal of World Business* 30, 3 (1995), 26–32.

Said, E., 'The Morning After' *London Review of Books*, 15, 20 (21 October 1993), https://www.lrb.co.uk/v15/n20/edward-said/the-morning-after.

Samara, A., *The Political Economy of the West Bank 1967–1987: From Peripheralization to Development* (London: Khamsin Publications, 1988).

UNCTAD, United Nations Conference on Trade and Development (UNCTAD) *Report on UNCTAD Assistance to the Palestinian People: Developments in the Economy of the Occupied Palestinian Territory, July 15* (Geneva: UNCTAD, 2011).

World Bank, 'Trade Options for the Palestinian Economy', *Working Paper no. 21*, 2001, https://www.un.org/unispal/document/auto-insert-197986/.

Fig. 14   Tom Hurndall, ISM volunteer in front of an Israeli APC at the Rafah
border, April 2003.

12. Evicting Palestine[1]

Penny Green and Amelia Smith

The state of Israel is premised upon ethnic cleansing and forced evictions. From the Nakba (Palestinian 'Catastrophe') in 1948 when historic Palestine was destroyed and replaced with a new state, forced evictions have been the mechanism and modus operandi of Israel's nation-building project.

At the turn of the twentieth century the vast majority of Palestinian people lived in Palestine, a land mass now divided into the state of Israel and the Occupied Palestinian Territories of the West Bank and Gaza Strip. At that time, 1.4 million Palestinian people lived in 1,300 towns and villages across the whole country. During the Nakba, 15,000 Palestinians were killed and 800,000 were driven at gunpoint from their homes into the West Bank and Gaza Strip, Jordan, Egypt, Syria, Lebanon and other parts of the world. Thousands more Palestinians were evicted forcibly from their homes but remained within the new Israeli-controlled post-1948 territory. Israel destroyed 531 Palestinian towns and villages, wiping them from the map. In 1967, following Israel's military occupation of the West Bank and Gaza Strip (since

---

1   This article is dedicated to Hashem Al-Azzeh, our friend and Palestinian peace activist who died in Hebron on 21 October 2015 from a heart attack induced by excessive tear gas inhalation. We first met Hashem during fieldwork in Palestine in 2014 and his life was a testament to peaceful resistance against forced evictions, occupation and the endless repressive incursions into Palestinian daily life by the Israeli state. He exemplified what Richard Falk has described as "the spirit of nonviolent Palestinian resistance that seeks to counterpose a heroic normalcy against the quotidian cruelties of the Israeli occupation". This chapter is extracted from an article first published in *State Crime Journal*, 'Palestine, Palestinians and Israel's State Criminality', 5. 1 (Spring 2016), pp. 81–108, https://doi.org/10.13169/statecrime.5.1.0081.

     https://doi.org/10.11647/OBP.0345.13

1948 respectively under the control of Jordan and Egypt), an estimated additional 300,000 Palestinians were displaced. According to a 2013 report from the Palestinian Central Bureau of Statistics 7.4 million (66 percent) of the global population of 11.2 million Palestinians have been displaced forcibly from their homeland.

Dispossession and displacement continue apace at the hands of what Oren Yiftachel describes Israel's 'ethnicization of contested territory and power apparatus'. In its 2012 submission to the United Nations Committee on Economic, Social and Cultural Rights, The Israeli Committee Against House Demolitions (ICAHD) revealed that since 1967, Israel had '...demolished over 28,000 Palestinian homes, businesses and other structures in the Occupied Palestinian Territory'.

Forced eviction has thus defined the Palestinian condition for the past sixty-seven years, not only as an historical tragedy situated in the ethnic cleansing and associated state crimes of 1948 but also as an ongoing form of persecution. Thousands of Palestinians throughout the Occupied Palestinian Territories and Israel have experienced eviction and displacement, many on multiple occasions.

The constant threat and reality of forced eviction results in a permanent state of insecurity, fragmentation, misery and fear for Palestinian men, women and children living in what was mandated Palestine and the Occupied Palestinian Territories.

Through the use of a number of case studies, we have documented a planned and intentionally complex set of criminal practices employed by the state of Israel to remove Palestinians from their historic lands. Those practices include: village destruction, house demolitions, the destruction of farmland and olive groves, land confiscation, access restrictions to natural resources, denial of residency rights and the denial of refugee return, all underpinned by a process now defined as Judaisation. These are facilitated through a range of formal and informal practices, notably discriminatory zoning and planning restrictions, the creation of militarised zones, forestation programmes, the illegal settlement programme, 'unrecognising' Palestinian villages, the separation wall, security checkpoints, service removal, a programme of Bedouin urbanisation, suppression of resistance and impunity for state and settler violence.

We examined forced evictions not only inside the Occupied Palestinian Territories of East Jerusalem and the West Bank (Gaza was closed to us) but inside that part of mandated Palestine which became Israel, where 1.4 million Israeli Arabs/Palestinians still live, many under threat of forced eviction.

Deviant Planning

In order to understand the continuing crisis of forced evictions of Palestinian communities in Israel/Palestine, it is necessary to understand the complex and fragmented structure of Israeli land, planning and housing control in the West Bank. This fragmentation is an integral component of 'Israel's matrix of control' defined by Jeff Halper as 'three interlocking systems: military administration of much of the West Bank and incessant army and air force intrusions elsewhere; a skein of "facts on the ground", notably settlements in the West Bank, Gaza and East Jerusalem, but also bypass roads connecting the settlements to Israel proper; and administrative measures like house demolitions and deportations.'

In 1996 the West Bank was divided into three distinct categories: Area A encompasses all Palestinian cities (and covers 18 percent of the total land mass of the West Bank) and is controlled by the Palestinian Authority (PA); in Area B (22 percent of the total land mass and largely rural) Israel controls all security while the PA controls civil affairs; and in Area C (comprising 60 percent of the West Bank) Israel controls both security and all land-related civil affairs. In 2014, according to OCHA, the Israeli authorities destroyed 590 Palestinian-owned structures in Area C and East Jerusalem, in the process, displacing 1,177 people. This represents the highest level of displacement in the West Bank since the UN began systematically monitoring the destruction of Palestinian homes and structures in 2008.

The possibility of Palestinian construction is restricted severely. In East Jerusalem the Israeli authorities have zoned only 13 percent of the annexed area for Palestinian construction, much of which is already built up, and only one percent of Area C (the most fertile land in the West Bank) is zoned for Palestinian building. According to the Israeli human rights organisation, B'Tselem, acquiring a building permit is virtually impossible for Palestinians — 94 percent of the 3,750 requests for planning permission made by Palestinians between 2010 and 2012 were rejected by the Israeli authorities. Palestinians wishing to extend their homes or expand their communities in order to accommodate family and population growth face impossible bureaucratic barriers and have no other option but to build without a permit in the certain knowledge that what is built will be under constant threat of demolition.

Areas A and B (home to the majority of the West Bank Palestinian population, i.e. 2.4 million people) have been carved up into 165 separate geographical areas with no territorial contiguity and are surrounded by Area C. (Maps of Areas A, B and C are available at https://en.wikipedia.org/wiki/West_Bank_Areas_in_the_Oslo_II_Accord.) This fragmentation, which resolutely restricts the possibility of demographic planning for growth, was to have been temporary while the transfer of governance from Israel to the Palestinian Authority took place. Twenty years later fragmentation remains a structural reality and an impossible barrier to Palestinian development.

The complexity of Israel's land, planning and security governance appears designed to obfuscate and deflect attention from its illegal and criminal practice of forced evictions. Yet as political geographer Oren Yiftachel reports, this complexity makes sense in terms of Israel's 'ethnocratic' state project: 'It's a way of managing a colonial situation through Judaisation internally and through a combined military sovereignty and Jewish settlement project in the West Bank' (interview, 24 March 2014).

Village and House Demolitions

House and village demolitions are a wretched and repeated fact of life for thousands of Palestinians and signal an intent on the part of the Israeli authorities to drive Palestinians from their homeland. Our data provides strong evidence that Israel has employed urban planning processes as weapons in advancing its concurrent goals of ethnic cleansing and Judaisation.

The case of the Palestinian village of Dahmash is emblematic. Dahmash lies some 20 kilometres from Tel Aviv and is located inside the 1967 borders of Israel. Its residents are Israeli citizens but as Arabs they are denied many of the basic rights of citizenship enjoyed by their Jewish Israeli neighbours. Dahmash is one of Israel's 176 'unrecognised' villages, a status which places it at constant risk of destruction. Israel refuses to recognise Dahmash as a residential village, claiming instead that it was built in an agricultural zone. (Around 90,000 Palestinian/Arab Israelis live in 176 'unrecognised' villages located largely, but not solely in Galilee (http://www.medea.be/en/countries/israel/unrecognized-arab-villages-in-israel/). In refusing to recognise Dahmash in this way, Israel also refuses to provide the basic services essential for community life. There is no sewage system or rubbish collection, no health services and no paved roads or public transport. There are no schools or nurseries. To be 'unrecognised' is also to be without an official address. Villagers are not permitted to use their Dahmash address on their identity cards because, officially, Dahmash does not exist; their existence can only be verified through the listing of a fictitious address, Ha'Heshmoniam Street in the nearby town of Ramla.

The seventy houses, home to around 600 villagers that make up the Dahmash community, are almost all considered to be 'illegal'. According to Arafat Ismail, the Head of Dahmash Village Committee, the village was targeted for demolition in 2004 when eighteen houses in the process of being built or extended were issued with demolition orders on the grounds that they were built illegally on agricultural land. Five of the houses were demolished in March 2006. The owners of the remaining thirteen continue to contest and resist the orders against them.

Originally the homes in Dahmash were built on land 'granted' to the Palestinians by the new Israeli state in compensation for the land and property from which, in 1948, they were forcibly displaced. The land, however, was zoned as 'agricultural' and those displaced were not entitled under Israeli planning law to build new homes there. Despite petitions by villagers to the regional planning office the Israeli government has refused to re-zone the land and legitimise the village. By granting compensatory 'agricultural' (rather than residential) land to the Palestinians they had forced from their legitimate homes and land the Israeli state was ensuring a life of marginalisation and insecurity for the displaced.

Successive local government planning committees in the regional centre of Ramla have rejected appeals by Dahmash residents to legitimise their homes by changing the zoning designation from agricultural to urban. New towns, they argue, are the province of the Interior Ministry. The regional planning committee also rejected an alternative claim to legality and security by the villagers; that Dahmash be re-designated as a neighbourhood of the existing towns of nearby Ramla or Lod. The Mayor of Ramla, Yoel Lavi, who sits on the Regional Planning Committee, dismissed the proposal with a violent counter-proposal. In 2006 he declared on Israeli television that he would, '[...] take two bulldozers, the kind the IDF uses in the Golan Heights, two border police units to secure the area and go from one side [of the village] to the other [...] when you give the first shock everyone runs from their houses, don't worry.'

According to a Human Rights Watch report, the Central Regional Committee for Planning and Construction rejected a plan submitted by Dahmash's residents on the grounds that it saw 'no justification for the creation of a new village in central Israel' (HRW 2010).

What central Israel can't justify is a 'new' Palestinian village, regardless of the fact that Dahmash's existence dates back to 1951. Jewish villages of the same age are welcomed. Listed on the Lod Valley Regional Council website are nine villages (eight of them moshavim or Zionist agricultural communities). All were built between 1948 and 1953.

While Jewish neighbourhoods flourish and develop, Palestinian communities face eviction, demolition and destruction. The practice of zoning appears to be used as a mechanism to deny Palestinian residents security of tenure, and the necessary urban status to obtain basic services. In effect, zoning has become a mechanism of violence, terror and marginalisation. Resistance to zoning brings with it the very real threat of violence and demolition.

Conquering East Jerusalem

The neighbourhood of Al-Bustan lying at the base of Silwan's densely populated Judean hills in East Jerusalem has 1,200 residents and 88 buildings. This is the area that Jerusalem Mayor Nir Barkat plans to destroy and replace with a Bible-themed tourist park. The forced evictions and house demolitions in Al-Bustan represent a clear plan to wrest land owned by Palestinians and bring it under Israeli control.

The fact that homes built before 1967 are 'legal' and cannot be destroyed and that it is legally impossible to destroy homes built without a permit more than seven years ago has not deterred Israel's expansionist plans. In 2004 East Jerusalem's City Engineer, Uri Shitreet, with the aid of statute (5)212 of the Israeli Laws of Building and Planning, proposed plans to prohibit the use of illegal houses ('use' of an 'illegal house' not being covered by the statute of limitations). By barring Palestinians access to their own 'homes without permits' and by then sealing off those homes, they could be declared as 'abandoned' or 'absentee' property and subsequently destroyed.

Abu Diab, who heads the Al-Bustan Residents' Committee, said that the people of Al-Bustan are afraid to go on holiday because they don't know 'if their houses will still be there when they get back' (Interview Abu Diab, 27 March 2014).

Victims of house demolitions in East Jerusalem speak of 'battalions' of armed and masked police storming their homes while they sleep; of being pushed, punched and abused; and of being photographed by soldiers as the bulldozers move in. Iyad Al-Shaer recently made the agonising decision to demolish the home he had built for his brother and his fiancée. 'I have two choices: I destroy it myself or they will come, demolish my home, then charge me for it. The second choice is that I go to court, pay fines, pay the engineer, pay the lawyer; at the end I know that I will lose. Palestinians; we always lose.'

According to the UN Office for Co-ordination of Humanitarian Affairs (UNOCHA) which monitors and maps house demolitions, East Jerusalem is experiencing an increasing number of demolitions and population displacement. In the ten years between 2004 and 2014, 516 housing units were demolished in East Jerusalem; 59 were carried out by the homeowners to save the amount that Israel demands for demolition. As a result, 2,028 people have been made homeless. The vast majority of these homes belonged to Palestinians.

The ultimate goals of land zoning, targeted planning laws and violent forced evictions have been reinforced by state-orchestrated physical changes to the built environment which have produced segregation of a kind witnessed only in Cold War Germany. The following section examines the impact of Israel's separation wall, illegal settlements and segregated road system.

Israeli Apartheid

It is clear that Israel's strategies and practices of urban planning and laws regulating land tenure have, alone, been considered inadequate for the task of displacing, marginalising and excluding Palestinians from their traditional lands. A striking feature of Israel's unique form of apartheid lies in its deployment of physical infrastructure as a further weapon of segregation and ethnic cleansing — most prominently the separation wall and a segregated road network. To understand the physical, demographic, social and economic impact of the separation wall we followed its contours as it snaked from Ramallah to Bir Nabalah. To follow the line of the wall is to experience a state of utter disorientation. It is very hard to make sense of it until one realises that disorientation and fragmentation are central to its purpose.

For Israel, the wall renders invisible the Palestinian population, annexes the illegal Jewish settlements to Jerusalem and at the same time separates Palestinian communities and their farmlands from the rest of the West Bank. The convolutions and incursions into West Bank territory that we observed are not irrational but designed specifically to accommodate Israel's future expansion of illegal settlements.

The separation wall is an 810-kilometre, grey concrete structure which winds in seemingly irrational convolutions through Jerusalem, parts of Ramallah, Qalqilya and the West Bank. In some parts it reaches eight metres high — obliterating all that is beyond. The wall separates Palestinians not only from Israel, but also from their Palestinian neighbours, from their friends and families, and in some cases encircles whole communities. It also serves to annexe the illegal settlements. In building the wall Israel has already, by stealth, seized another 12 percent of Palestinian West Bank territory. As a result, 211,000 Jewish settlers living illegally on land confiscated from Palestinians have also been effectively annexed to Jerusalem.

The data we gathered demonstrates unequivocally that this wall or barrier is not about security as the Israeli state claims, and it is most certainly not about protecting Israelis from Palestinians. Rather, its path is designed to connect and annexe the illegal settlements (built on Palestinian land) to Israel. According to President of the International Committee of the Red Cross (ICRC), Peter Maurer, 'the Barrier cannot be justified as a security measure' because it consolidates and perpetuates the illegal presence of settlements.

The wall has separated hundreds of thousands of Palestinians from Jerusalem and in doing so has wilfully and forcibly altered the city's cultural and demographic composition. We interviewed many for whom the wall has made family life and friendships difficult if not impossible: At Shaikh Sa'id checkpoint an elderly man reported, 'Before the wall it would take me just 10 minutes to reach my daughter and her children; now it takes me between an hour and an hour and a half depending on traffic at the checkpoint.' He pointed to the village of Jabal Almokabir in the distance. The wall, he said, has isolated the two villages from each other.

The wall is chequered with watchtowers and its 30–100-metre 'buffer zone' accommodates military patrols, surveillance equipment and electric fences. There are 634 checkpoints along the wall, 34 of them fortified. The wall and these checkpoints severely limit the capacity of Palestinians to live and work freely. Rather, they have created permanent Israeli control over the daily lives of Palestinians. Thousands must queue in the metal corridors of Eyal, Qalqilya, Tarqumya or any of the West Bank's checkpoints serving as major entry points for those Palestinians with permits to work in Israel. The checkpoints resemble cattle yards, with yellow barriers, metal holding pens covered with razor wire, long, narrow, metal-fenced inspection lanes and iron turnstiles. Workers at Tulkarem 'Terminal' begin arriving as early as midnight, hours before the checkpoints open at 4 a.m. By 3.30 a.m. thousands of workers are edging forward in a process that will take them at least two hours, simply to arrive at work on time. The experience is dehumanising and, at the same time, a very clear assertion of Israeli power over Palestinian movement. The wall has also separated many farmers from their land and while agricultural 'gates' exist, they are often opened only at the whim of the IDF soldiers who control them (interview with Jamal Juma, 25 March 2014).

The wall is supplemented by an apartheid system of modern, direct roads, bridges and highways linking the illegal settlements to west Jerusalem; there are 1,661 kilometres of roads on which it is strictly forbidden for Palestinians to travel. They must instead rely on a system of 44 tunnels linked by roads in poor repair which wind beneath the illegal settlements and link the 22 otherwise fragmented and isolated Palestinian villages through slow and circuitous routes.

The Stop the Wall Campaign estimates that the wall, when completed, will have annexed around 46 percent of the West Bank and isolated 78 Palestinian villages and communities in which 266,442 people live. As a result, some 257,265 Palestinians will be living in villages surrounded by the wall, settlements and settler-only roads; 8,557 Palestinians will be living in villages trapped between the wall and the Green (1949 Armistice) Line; and 6,314 Palestinians will be threatened with expulsion. The Palestinians of East Jerusalem will be totally isolated from the rest of the West Bank.

All roads and checkpoints leading from Israel toward Palestinian communities declare Israel's infrastructural commitment to apartheid: ubiquitous and alarmist red and white road signs provide a warning, a distorted reassurance to Israelis that separation is a necessary protection: 'This Road Leads to Area A under the Palestinian Authority. The entrance for Israeli Citizens is Forbidden, Dangerous to Your Lives, And Is Against Israeli Law.'

Perhaps one of the most disturbing of these pretexts for the collective punishment of Palestinians, and one which demonstrates just how unjust this collective punishment is, is the Baruch Goldstein massacre which took place in the Ibrahimi Mosque, one of Hebron's most cherished sites, located in H-2. In 1994, during Ramadan, Goldstein opened fire on Palestinians praying inside the Ibrahimi Mosque, killing 29 and injuring a further 125. Eventually, survivors of the tragedy overpowered him and beat him to death. After this the mosque was divided and Muslims were delegated one area to worship in and Israeli Jewish settlers a much larger portion. Inside the mosque today, through bulletproof glass at the back, it is possible to see illegal settlers praying in the other half of the building. In the middle of the two sections is the cenotaph of Abraham, whose birthplace is said to be Hebron. Goldstein's tomb is located on a hill overlooking the city, the epitaph reads: 'He gave his soul for the people of Israel, its Torah and Land.' Palestinians have paid the price for his actions ever since whilst the settlements, and those that reside in them, remain (Klein, 2013). The massacre sparked protests across the West Bank and the Gaza Strip. Twenty-five Palestinians were killed by the Israeli army during these protests (972 by 2014).

Not only are settlements a method used to transfer the Israeli Jewish community onto Palestinian land, but, as the case study of Hebron demonstrates, restrictions are placed on Palestinians to protect these settlements, which makes life so intolerable for Palestinians that they leave.

King David in Silwan

In 1967 Israel occupied East Jerusalem and declared the city Israel's 'eternal, undivided capital'. The Knesset's 1980 Jerusalem Law states, 'Jerusalem, complete and united, is the capital of Israel.' The international community, however, consider East Jerusalem to be occupied territory and the capital of a future Palestinian state. United Nations Security Council Resolution 478 rendered the Jerusalem Law to be 'null and void' with fourteen votes to none (the US abstained) but this has not stopped Israel expanding the Israeli Jewish population in East Jerusalem and forcing the Palestinian population out. Silwan in East Jerusalem, used as a case study in this section, has become a centre of the conflict between the expansionist aspirations of the Israeli authorities and the struggle of Palestinians living there defending their rights. Despite Palestinian resistance in Silwan the Israeli authorities pursue their goal. They do so under the cover of excavation work; the search for ancient Jewish temples lends legitimacy to their claims that Jewish Israelis have a historical right to this land.

When we visited, Silwan was celebrating the release of Palestinian prisoner Mohammed Siyam, aged thirteen; Mohammed was being carried down the central street on the shoulders of his friends, brandishing a white and yellow flag and wearing a matching headband. Mohammed's arrest was part of the information-gathering process, the collective punishment imposed on Palestinians, by Israeli authorities seeking expansionism in the area. Mahmoud Qaraeen, co-founder of the Wadi Hilweh information centre that monitors Israeli encroachments in Silwan, told us that arresting Palestinian children is part of the clampdown on activists in Silwan: 'In the beginning they arrested activists, demolished houses, gave house owners more demolition orders. [They used] many tools. But in the last three years they found that the best way to stop the Palestinian movement in East Jerusalem is to arrest the children', he says (Interview with Mahmoud Qaraeen, 23 March 2014).

Children like Mohammed get in the way of Israel's strategy of expanding the Israeli Jewish population in East Jerusalem and reducing the number of Palestinians living there, a strategy they pursue by isolating the area from the rest of the West Bank and other Palestinian cities, demolishing houses, enlarging settlements, establishing tedious bureaucracy and redrawing the city's boundaries with the help of the separation barrier (B'Tselem, 2005).

One blueprint for this process of Judaisation and de-Arabisation is a document called the *Jerusalem Master Plan*, devised by former Israeli Prime Minister, Ehud Olmert when he was mayor of Jerusalem. Though it has not yet been officially approved, it is a reference point for planning decisions in Jerusalem, and the first of its kind since 1967. On the surface the master plan appears to call for more housing for the Arab population in the city. But a closer examination of plans for the Old City, which is located within East Jerusalem, reveals an intention to decrease the population of the Muslim and Christian quarters whilst offering sixty site plans for buildings in the Jewish quarter.

The Old City houses many sites of religious importance: the Dome of the Rock and Al-Aqsa Mosque for Muslims, the Church of the Holy Sepulchre for Christians and the Temple Mount and the Western Wall for Jews. Yet underneath Al-Aqsa Mosque (the third holiest site in Islam) and the Old City, excavations are being carried out by Israeli authorities in search of the remains of ancient Jewish temples. Likewise, excavation work is taking place in Silwan under the archaeological guise that it was once the home of King David. The settlers that move into settlements in East Jerusalem claim a biblical right to this land; archaeological claims that East Jerusalem once housed Jewish temples and Silwan was once home to King David serve to legitimise such claims and provide a cover for the underlying political agenda: removal of the Palestinian population.

The organisation driving the work to discover King David is Elad (Hebrew for 'To the City of David'), pioneered by David Be'eri in 1986. According to its website, 'Ir David' or the 'City of David', is the actual location of the biblical city of Jerusalem captured by King David over 3,000 years ago (The Ir David Foundation). In an interview with journalist Lesley Stahl about his aspirations for the site, Doron Spielman, international director of development for the City of David, argued that because King David conquered Jerusalem for the Jewish people in 1010 BC, it belongs to them today.

In the centre of the King David complex lies the Abbasi Palestinian family home comprised of nine flats and two warehouses. Mahmoud explains that Be'eri once brought groups of visitors to Abbasi's home, to whom he would sell oranges, lemons, coffee and tea. The two became close friends, eventually visiting each other's families. Abbasi began to trust him and would tell of his secrets; the history of the house, how one of his brothers lived in the US and the other in Jordan. 'David Be'eri started to collect this information to keep it in order to use it against him by the Absentee Properties Law', explains Mahmoud. The 1950 Absentee Properties Law authorised the transfer of land to the State of Israel if the owner was absent. This meant that thousands of Palestinians, who were forced out of the country during the 1948 Nakba when Israel was established, could not return to their homes. Eventually, in 1991 Be'eri came flanked by a member of the Knesset and a group of settlers in the middle of the night to occupy part of the house and over the following twenty years took all the parts that belonged to Abbasi's absent brothers. Now Abbasi has seven cameras at the entrance to his home and if he travels requires a permit to leave and return. If guests visit, they are obliged to leave their names with the authorities (Interview with Mahmoud Qaraeen, March 2014).

According to Mahmoud, and other scholars including Yonathan Mizrachi, a former archaeologist for the Antiquities Authority, there is no physical evidence that King David was ever on this site. Even if there was this would not be a pretext for pushing Palestinians off their land. 'The British Mandate did a lot of excavations around here but they didn't find anything that linked to the City of David. If they found something it's not really so bad for us, if King David lived here we would be proud. It doesn't give them the reason to occupy our land', says Mahmoud (Interview with Mahmoud Qaraeen, 23 March 2014).

Back on the development itself is another house whose Palestinian owners are in Jordan. Settlers have taken over the roof and built a cinema, whilst a Palestinian family, sitting tenants, live downstairs. In total there are 550 security cameras placed around the City of David. 'From this point you can imagine the life of the Big Brother show', says Mahmoud. The extraordinary surveillance presence strongly suggests that the illegal settlers are being protected from 'dangerous' outsiders, a perception which is taking its toll on the Palestinian tourist industry and the country's economy. Mahmoud explains that a bottle of water in Silwan costs three shekels, but in the City of David it is twelve shekels. Still, people would rather pay four times the price and buy it in 'safety'. 'From 1991 until today we didn't earn anything from tourism', he says (Interview with Mahmoud Qaraeen, 23 March 2014). It is a strategy and part of a deliberate, ongoing attempt by the Israeli government to demonise Palestinians. In February, Netanyahu said he wanted to surround Israel with fences and barriers, 'to defend ourselves against wild beasts'.

Judaisation is the mechanism behind Israeli expansionism (or settler colonialism) and the eviction of Palestinians from their land because Israel's ultimate goal is to create an Israeli Jewish majority whilst reducing the Palestinian population. The 'discovery' of ancient Jewish temples attempts to provide a cover for such expansionist aspirations. Meanwhile, Palestinians who resist these aspirations are punished.

The Jewish National Fund, Planting Trees to Cover up Palestinian Villages

The Jewish National Fund (JNF) is an organisation that takes advantage of a complex web of laws to take land from Palestinians, exclude non-Jews from using it and then prevent them from returning. To do this, the JNF helps Israel build settlements, control natural resources to their own ends, construct dams, water reservations and parks. Canada Park, one of Israel's most popular national parks, was built by the JNF on the top of the remains of three Palestinian villages. During the Six-Day War, the land under what is now Canada Park, home to three Palestinian villages, was captured and razed to the ground and up to 10,000 people were expelled and almost 1,500 homes demolished. The park was built on the remains of Imwas, Yalo and Beit Nuba to avoid Palestinians returning to the site of their devastated villages, yet despite its history there is nothing at the park to tell visitors about these three villages, nor that it has been built on the wrong side of the Green Line outside Israel's internationally recognised borders.

As a result of the Jewish Agency Law passed in 1952 and the Jewish National Fund Law passed in 1953 by the Knesset, a special legal status and role was created for the JNF in the development of Israeli land regime and policy. The JNF was declared an Israeli institution and the Knesset detailed its part in the design and administration of public land in Israel. Land was taken away from Palestinians through the 1950 Absentee Properties Law and the 1953 Acquisition of Land Law and transferred to the JNF. It was now to be used for Israeli Jewish citizens only. All over Israel there are forests abundant with fruit trees and cactus plants, built on land reassigned to the JNF. In total, more than 500 Palestinian villages, some 2,000 years old, have been depopulated, destroyed and buried under their parks and forests. As documented by Dan Leon in the Israel-Palestine Journal, the land acquired by the JNF has grown from 22,363 dunams in 1920 to some 2.6 million dunams today. 'Since its foundation, it has purchased 2.6 million dunams (one dunam is a quarter of an acre) of land all over the country for 1,000 settlements (including the kibbutzim and moshavim), planted 240 million trees and built 150 dams and water reservoirs and 400 parks'.

As part of their afforestation plan, the JNF — 'the guardian of the land' by their own admission — has planted many trees on Palestinian ruins in the Naqab. Though their website claims that 'when the pioneers of the State arrived, they were greeted by barren land', in reality those 'pioneers' uprooted many indigenous olive trees and planted pine and cyprus trees, chosen because they grow quickly. In the unrecognised village of Al-Araqib the human cost of the JNF's forestation projects are clear. In 2006 the JNF began planting the Ambassador's Forest here and invited heads of diplomatic missions and ambassadors serving in the country to plant trees (Israel Ministry of Foreign Affairs, 2005). Aziz, son of the village head Sheikh Sayakh, shows us the trees, which are starting to grow in between the stones left from his original home and the stumps of olive trees that belonged to his family. 'Every tree they plant here is like an Israeli criminal policeman who is rooted in our land', he tells us. 'They want us to hate the land but they will never be able to do that. This is my life' (Interview with Aziz Al Turi, 26 March 2014). The trees they plant restrict the movement of Bedouins and prevent evicted Palestinians from returning to their land, whilst ridding the area of any trace of the people they evict.

Conclusion

Under international humanitarian law (specifically the 1949 Fourth
Geneva Convention and Additional Protocol I) Israel, as an occupying
power, is obliged to protect the civilian population and administer the
occupied territory for the benefit of civilians living there. Our research,
however, documents policies and practices related to forced evictions
which are not only *not* to the benefit or protection of the occupied
Palestinians, but which expose Israeli state criminality on a structural
scale. Israel's practice of forced evictions, mass forced displacement,
house and village demolitions, institutionalised discrimination, land
grabbing, resource theft and the movement of settlers into the occupied
territory are, it is argued, designed with the deviant organisational goal
of expanding Israel's colonial control and annexation of Palestinian
territory.

The techniques embodied in the destruction-displacement cycle,
outlined above, are intertwined and clearly serve Halper's 'matrix of
control'; yet whether by demolishing someone's home to make way for
Jewish-only housing or by cutting off Palestinian water supplies, the
effect on the people is nearly always the same: psychological trauma
and the thwarting of Palestinians' potential to live as free people.

One need spend only one day in Palestine to understand the nature
of Israel's project of dispossession. Yet in between the endless rows
of settlements that continue to transform the landscape, behind the
separation wall and beyond the signs that declare Palestinian land as
closed military zones, the warmth, dignity and strength of the people
who live there remain. For Palestinians the struggle against forced
evictions and the programme of ethnic cleansing is more than *hudud*
(borders); it is about their very *wujud* (existence) in their ancestral
homes.

Fig. 15 Tom Hurndall, Hamas funeral march for Palestinian killed in an Israeli airstrike, April 2003. All rights reserved.

13. Resisting Cybercide, Strengthening Solidarity: Standing up to Israel's Digital Occupation

Miriyam Aouragh

Over the years, the political impact of digital media as tools for 'citizen journalists' has grown substantially. It is this arena that Tom Hurndall was navigating with his photo journalism, bearing witness to the destruction, occupation and resistance in Palestine. In the years since the Second Intifada (2000–2005), we have seen digital technologies become a key tool for solidarity groups across the world.

Mainstream media have come to function as gatekeepers by determining what stories are aired or properly contextualised. Thus, the Internet has influenced Palestinian politics by disseminating textual, visual, and audio narratives beyond the confines of censorship of commercial media and political elites. More than a decade later, the Internet has by now grown into a counter-public space for Palestinian liberation politics.

The relationship between technology and politics is multivalent and in contrast to a technologically deterministic view, reality is messy. Political change ultimately must emerge from human decisions and practices, themselves based on historical conditions. This implies great contradictions and therefore requires a nuanced approach. The Israeli state and its international supporters deploy the same technologies for instance. In fact, they have a far greater advantage than Palestinians.

 https://doi.org/10.11647/OBP.0345.14

There are two sides to this, simply put, the material and the immaterial. The immaterial is found for instance in the effort to mobilise pro-Israel sentiments. I have discussed this Israeli public diplomacy through social media as a form of *Hasbara 2.0* (Aouragh, 2016). The material side has to do with the warfare and surveillance — the destruction and violence so to speak — which I have framed as *Cybercide* (Aouragh, 2015).

I will return to this later. But first, if we agree that social media has affected the basic algorithms of resistance, we need to contextualise this resistance and media. Media and information studies researchers can benefit from historians of European and US Empire who have documented the ways in which Western technological advances are often based on particularly violent experiments in warfare and of counter-insurgency developed in the Third World. Rashid Khalidi (2006) writes about French and British air bombardments, and this became the basic knowledge for textbooks on aerial bombardments. It was indeed in the early postcolonial era, across the Third World, when the village and slum became a social laboratory for research. That is not all; the idea of individual rights associated with access to media and information technologies was part of the tightening grip of postcolonial states in regulating media and information. For this to become clear, we need to relate to the political-economic context, for Information and Communication Technologies, ICTs, are not operating in an immune field or vacuum.

Technology as a commodity (infrastructures) and as capital accumulators (ownership, profit) are protected through an inherited inequality between North and South. This meant a late and very uneven development of post-independent states' own infrastructures. Neoliberal multinationals (e.g. 'public private partnerships') are state-protected corporations that can behave like cyber Gods, like anonymous entities they can for instance allocate URL (Uniform Resource Locator) names, refuse political website addresses, and under the guise of national security or privacy laws some nations are rejected while others are included. Palestine is a case in point. In the case of finding a generic URL-based naming system, it took Palestinians many years of negotiation (and pleading) to get the Internet country code top-level domain — the sovereign .ps domain — assigned.

Thus we have here a combined problem of being bound by neoliberal rules in the ICT sector at large, while being disadvantaged by a forced, uneven inheritance of colonial infrastructures. This political economic approach helps to demystify the diffusion of technologies and instead to frame them as part and parcel of the expansion of capitalist market systems and geopolitical interests. This is nowhere as clear as in Palestine. But the struggles against occupation must be situated within the structure of *settler* colonialism for, as scholars have argued, Palestine is not colonised in the 'common sense' of the word (Salamanca et al., 2012). Palestine, both in its abstract sense as a nation and as a territory in the concrete physical reality, faces colonial subjugation. This is motivated by the need to empty the land of its inhabitants, rather than 'civilising' the people as part of the pretext to extract the land and exploit the people.

But what does this mean concretely for online politics? On the most basic level, it means that technology has been part of the underlying reality within which Palestinian resistance operates. In other words, the Palestinian political landscape mediates between settler colonialism and cyber-colonialism.

Cyber-colonialism

The Internet had become increasingly incorporated into Israeli military strategies — prohibiting, removing, and destroying the Palestinian Internet. This is regarded as the (uglier) façade of the more latent hasbara policies, a destructive condition that I began to understand in connection with what was termed Israeli *politicide* by Baruch Kimmerling (2003).

This cybercide is intimately embedded in military procedures: employing the Internet is not a random move. The Information and Communication Technology (ICT) sector itself is part of the military industrial complex. The urge to control the politics of mediation while simultaneously conducting cyber warfare was most clearly seen for the first time during the July 2006 war on Lebanon. Two and a half years later, Israel organised the military invasion of Gaza (Operation Cast Lead) — one of the bloodiest to that date in the Occupied Palestinian Territory (OPT) — where its Internet skills were significantly stronger. Then it took even further measures when it stormed the Mavi Marmara (one of the solidarity flotilla ships sailing toward Gaza carrying tonnes of aid) on 31 May 2010. In a sense, this was a tipping-point. Israeli paratroopers were dropped on the ship from their helicopters, they confiscated laptops and mobile phones from activists aboard the ship. Israel had already tried to block cellular and radio communication. An outcry was expected and therefore it was imperative to limit the impact of the killing of unarmed civilians in international waters. Adi Kuntsman and Rebecca Stein analysed the Israeli military tactics during the attack on the Mavi Marmara flotilla (Kuntsman and Stein, 2015). And what is interesting about this case is that one of the passengers had managed to smuggle out a digital tape of the first moments of the attack. Once out of the country, the footage was uploaded online, and a different version of what had happened appeared, one that refuted the 'self-defence' rationale underlying Israel's versions.

It is important to understand the relationship between the Internet and politics through on-the-ground practices. When we expose the economic and territorial structures that shape and negate Palestinian resistance, tangible frustrations of Palestinian cyber-activists become clear. This is why we should always relate back to settler colonialism as a dynamic and multi-layered phenomenon, which includes online and offline features and is both political and economic. This is the case with what can be called 'cyber-colonialism'.

Throughout the past twenty years, the Israeli army has jammed and hacked telephones, Internet, and broadcast signals. Occupation forces have destroyed infrastructure almost continuously, the Israeli army intentionally and repeatedly severs the only landline connection between southern and northern Gaza and has dug up cyber-optic cables in the West Bank, or uprooted transmission towers.

The challenge of Palestinian activism is therefore equally dynamic and multi-layered. It entails manoeuvring between online and offline organising as well as attempting to circumvent crackdowns on those practices, as when the Israeli army engages in acts of cybercide by destroying hardware, bombing broadcasting stations, ransacking IT forms and even via remote-control killings of Palestinian protesters.

During fieldwork in Palestine in 2012 the Stop the Wall office was raided by the Israeli military: computers, hard disks, and memory cards were stolen. Not much later, Israeli soldiers confiscated the computer of

Addameer, a prisoners' and human rights organisation. As a consequence, activists and everyday users alike are well aware that the Internet is constrained by Israeli military, economic, and 'security' policies. Among Palestinians there is widespread awareness that their Internet usage is under surveillance. Israeli security forces have used confiscated personal communications to blackmail others into collaboration. This threat constantly hangs like a Damocles Sword above the computer screens of activists. The Internet is used at one's own risk due to a combined impact of surveillance and intimidation.

The difference between the Internet as a *space* in which to mobilise solidarity and as a *tool* by which to organise protest is starker than anywhere else, predominantly because Palestinian infrastructures are so clearly compromised. Although used efficiently for international mobilisation, it is noticeable that the Internet is not the *primary* tool for persuasion — other spheres and mediums such as satellite television, mosque announcements, university campus gatherings, and posters are often as important to fulfil this need.

Therefore, to be relevant for Palestinian activism, online politics must facilitate offline mobilisation and long-term strategies. Grassroots campaigns demonstrate that the Internet has empowering characteristics and is significant for activism. However, this is precisely why they are also violently targeted and their equipment destroyed during raids. In other words, the disempowering materiality of technology shapes that very empowering activism.

Thus, cyber-colonialism functions through a double-layered mechanism, involving overt and covert control, and combines latent and manifest methods, and is concluded by a politics of controlling, altering, and deleting. The relationship is dialectical: the implication of the *online* must always be addressed by what it means offline. Within the Palestinian realm today, offline activism is marked by colonialism on the one hand and an oppressive internal authority (Palestinian National Authority) on the other. Does this mean that Palestinian resistance will always be the weaker party?

Meticulous Strategy, Magnificent Failure

For Palestinians, cybercide and especially *hasbara* (Israeli state propaganda) mediates not only the exercise of power over life and death, but over truth itself. It is difficult to mask images of conflict when one perpetually is involved in wars. The underlying truth of colonialism, obscured by an ideological bias, does not allow *hasbara* to arrive at the most logical explanation that would be in tune with most public relations approaches or media analyses. However, the overall impact of the Palestinians on social media outweighs that of Israel, defying the mathematical logic that one might presume applies. That an opponent with more resources, superior access to intelligence and crucial international backing is not able fully to impose its will is an important confirmation of the efforts of activism and power of solidarity.

It is important to remember that the grassroots struggle against Apartheid South Africa took many decades; without all of the initial cracks in the projection of white supremacy by solidarity groups both big and small around the world, a collective that managed to pressure international governments to end their diplomatic and economic support for South Africa would not have emerged.

The lacuna between Israel's desired public persona and its actual international perception continues to deepen, and pro-Palestinian movements are gaining public support. There is a parallel common sense seeping through, one that defies many of *hasbara*'s attempts to 'explain' it all away. This 'common sense' is captured by the words chanted in the streets of many capitals across the world in July and August 2014: 'In our thousands — in our millions — we are all Palestinians.' This striking chant proclaims that (pro-)Palestinian public diplomacy, which clearly does not rely on government interventions, is an international people's objective. The basic fact, therefore, is that every time Israeli propaganda becomes more masterful in its techniques and receives more budgets, it ends in disappointment. Paradoxically, grassroots diplomacy — a public relations that is formed by universal principles of justice and equality — offers qualities that money cannot buy.

One of those qualities was Tom Hurndall. The Palestinian cause and its great 'sumud' and courageous resistance had become visible for a new generation during the outbreak of the Second Intifada.

Palestinians sparked hope and rebellion, and they inspired Tom. He in turn represented a peaceful and strong humanity which continued to inspire many of us when we heard of his tragic end, fatally wounded by the Israel Defence Forces whilst protecting Palestinian children in Gaza. He died on 13 January 2004. This was my message at the time.

Dear family and friends of Tom,

Despite nine months in a coma, Tom's death took us by surprise. It left us in a moment of retreat. Stunned while staring at the television screen. Upon hearing the news of his passing, many thoughts crossed my mind. I am sure that others felt similar emotions, ranging from anger to sadness and settling on renewed determination.

Tom's death was the result of a cowardly act. Of viciousness. Itself the result of an entrenched racist and oppressive system. Tom's killing revealed not only the mercilessness of the tactics used by the Israeli army, but also disclosed the hypocrisy and compliance of our own Western governments.

Tom symbolized the peaceful, yet at the same time strong, will of humanity. That is more than can be said of the many "Coalition Forces" army casualties in Iraq who receive elaborate memorials and media coverage. We remember the double standard when an Israeli bulldozer crushed the young American peace activist Rachel Corrie to death in Gaza. Not long after that dark day in March, all media spotlights and patriotic rhetoric were focused on another young American woman: Private First Class Jessica Lynch, an injured war heroine 'rescued' by Special Forces in an aura of Hollywood style triumphalism. Not yet a year since her ordeal, Ms. Lynch has already been featured as the subject of books, a made-for-t.v. movie, and several nationally broadcast interviews.

This tragedy reminds us of the Orwellian axiom that 'Who controls the present controls the past, and who controls the past can control the future.' As we gaze at our television screens, we see how chillingly accurate this formula is when Israeli spokespersons change the logic of language by redefining a permanent apartheid wall as a 'terror prevention fence'. Most of the peace activists currently in Palestine are doing all they can to resist that wall. And they should, because it is like a poisonous snake that slowly penetrates, encircles, strangles and then swallows what is left of Palestine.

Fatalist though it may sound, given the current political realities it is just a matter of time before the next victim, another Tom Hurndall or Rachel Corrie, or an Israeli protestor, will fall (and be commemorated by us) while resisting that snake in disguise. And it is inevitable, too, that the next person killed by the Israeli Army will be blamed for their own death in the mainstream media. The ruling ideas are indeed the ideas of the ruling class.

Yet, times are changing. The thick wall of ideological domination, protected by military supremacy, which separates us from what could be a better world is starting to show cracks. Not only does the dissemination of alternative information through the Internet and satellite television give us a voice and thus a tool to organize, modern mass media are also enabling millions of people throughout the world to become organized and to actively take to the streets, motivated by an international level of solidarity never before seen. Tom was certainly a key player in this new global politics.

The struggle for justice would be stronger if Tom were still with us. But I believe that his selfless actions and the ultimate price he paid sparked a desire to know, struggle, act; to help bring about a revolution in perception and action concerning Palestine.

We don't need elaborate memorials or long speeches from the same establishments that continue to back Israel and provide it with the very weapons and bulldozers that cause death and destruction. What we do need is hope and will to make a difference.

One can only feel astonishment at the bald contradictions and injustices of the current world order, and horror at the astronomical prices that must be paid to support this unbalanced system. The latest bill for maintaining power in Iraq, after a war that was based on lies and deceptions, is illustrative. For a war that only ideologically deranged neocons [neoconservatives] and corporate interests are still willing to defend, Bush needs an extra $86 billion just to hang on. At the same time, we live in a world where 799 million people suffer from famine; 115 million children can't afford to go to school; more than 30,000 people die from hunger and poverty-related disease every single day. The UN estimates that $9 billion are needed to provide basic education for all the worlds' children and $36 billion to provide clean water and basic healthcare for all.

While gazing at the news of Tom's death, and looking at the picture of his gentle face again, it became clearer than ever before that the priorities of Bush, Blair, and Sharon are anything but the priorities of ordinary people trying to make a living and to live in peace. Since the result of these global contradictions will be increasing political instability on a global scale, priorities must be set with regard to our own individual choices. Indeed, it is not enough merely to analyze the world, the challenge 'is to change it' as Marx observed over 150 years ago. Although it won't be easy we will have to make our own history.

Tom made a choice; Tom made history. It is people like him, Rachel, and many others who personify a new generation unwilling to blindly accept the world as it is, but who instead take risks and work together to forge new protest movements. People like Tom actively helped to universalize the Palestinian struggle, who together with millions of others in Washington, London, Paris, Genoa, Porto Allegre, Cairo and Ramallah showed that the Palestinian flag can become a symbol that binds us together. As the late Edward Said said, Palestinians by themselves cannot defeat Zionism and its US backers.

To pay tribute to the many Toms and Rachels of Britain, to Gaza, Jerusalem or Shatila camp, I conclude by saying to those who have been taken from us: 'You will never be forgotten and we will complete what you started.' And to all those still fighting I say 'We are with and beside you, no matter what.' And to all those who are not yet part of the struggle for justice, I implore: 'Join the struggle, because united we will stand and divided we shall fall.'

I hope that on the coming international anti-war day planned for 20 March 2004 in all major cities around the world, that pictures of Tom, Rachel and so many other heroes — people who made history by making choices — will be carried in our hearts, minds, and on our banners.

With comradely, loving, and respectful feelings,

Miriyam Aouragh

Bibliography

Aouragh, M., 'Between Cybercide and Cyber Intifada: Technologic (dis-) Empowerment of Palestinian Activism', in: Jayyusi, L., & Roald, A. S. (eds), *Media and Political Contestation in the Contemporary Arab World: A Decade of Change* (New York: Palgrave Macmillan, 2015), pp. 129–60, https://doi.org/10.1057/9781137539076_6.

Aouragh, M., 'Hasbara 2.0: Israel's Public Diplomacy in the Digital Age', *Middle East Critique*, 25:3 (2016), 271–97, https://doi.org/10.1080/19436149.2016.1179432.

Kimmerling, B., *Politicide: Ariel Sharon's War Against the Palestinians* (London: Verso, 2003), https://doi.org/10.1525/curh.2005.104.678.25.

Khalidi, R., *The Iron Cage: The Story of the Palestinian Struggle for Statehood* (Boston: Beacon Press, 2006).

Kuntsman, A. and Stein, R.L., *Digital Militarism: Israel's Occupation in the Social Media Age* (Stanford, CA: Stanford University Press, 2015), https://doi.org/10.1515/9780804794978.

Salamanca, O.J., Mezna Qato, M., Rabie, K. and Samour, S., 'Past is Present: Settler Colonialism in Palestine'. *Settler Colonial Studies* 2.1 (2012), 1–8, https://doi.org/10.1080/2201473x.2012.10648823.

Fig. 16 Tom Hurndall, ISM volunteer in the street on the Rafah border with IDF
vehicle, April 2003.

14. Israel's Nation-State Law and Its Consequences for Palestinians

Salma Karmi-Ayyoub

I will take this opportunity to discuss Israel's nation-state law, passed in July 2018. Firstly, I will outline what the law says and what its effects are. Secondly, I will suggest that the law establishes Israel as an ethnocratic, as opposed to a democratic, state, that the law is in violation of international law, and that it paves the way for Israel to practice apartheid. Finally, I will examine the political context in which the law was passed and argue that, whilst the law is fundamentally a misguided attempt by Israel to respond to a crisis of legitimacy, it must be resisted as it represents an entrenchment of Israel's discriminatory regime against Palestinians, and contributes to the erosion of Palestinian rights.

Israel's Nation-State Law

On the 19 July 2018, the Israeli Knesset passed the 'Basic Law: Israel — The Nation-State of the Jewish People' ('the nation-state law'). The document is here: https://m.knesset.gov.il/EN/activity/documents/BasicLawsPDF/BasicLawNationState.pdf. The law contains the following provisions:

- the 'Land of Israel' known as 'Eretz Israel' is the historical homeland of the Jewish people;

  https://doi.org/10.11647/OBP.0345.15

- the State of Israel is the nation state of the Jewish people, and the realisation of national self-determination in the State of Israel will be exclusive to the Jewish people;
- immigration leading to automatic citizenship is exclusive to Jews;
- 'Greater and united Jerusalem' is the capital of Israel;
- Hebrew is the official language of the state, and Arabic will have special status;
- the state will act to encourage, consolidate and promote Jewish settlement, and the state will work to foster ties with Diaspora Jewry.

The Constitutional Status of the Nation-State Law

The nation-state law is a constitutional law which determines the way the state of Israel is defined. In particular, the law determines the identity of the political community that constitutes the locus of sovereignty of the state — that is the people that the state is meant to serve and to represent — as well as defining the aspirations and visions of that political community, and its cultural identity (in terms of language, religion and symbols). It also determines how all other laws, policies and practices of the state must be interpreted and applied.

Confirming the law's constitutional status, a report commissioned by the Israeli Justice Minister in 2015 into the implications of the nation-state law concluded that the law was not merely declaratory — grounding into law already-existing policies and practices of the state, as had been argued — but that it amounted to a 'constitutional anchoring of the vision of the state'. As a result, the report advised against the enactment of the law because it was obvious to the author that such constitutional anchoring should only be done in the framework of constitutional politics, and when it enjoys the support of a large sector of society. By contrast, the report noted that such a process had not taken place in Israel at the time the law was proposed, and therefore recommended against the law.

The Nation State Law Makes Israel an Ethnocracy

Let us now look at the law's provisions in more detail. The law stipulates in Article 1:

(a) The Land of Israel (Eretz Israel) is the historical homeland of the Jewish people, in which the State of Israel was established;

(b) The State of Israel is the nation-state of the Jewish people, in which it realizes its natural, cultural, religious and historical right to self-determination;

(c) The realization of the right to national self-determination in the State of Israel is unique to the Jewish people.

In defining the state of Israel as the 'nation-state of the Jewish people' alone, and stating that the Jewish people have an exclusive right to self-determination, the law provides that the political community that the state serves and represents, is one ethno-national group only — the Jewish people — as opposed to all the national groups or persons residing in the territory subject to the state's constitutional order.

A comparative study commissioned by the Knesset found that there is currently no constitution in the world that appropriates the state exclusively for one ethnic group. Rather, constitutions generally adopt one of two ways of dealing with different ethnic groups within the territory of the state: the first is to define the political community of the state as containing the main national groups who are specifically recognised; the second relies on a territorial nation-state model, where the sovereign is defined as comprising all the residents of the territory of the state.

The fact that the nation-state law provides that Israel is the nation state of only one of the national groups within its territory, and establishes Israel as an 'ethnocracy' rather than as a democracy, it would be tantamount to, for example, Britain defining itself not as the state of the British people, but as the state of 'the whites or 'the Christians'.

Furthermore, it is clear that the ethnocratic effect of the law is deliberate. During the drafting of the law, the legal advisor to the Knesset put forward an alternative proposal, which would have included the principle of equality and a provision that the state belonged to all of its citizens. The proposal was explicitly rejected by Knesset members.

The Knesset's legal advisor explained after the law was passed, 'We [...] recommended during the discussions in the committee that it would have been appropriate, as has been done in other constitutions, [that] alongside the mention of the Jewish nation there be a mention of the issue of equality and the issue of the state belonging to all citizens, [but] the committee chose not to make this into a law.'

The Law Ensures Exclusive Jewish Self-Determination and May Amount to Annexation

Article 1 of the law also provides that Jews have an exclusive right to self-determination in the land of Israel. Therefore, it denies any right of self-determination to Palestinians in the same country.

Furthermore, although the law does not explicitly define the territory of the state of Israel, it refers both to 'Eretz Israel' (Greater Israel which encompasses the whole territory of Mandate Palestine) and to 'the State of Israel' without distinguishing between the two. This means the law may be interpreted as applying both in Israel within the 'Green Line' ('Israel proper'), as well as in the occupied Palestinian territories and if this is correct, the law could amount to an act of annexation.

How the Nation-State Law Violates International Law

Having looked at the provisions of the law in more detail, we are now in a position to analyse the ways in which the law can be said to be in violation of international law.

Firstly, the law is in conflict with international human rights law. The latter provides that all persons have a right to equality, and to be free from discrimination on ethnic, national, racial or religious grounds, and, furthermore, that states have a duty to treat equally all individuals within their territory or subject to their jurisdiction. The nation-state law, because it defines the Jewish people as the only ethnonational group represented by, and therefore served by, the state, effectively mandates the unequal treatment of Jews and Palestinians by the state. Indeed, the law provides that many state functions are reserved exclusively for the benefit of Jews such as, for example, Jewish settlement and citizenship and, therefore, rights to nationality and land. By contrast, Palestinian rights are not mentioned in spite of the fact that they make up roughly 50% of the population of the territory which Israel controls. Thus the law breaches the obligation contained in international human rights law of non-discrimination and equality of treatment.

Secondly, the law violates the Palestinian right to self-determination in that it reserves self-determination rights exclusively to Jews. International law has recognised that Palestinians have a right to self-determination through the creation of an independent state in the West Bank and Gaza Strip, and that all peoples, generally, have a right to self-determination, with no one nation having a right to rule over another. The nation-state law violates international law through these principles by providing that the self-determination of Jews is an exclusive right.

Finally, the law creates the foundation for the practice of apartheid in Israel. Apartheid is defined as the perpetration of inhumane acts, as part of an institutionalised regime of racial discrimination, which has the purpose of ensuring the domination of one racial group over another. Many commentators have suggested that the discriminatory policies and practices of Israel, which include the indefinite occupation of the West Bank and the Gaza Strip, the fifty or so laws that discriminate against Palestinian citizens of Israel, and the policy of denying nationality and the right of return to expelled Palestinian refugees whilst promoting Jewish emigration to and citizenship of Israel, mean that Israel is already a state that practices apartheid. However, the nation-state law effectively elevates the supremacy of Jews over other ethnic groups in Palestine to a constitutional value, establishing a legal framework for the practice of apartheid.

The Broader Context

All of this begs the questions: why was the nation-state law passed, and how does it fit into the broader political context?

There is no doubt that Trump's presidency in the US emboldened Israel to pursue its most extreme agenda. Indeed, the nation-state law was passed in the context of the acceleration of other Israeli policies which all, in one way or another, have sought to extinguish the main demands of the Palestinian national movement, and thus to ensure the supremacy of Jewish nationalist aspirations in Israel/Palestine. These polices include expanding settlements in the E1 area of the West Bank, thereby ensuring a lack of territorial contiguity of a future Palestinian state, solidifying the Jewish presence in Jerusalem to ensure that the city cannot act as a future capital of Palestine, and pressuring UNRWA (the UN's Palestinian refugee agency) to stop defining the descendants of expelled Palestinians as refugees with a right of return to their homes in what is now Israel.

However, it is also important to understand the passing of the nation-state law as a response to a crisis of legitimacy that Israel correctly perceives itself to be suffering from, both domestically and internationally.

This crisis of legitimacy is caused, firstly, by Israel's continued colonisation of Palestinian land and the failure to bring about a two-state solution. This has created a situation on the ground in which Israel controls all of the territory of Mandate Palestine, a territory inhabited by approximately equal numbers of Palestinians and Jews, but in which Palestinians are denied all or most of their human rights. This unacceptable situation, which many commentators consider to amount to apartheid, presents a clear challenge to Israel's legitimacy, as well as threatening Israel's viability in practice as an exclusively Jewish state.

Secondly, civil society activism, and in particular the Boycott Divestment and Sanctions movement, have successfully raised awareness of Israel's crimes and violations of international law, eroding Israel's legitimacy in the international arena and causing ever-more vocal calls for Israel to either transform itself into a state for all of its citizens, or to give up its rule of occupied Palestinian territory, thus enabling a Palestinian state to emerge.

I believe that Israel is keenly aware of the contradictory position into which its policies have placed it, and which means it cannot be a democracy with international legitimacy, while at the same time presiding over an apartheid reality on the ground. I believe that Israel has responded to this paradoxical situation by passing the nation-state law. It is as if Israel's leaders believe that by codifying Israel's exclusively Jewish character into law, this will help stem the threat to the Jewish character of the state, as well as somehow putting a stop to the legitimacy crisis that Israel faces.

Conclusion

The nation-state law establishes Israel as an ethnocracy as opposed to a democracy. It entrenches Israel's discriminatory regime, and it supresses the Palestinian right to self-determination. The law will undoubtedly contribute to the further erosion of Palestinian rights. It is important for those who care about the Palestinian cause to understand what the nation-state law represents, and to help Palestinians resist it by advocating for the international community to take action to bring an end to Israel's discriminatory policies and practices.

Fig. 17 Tom Hurndall, Flags burnt at funeral for Palestinian killed in an Israeli airstrike, April 2003.

15. The Crafting of the News: The British Media and the Israel-Palestine Question[1]

Tim Llewellyn

I want to start by saying two basic things to map out my thesis, if you like, about the British media coverage, particularly the broadcasting media coverage of the Israel/Palestine question over the past forty years or so. The first thing I want to say is that journalism is not a perfect art, a perfect form. News editors are faced everyday with myriad stories. They have to make instant judgements, important stories fall by the wayside and are ignored. Many other things operate to take our interest, which is in Palestine and Israel, out of focus for a while. But the main point I want to make is that when the story is covered, as it is from time to time now, and as it used to be more consistently, it should be covered properly.

And my case is that over the past twenty years now, the BBC particularly, but the other broadcast media as well, and to some extent, newspapers which had been sympathetic to the Palestinian cause or Palestinian legitimate aspirations for equal rights, have not done the job properly. As to the BBC, I say this not because I am anti-BBC, and not because I'm a resentful ex-employee. I still admire the BBC. And I think the institution should remain. But it does not do the Israel/Palestine job properly. It listens to the voices of government and it takes into account the voices of pressure groups instead of listening to public opinion,

---

1   This is extracted from a talk given online on 13 August 2020, which is available at https://balfourproject.org/tim-on-media/.

    https://doi.org/10.11647/OBP.0345.16

which as we know, steadily over the past twenty-five years or so, has moved away from open support of Israel and taken, especially in Britain and in Western Europe, the Palestinian cause seriously.

History

That's my basic thesis. I want to go back now a little bit into the history of this whole affair. In the 1950s and '60s, the Palestinian identity had more or less disappeared from the public discourse outside the world of the Palestinian Arabs themselves. The word just was not used. It was not an issue. After 1948, unfortunately, the Palestinian Arabs, the refugees, the ones still hanging on in Israel, those treated as second- and third-rate citizens, were regarded as Arabs, Arab refugees. They were not called Palestinians and there was no Palestinian cause as such that we heard about in the West. The media coverage of the Middle East in those days, in the fifties and the sixties, was very much a coverage of Israel against the Arabs. Plucky little Israel fighting off the great hordes of the Arab masses, who were, we were led to believe, about to descend on plucky little Israel and eliminate it at any moment, if they were given half a chance.

This was of course exacerbated by the West's relationship with Gamal Abdel Nasser, the great foe, the great fear in the media and in government circles in the West, especially after what happened, the Suez crisis, was Arab nationalism. The governments in the West chose to see Arab nationalism not as a legitimate enterprise in itself, which it obviously was, but as an arm of some kind of global Soviet-inspired revolution. In the American view, it came under the heading of the Eisenhower Doctrine, you were either with us or against us. And because Nasser's Egypt and Syria, and after 1958, Iraq, were countries that in their different ways were backing Arab nationalism, the Arabs were seen vaguely as troublesome and possibly pro-Soviet.

These are very broad brushstrokes, but that was the way the Western media, and the BBC included, tended to see it. In 1956, for instance, the *Guardian* was against the Suez conspiracy between Britain, France and Israel to attack Egypt. The *Guardian* and those who opposed the conspiracy, including the Leader of the Opposition, Hugh Gaitskell, whose opposition speech was controversially carried by the BBC, chose to take as the object of criticism the British and the French. Israel very largely escaped criticism. As someone who wrote a book about the *Guardian* at the time said, The *Guardian* was more interested in saving Israel from itself than actually criticising Israel. The *Guardian*, by the way, had a long history of involvement with Zionism. CP Scott, the legendary editor of the *Guardian*, the *Manchester Guardian*, as it then was, Manchester being a strong centre of British Jewry, British Jewish art, business, industry and influence, was very close to the Zionists. And in fact, he was the one who befriended Chaim Weizmann and introduced him to the prime minister of the day, Lloyd George. CP Scott played a big part in pushing the Zionist case in Britain at a crucial time.

However, that is the broad look of the British coverage of the region at the time. No Palestinians, but Arabs, deeply suspect for being possibly pro-Soviet. That was really the way in which the coverage was delineated. It was very much part of the Cold War attitude.

Broadly the Palestinians weren't getting a look in. Palestinian nationalism itself, though, was beginning to emerge inside the Middle East, in Kuwait. Yasser Arafat had created Fatah in 1959. In 1963 or '64, the PLO had been created very much under the Egyptian umbrella. Yasser Arafat didn't take it over until the mid-sixties. The seeds of Palestinian nationalism were being sewn but they weren't being shown in the media.

Another big problem for the media in those days was in Israel itself, and this was true, well after the '67 War, when things began to change. Most of the operators there, most of the journalists in Israel were residents of Israel. Many of them were Jewish Most of them actually were Jewish. Many of them were Jewish residents of Israel, if not citizens of Israel. The BBC correspondent from 1967 onwards, for another fifteen years or so, was an excellent correspondent called Michael Elkins, but he was definitely a Zionist. He was a man who had gone to Israel to escape persecution in America of allegations that he was a communist. His heart was in Israel. His family were in Israel. He believed in Israel. He was an excellent reporter on Israel. But like many of his colleagues, he did not, even after 1967, spend much time in the West Bank and had no great empathy for it. He reported Israel and did it very well. And I think this was true of many of the other reporters that the major British media relied on.

1967 changed everything, of course. In 1967, the Israelis occupied the Gaza Strip, East Jerusalem, the West Bank, and the Golan Heights. They annexed later on East Jerusalem and the Golan Heights, and they still hold onto and threaten to annex most of the West Bank. And of course they still occupy Gaza in the sense that they are responsible for it, although it's under a dreadful siege.

The point was, this was in a sense, a terrible mistake for the Israelis because when they invaded the West Bank and the Gaza Strip, what they did was they brought to the attention of the world a problem which had lain fallow since 1948 and the world began to pay attention to the fact that there were such things as Palestinians, that there was a Palestinian nationalism and that it was a force to be reckoned with.

Now, at first, it didn't get off the ground very well. I want to give you some examples of the way the British media particularly, and the BBC, ignored this, or rather, didn't ignore but slighted this fateful position that the Palestinians were in. Reporters started to go to the West Bank from Jerusalem and from London. And to give you one example, one of my great heroes was a doyen of Middle East reporting in the sixties. He had been on the staff of the *Guardian* but by now he was a freelance. His name was Michael Adams. His son is Paul Adams, who now is a diplomatic correspondent for the BBC and is himself an expert on the area. Michael Adams went to the West Bank in 1968 to have a proper look at the way in which the Arabs and the Palestinians were being treated. And he didn't like what he found. Other reporters found the same. He wrote three articles for the *Guardian*. The then editor Alastair Hetherington, who himself was very pro-Israeli, but not perhaps as much as CP Scott, but certainly in that great *Guardian* tradition of being very much on the side of Israel and Zionism, didn't like this, that's to say the first three articles, but he printed them.

The Fourth Article

This is quite close to my heart because I had similar trouble with this same story thirty years later. This fourth article was about three villages in the West Bank, just north of Jerusalem. One of which you'll be familiar with, from the Bible Emwas, which in the Bible was called Emmaus. These three villages were obliterated by the Israeli army long after the fighting stopped. The Israeli reason for this was that they felt that the position of these three villages, which was in a position north of and overlooking the main highway between Jerusalem and Tel Aviv, was militarily suspect. So they kicked the villagers out. They made them march to Ramallah about fifteen miles away, and they razed them. They flattened the three villages. If you go there now, as I've gone there, you can still see the ruins under the foliage, but there's nothing there. These villages ceased to exist. The *Guardian* refused to accept this article. It was too much for Alastair Hetherington. Michael Adams then took it to *The Times*. *The Times* set it in type, as they did in those days, but in the end refused to run it. In the end *The Sunday Times* ran it.

Likewise, the foreign editor of *The Times*, who I used to know quite well, a very mild-mannered man, nearing retirement then in 1968, called EC Hodgkin, Teddy Hodgkin, also went to the West Bank and, in his erudite way, he was an expert on the Middle East...he'd covered the original United Nations General Assembly meeting, which partitioned Israel in 1947. Teddy went and wrote an article for *The Times*, which they published, and which was highly critical of the way Israel was behaving to the refugees in the West Bank and in East Jerusalem. There was uproar. Emanuel Shinwell of the Labour Party, a very famous MP at that time, very well thought of, very highly regarded, but an archetypal vitriolic Zionist, cursed Teddy Hodgkin, this very mild-mannered Englishman, as a vicious antisemite in the Houses of Parliament, a terrible libel of course, which Hodgkin was able to do nothing about.

A little later, *The Times* decided to publish a supplement, which was organised and paid for by the Arab League. And it did publish four pages within which was an Arab's explanation of what was happening in the Middle East and in the West Bank of the occupied territories. At that stage, *The Times* did publish that supplement. It was paid for. They more or less had to. But the editor, William Rees Mogg, father of our famous Jacob, decided at the same time that he should write an apology in the leader columns for this article, dissociating *The Times* from it in some strange way. He was publishing it, but he didn't like it, is what he wanted to tell the readers. So it was for *The Times*, but not of *The Times*. And he authorised his correspondent then in Jerusalem to write a piece from Israel, which they printed on the front page.

So you can see that even after the Israeli occupation, although there were murmurs and the beginnings of discussion about the condition of the Palestinians on the West Bank, it was a hard job for the journalist.

I want to give you one example of the way the BBC covered the story at the time, because like now, whenever the Palestinian question came up in the late sixties on programmes like *The World at One* or other current affairs programmes on television, the Israeli point of view prevailed. There was the usual predominance of Israeli spokesmen over Palestinian spokesmen. There was the usual acceptance of the Israeli point of view as being more valid than the Palestinian point of view. There was an imbalance, which I maintain has continued almost ever since, with a gap, which I shall explain. At that time, Christopher Mayhew, a colleague of Michael Adams, a Member of Parliament at that stage, had been in the Foreign Office, he'd quit the Foreign Office over Suez, he wrote to the BBC Secretariat complaining about the imbalance of coverage. This was in 1968. He got this reply from the BBC Head of Secretariat. And I think you should read this very carefully because it's indicative of the way the BBC still thinks:

> Journalists doing an honest job in this country have to take account of the fact that Israeli or Zionist public relations are conducted with a degree of sophistication, which those on the other side have rarely matched. An accurate reflection of publicly expressed attitudes on the issue may well inevitably reveal at times a preponderance of sympathy for the Israeli side.

In other words, said Mayhew and says Tim Llewellyn, the BBC view is that it should not concern itself with striking a balance, but reflect the greater power of the Israeli lobby.

And it's interesting, thirty years later, I had a very similar conversation, this was in about 2003 or 2004 during the Aqsa Intifada, when things were going very badly and the reporting by the BBC had, once again, deteriorated. I'm going to read what I wrote not long ago about this. I heard a similar view put by a senior BBC news executive with responsibility for Middle East coverage. And I was, like Mayhew before me, complaining about BBC bias and coverage of the second Intifada of 2000 to 2005. I put it to him that if the Palestinian side were not coming up with articulate spokesmen in modern studios in easily accessible locations like West Jerusalem, London, or New York, it was up to producers and reporters to dig them out, find ways of representing Palestinian representatives, commentators on Palestinian views, and put them on the air in the interests of impartiality. The executive's rejoinder to me was in the same vein as the secretariat had replied to Mayhew, thirty years earlier. He said that if the BBC reporters and producers and editors did that, we would be doing the Palestinians' job for them.

So, the situation at the end of the 1960s was that the Palestinians were beginning to put themselves on the map. They were doing it in many different ways, but the reporting of their case was still very tricky and still regarded with the greatest suspicion by the organised forces of the British media, the BBC particularly.

Of course, the Palestinians had their own difficulties. First of all, one way they were putting themselves on the map was in creating enormous difficulties in the Middle East itself. There was Black September in Jordan. There was the move to Beirut where they started to cause difficulties for the Lebanese government, after they'd been thrown out of Jordan, bringing their army into Lebanese territory, next door to Israel. And we know what came of that.

So the Palestinian image was being put forward, but sometimes in a negative way. However things did begin to change on other fronts. And I think this is very significant. In the 1970s, a number of different things were happening. The Palestinians were becoming recognised as a people with a cause, and more and more writers were beginning to take up that cause. The mood of the Western world at that stage was, especially among younger people, but among many politicians, somewhat revolutionary. It was the era of Vietnam. *Les évenèments* on the streets of Paris. There was a movement that said that the Third World, as we called it then, had to be heard. There were injustices that outlasted the end of colonialism. Colonialism was continuing in a new form. The French had only just got out of Algeria, leaving chaos behind them for a while. So there was a different mood abroad.

Secondly, the Palestinians themselves, although their name was in lights for hijacking, for the dreadful occurrences of the murders in Munich in 1972, the attacks across the Israeli border, the Palestinians would be making their case diplomatically. In 1973, the Arab States nominated the PLO and Yasser Arafat as the representative of the

Palestinian cause, which was a massive step forward because many of the Arab States were deeply suspicious of Yasser Arafat.

In 1974 in November, Yasser Arafat addressed the United Nations General Assembly. He made his famous 'gun and the olive branch' speech, in which he said that if he was accepted diplomatically, if the world looked on the Palestinians with grace and favour, he would reply by being a diplomat himself. And we started to hear the first murmurs of the idea of a two-state solution. Of course, this was rejected by Israel, but the European powers were beginning to listen.

In 1973, Egypt attacked across the Suez Canal, into the occupied Sinai Peninsula and pushed the Israelis back. It looked like a defeat at first. The Israelis came back but the Arabs proved that they were a force to be reckoned with. Later on, in those seventies, there was the Camp David Peace Agreement, when Israel signed a peace treaty with Egypt. This was not actually good news for the Palestinians, but it all helped to change the mood.

And the reason I'm talking about this is that during that period, interestingly, the BBC's attitude — and this was about the time I joined them, as the mood of the politicians began to take into account the Palestinians — towards the reporting began to change.

When I arrived in the Middle East in 1974, I was able to report without fear or favour from the Arab side about what the Israelis were doing. I remember one of the first stories I ever wrote was about how the Israelis had blown up the Syrian town of Kuneitra, on the Golan Heights. The story they were putting out was that Kuneitra had been destroyed by shelling, but it was obvious when we went into there, in spring of 1974, this is after the October War in 1973, that the place had been blown up as the Israelis left, and this proved to be true, and the UN confirmed it. That story was used without fear of favour.

Changing Mood

The mood was changing in the media. The Palestinian case was to be accepted. But at the same time, suspicions of what Israel were doing were growing and the old full-hearted support for Israel was dropping. So you see here, I'm showing parallel lines: as the government shifts, so does the BBC, and so do many of the other elements of the media.

We come to the fact that also at that time, the nature of the press corps in that area was changing. From the seventies onwards, and particularly as the 1980s approached, the newspapers and the BBC started to change their personnel. A whole new generation of younger reporters was beginning to emerge, both in Beirut, where the reporters like myself mixed with the Palestinians, civilian and PLO. We didn't always get on terribly well with the PLO. They were quite rightly suspicious of anything Western, but we understood what was going on. We heard the Palestinian side of the story, and we were able to write our stories in a much more sensitive way about why the Palestinians were behaving the way they did and why they wanted their rights.

At the same time, in Israel, the newspapers and the BBC were beginning to get worried about the fact that so many of their reporters there were actually Jewish and Zionist, were supportive of Israel, were residents of Israel. And over the years, the foreign media gradually moved in excellent reporters from outside. Sometimes they were Jewish, sometimes they were not, but they were outsiders. They were people coming from Britain, from France, from Scandinavia, from Germany, from the United States, and people who took a different view of Israel, people who had a more objective view of Israel.

This made an enormous change. In the early eighties, people like Ian Black of the *Guardian*, a superb reporter who speaks Arabic and Hebrew, made a tremendous difference to the way the West Bank and the whole Israel/Palestine issue was being reported. And so we see gradually that under this kind of umbrella of overall British government approval, and of course the same is true with other European governments, to a certain extent, the French particularly, not so much perhaps the Germans, but the reporting became more balanced.

One big event, which is probably largely forgotten now, which helped this process was that the EEC — that's the European Economic Community, which had nine members, of which the United Kingdom was one — made its famous Venice Declaration in 1980, in which it more or less recognised the Palestine Liberation Organisation, which was a big step at that time. And in a sense, in a sideways way, was critical of the Camp David Agreement, in which Israel had made peace with Egypt, without mentioning really in any significant way, the Palestinians, and left the rest of the Arab world in the lurch, emphasised the fact that the Palestinian question had to be looked at.

And so we have over that period between, I would say, 1974 and the Oslo Agreement, a growing feeling in government circles and in the West in general, less so in the United States, of course, who paid some lip service to this, but the Israeli lobby held on strong there. But certainly, as regards British journalists, the movement was in tandem with government thinking. Even under Mrs. Thatcher, junior ministers, like William Waldegrave and David Mellor, very different people who used to come out to the West Bank — I met them there — were very critical, openly critical of Israel, as indeed was Robin Cook ten years later, under Tony Blair. It would never happen now. But the mood was changing.

At the same time, the Israelis were making fantastic mistakes. Let's just take a couple of them. People were becoming aware of Israel's aggression in Lebanon, and the fact that in 1978, Israel had actually occupied the South of Lebanon. People talk as if Israel started to occupy it in 1982, but it didn't. It started in 1978. That started to arouse problems. Many more press people came out because there was a UN force there, Irish journalists, Norwegian journalists came out. All sorts of people who would not normally have gone to the Middle East were attracted because of the presence of their countries' soldiers on that tense border between Israel and Lebanon. And not surprisingly, because of the aggressive tactics of the Israelis, these reporters began to find out that the Palestinians and the Lebanese and the South were actually human beings, were oppressed, were having great difficulties under the Israeli thumb, and that the Israelis did not play cricket, to say the least.

So the mood started to shift yet again, but the biggest fundamental mistake the Israelis made was their invasion of Lebanon in 1982, which ended alas in that massacre, which I covered, which I was the first to get the news out about for the BBC, the Sabra-Shatila massacre. The Israelis did not carry out that massacre, but they allowed it to happen. It could not have happened without them. That, on top of a whole summer of Israeli bombing of civilian targets in Lebanon, of the Lebanese and the Palestinians and the ultimate invasion of Beirut itself, the massacre and the long and bloody and tedious withdrawal of Israeli soldiers back down through to the South, which they hung on to for another eighteen years, cast the Israelis in a terribly bad light, and they did not handle it well. They came in for enormous criticism at home as well.

Now I was covering the Middle East at that time. So were my colleagues, many fine reporters like David Hirst at the *Guardian*, Robert Fisk of *The Times*... The *Washington Post* reporters won a Pulitzer Prize for their reporting on Sabra-Shatila. We can see how Israel was really under the media gun. Things weren't perfect, don't get me wrong. Israel's support in America remained strong and it still remained strong, but somewhat subdued, in Britain.

I remember coming back after Sabra-Shatila, and my stories had run without any demur, there was no question. And so it went throughout the 1980s. You start to see the pattern.

What changed though — and there's a lot more detail to this, which you can ask me about — what really changed I think was in 2000, the mood in the British government changed. Tony Blair was a strong supporter of Israel. Gordon Brown was a strong supporter of Israel. The attacks on the Twin Towers cast a great shadow over the Arab and the Muslim world, for all the wrong reasons, but it did. The Second Intifada, which was a violent Intifada on both sides, was very badly reported. The BBC hedged its bets, it made terrible mistakes in its reporting. The reporting of that Second Intifada, well, I thought was disgraceful and I said so publicly. It was terribly unbalanced. The language used to describe the way Palestinians behaved and the way Israelis behaved was very different.

I'll just give you one example. Just before the Intifada started, there was an attack on Israeli Palestinians inside Israel itself. In October 2000, Israelis in a mob stabbed two Palestinian Israelis to death south of Tel Aviv. In subsequent violence, thirteen Israeli Palestinians were reported killed. The BBC and ITV reporting was muted. After these attacks, two Israelis held prisoner in a Palestinian police station in Ramallah were killed by a crowd of Palestinians who thought they were undercover agents. Now the language used to describe them was extraordinary. They were 'killers'. There was 'rage in their faces'. The descriptions of these acts were much more colourful and vivid than they were about the killers of the Arabs inside Israel. There was a terrible imbalance in the way cause and effect were described. Israelis were always retaliating for Palestinian attacks. And that's something that still holds true today.

In 2001, the Israelis assassinated a Palestinian leader of the PFLP, firing a rocket through his office window in Ramallah. A month or so later, in a hotel in East Jerusalem, the PFLP assassinated the Israeli tourism minister, shooting him dead inside a hotel inside the West Bank. Now, when that happened, I recall the reporting of the death of the Israeli minister, who was a hardliner, made no mention of the fact that this was an answer to a murder of a Palestinian in the weeks before. And continually we found that there is what I call a spurious imbalance, a spurious equivalence in the way the two sides were reported.

The Palestinian-Israeli conflict is described as a war, it takes on warlike terms. One side against the other side, as if there were two equal sides involved in all this.

That's been the nature of the reporting, I think ever since the beginning of 2000 and the Second Intifada. The Israelis regained their strength, their power over the media. And what we've seen in the past few years, unfortunately, with all the protest against this, the board of governors at the BBC reported in favour of these criticisms of the BBC and other broadcast media in 2006. But it did no good. The BBC took absolutely no notice of it. In fact, they got worse, and we see to this day that the reporting is still either missing completely or biased against the Palestinians.

I'll give you one example. I want to read to you from an interview, and this is typical, which John Humphrys did with a BBC correspondent in Jerusalem after there had been attacks in Jerusalem against settlers and other Israelis. This is how Humphrys began his conversation with this correspondent. Humphrys speaking, 'yet another attack on Israelis last night, this time an Arab man with a gun and a knife killed a soldier and wounded ten people. Our Middle East correspondent is (I'll leave his name out to save his face). The number is mounting. Isn't it? The number is about fifty now, isn't it?'

Not only does Humphrys's introduction make it sound as though only Israelis are being attacked. He implies that the fifty who'd been killed since the beginning were all Israelis. The correspondent doesn't correct him. He says, 'yes, we think around fifty, over the course of the last month or so, John.' In fact of the fifty dead, all but eight were Palestinians.

So you see this tremendous imbalance of cause and effect, of who's doing what to whom, and the lack of explanation why. That same correspondent I heard recently, after more attacks in Jerusalem, was asked why these young Arab men, Palestinian men were carrying out these attacks. He had no answer. He said he didn't know. That is quite pathetic. Without, in any way, excusing these attacks on Israelis, on settlers, there is an explanation and he could have found it out by ringing up any of a dozen easily accessible Israeli and Palestinian social workers, sociologists, commentators, and experts inside East Jerusalem within a few minutes.

Antisemitism

So there's a lackadaisical air about the BBC reporting, but it is I think, deliberate, that they would rather not explain things and they would rather avoid the wrath of the Israeli lobby. And then one of the big things that's made all this worse over the past decade or so is the virulence now with which the friends of Israel and Israel itself are pursuing the idea of antisemitism, so that any criticism of Israel is antisemitic.

This is sticking. This is serious. Nobody at the BBC, no executive, no producer, no editor, no reporter, no one sitting at their desk likes to be called an antisemite, whatever the truth of the accusation. Most of them have no more clue about how to handle this than Jeremy Corbyn and his friends were able to handle the assault on them. This has been a very significant move.

At the same time, our government shows no signs of shifting its view of doing anything about the current threats against the Palestinians, their situation, the threat of annexation, the movement of the American embassy to Jerusalem and so on.

So in that atmosphere, what the BBC does now, I think, is to avoid the issue if it can. The *Guardian*, it was said, was very glad in 2005, when the Iraq War took place and took the focus away from Palestine and therefore took away a lot of the pressure, which it had been getting for its reporting of the Second Intifada.

I think what we've seen in the past few years is the Arab Awakening, the civil war in Syria, the dreadful after-effects of the war in Iraq, and now of course we have domestic issues like Brexit, and then COVID-19, and these have been a great relief for the BBC, a reason to ignore the Palestinian question. I don't blame the reporters so much in this, as I blame the system. The reporters report in the way they know they will get on the air. That is to say they will report the way I've been describing, which is to continue the spurious equivalence, pretending that the talk about one side and the other is a way of getting at the truth.

I'm going to leave it there because I think I spent far too much time on the background, but I think I've made the essential point. The BBC especially shifts with the government thinking, and the effectiveness of the friends of Israel and their supporters is crucial in this, and allegations of antisemitism are as crucial as anything.

Media

Well, I think my own feeling is of course online. If you read online websites like *Middle East Eye, Electronic Intifada, Middle East Monitor, Mondoweiss*, you'll find fair reporting of not just the situation on the ground in Palestine, but also the background to it and the lobbies and the various pressures, et cetera, et cetera.

As to the mainstream media. I don't think anybody in Britain is doing a good job with them. And frankly, the *Guardian* did for many years, the *Guardian* was at the forefront. Even when the BBC was good, the *Guardian* was always even more on the ball. And the *Guardian* remained on the ball in the 2000s, long after the BBC had given up the ghost completely and was reporting it as a kind of table tennis match between Israel and the Palestinians. The only channel I watch now is Al Jazeera. But other people may watch others.

I mention these because I think they're reliable. I've been in journalism now for, I dread to say it, more than sixty years. And I think I know what is authentic and what isn't. I've been following the terrible events in Beirut and Al Jazeera has done a brilliant job. None of these spurious allegations about nuclear missiles are being reported, or taken seriously, as they shouldn't be, but the reporting on the background is very good.

I think the British government has an influence, not so much directly. I don't think anybody rings up from Number 10 to some sort of commissar at the BBC or ITV or Sky and tells them the menu for the day. But I think that these broadcasters, especially the BBC, which is very vulnerable, look at what happened in 2005 when they lost the director general and the chairman in one fell swoop over their reporting of Iraq, after their critical reporting of the dodgy dossier. That was another great setback for the BBC. However, to answer the question, I think that the BBC watches the government very closely, but certainly not MI6 or the Foreign Office. The Foreign Office itself has lost a lot of its power, a lot of its weight, unfortunately. And if you go to the Foreign Office for a briefing about Palestine, you probably get a very sympathetic version of the Palestinians and what's happening. So I would say the answer briefly is that neither of those institutions are really what matter.

This business of the way the Palestinian question has been ignored and is being ignored now is very important. And especially in view of the concentration, quite rightly so, that we've had recently on Black Lives Matter and Britain's past colonial excesses. Now it seems to me that it's not at all rare on the BBC or on ITV or on Channel Four to see factual and fictional pieces about the horrors of the British experience, the Indian experience of the British Raj, the Amritsar Massacre, the Bengal Famine, the terrible effects of Partition. They're constantly on our screens, we are very conscious of our dreadful colonial heritage as regards India and Africa.

And now with Black Lives Matter, quite rightly, we're examining our whole relationship with black British people. The Windrush affair has brought it into the forefront. And all these things are quite valid. The Balfour Project is very aware of this, and that's why we asked our last speaker, Sarah Helm, to touch on this. Because despite all this soul-searching about the British Empire, the one legacy of the British Empire which still hangs on to the great detriment of the people there and us all, and I reckon eventually to Israel itself, is the Balfour Declaration and its consequences. We made Israel. There's no question about it. Israel would not have happened without British interference, British takeover of Palestine, the finagling of the Mandate and all the rest of it. And the savage putdown of the Palestinian rebellion in 1936.

Conclusions

Keep complaining at the end of every BBC programme, radio or any other media outlet. Who wrote it? Who produced it? Take the names, write to them directly, write to the complaint system. Follow the rules. They are onerous, and the chances are as ever, and as I found my cost, you'll get the run-around. Your complaints will be disagreed with rather than fundamentally challenged. And it's a depressing experience, but it has to be kept up. Because if you don't challenge, if you don't keep at it, nothing will ever happen. It's a depressing prospect, but I'm afraid, that is the way: to keep at the BBC, to keep at your MP. The BBC represents you, not the government, not Israel. The BBC is actually listening to Israel instead of listening to the British people. That's what you have to remember, and that is outrageous.

Fig. 18 Tom Hurndall, Memorial to Rachel Corrie at the Rafah border, April 2003.

16. Palestine is a Four-letter Word: Psychoanalytic Innocence and Its Malcontents[1]

Lara Sheehi

In *Can the Monster Speak?* (2021: 96) Paul B. Preciado punctuates his rousing call to psychoanalysts: 'my mission is the revenge of the psychoanalytic and psychiatric "object" (in equal measure) over the institutional, clinical and micropolitical systems that shore up the violence wreaked by the sexual, gender and racial norms. We urgently need clinical practice to transition. This cannot happen without a revolutionary mutation in psychoanalysis, and a critical challenge of its patriarchal-colonial presuppositions'. Preciado summons us to something very specific. It is not abstract or theoretical. It is material and technical. If psychoanalysis is to transform itself from a disciplinary practice of quiet (and often explicit) violence, we are asked to confront the dynamics and paradigms that objectify rather than liberate.

1   My immense gratitude to Ian Parker without whom this piece would not have come into existence and whose fierce solidarity is moving, even across the distance. Thank you, also, to Manchester Metropolitan University for holding the Hurndall Memorial Lecture at which I was generously invited to speak. Most movingly, I want to thank and extend my deepest love and solidarity to and with the Hurndall family — it is a moving honour for me to carry Tom's legacy in print — a responsibility I take seriously and with the militancy that does his life justice. My own commitment to revolutionary love is daily stoked by my partner and co-author, Stephen Sheehi — thank you for lending your heart, comradeship and brilliance to this piece and to our book. A brief portion of the vignette on 'collapsing psychoanalytic space' appeared in Sheehi, L. (2018). 'Palestine is a Four-Letter Word', *DIVISION/Review, 18*, pp. 28–31.

https://doi.org/10.11647/OBP.0345.17

What follows in this chapter is an account of how contemporary psychoanalysis resists, subverts, and defangs such a possible revolutionary mutation and threats of transformation. But also, more importantly and simultaneously, this chapter highlights the real-time transformation of the field by Palestinian clinicians who wilfully enact and materialise the promise of mutation, and indeed liberation, across Palestine.

To map out the counter-revolutionary forces that attempt to upset the life-affirming mutation happening in Palestine, I will use work that my partner and co-author, Stephen Sheehi and myself outline in our book, *Psychoanalysis Under Occupation: Practicing Resistance in Palestine* (Routledge, 2022). Importantly, our work and book utilises a decolonial feminist solidarity-building approach to map out, discuss and platform the work of our Palestinian colleagues, not as they are interpolated by and through settler-colonial logic, nor through what Françoise Vergès (2021) identifies as 'femoimperialism' (17) or 'civilizational feminism' (4). Rather, we approach Palestinian clinicians through the understanding of them, following Sara Ahmed (2014), as 'willful subjects'.

Heeding Ahmed (2014: 1–2), we see in Palestine that 'willfulness is a diagnosis of the failure to comply with those whose authority is given [and]... involves persistence in the face of having been brought down'. It is not coincidental that a decolonial feminist 'style of politics' guided our book, especially since decolonial feminist and queer methodologies affirm that cis-heteronormative patriarchal structures, including all forms of capitalism, colonialism, and settler colonialism are the problem. It is not coincidental then that these systems themselves structurally and persistently identify *wilfulness* as the central problem, a problem of resistance.

Here, I am also heeding what Mamta Banu Dadlani (2020) invites us to do, psychoanalytically, in her own internalisation of Ahmed's (2019) call to 'queer' spaces, theory and action. My approach in this chapter parallels Dadlani's approach. She reminds us that 'queer use is a dangerous task, as it involves a lack of reverence for what the colonizer has gifted. By attending to what one is supposed to pass over, creatively engaging with what is left behind, and finding value in what is discarded... one falls out of compliance, and queer use becomes an act of destruction and vandalism of normalized use' (Dadlani, 2020: 124). In Palestine, we remain invited into this type of world, into a process, mutation and liberation by Palestinian clinicians, comrades and colleagues. These clinicians assert themselves daily as defiant, unassimilable 'problems'. They are clinicians who 'fall out of compliance' because they engage in acts of refusal that alert us to their wilful self-affirmation, individually and communally. In their affirming acts of refusal, both in the street and in the clinical spaces, they 'speak life', as Nadera Shalhoub-Kevorkian says, and they 'speak Palestine'. In doing so, they insist on the power of liveability.

In psychoanalysis, in a parallel to that which Preciado and Dadlani alert us, wilfulness is largely problematised. Indeed, in psychoanalytic parlance, what Dadlani (2020) especially also dares us to do is attend to the ideological underpinnings of patterns that replicate themselves along always-already fault lines, the violence of which is structured to fall on certain bodies before others. This distribution of violence, vulnerability, and precarity is never coincidental but rather reifies the very structures that created these conditions/possibilities of oppression.

This is how Palestine emerges as a four-letter word in psychoanalysis.

Vignette One: Collapsing Psychoanalytic Space

I presented at the 2017 Society for Psychoanalysis and Psychoanalytic Psychotherapy (SPPP) Spring meeting in New York City as a part of a panel that we simply called, 'Talking About Palestine in Psychoanalysis'. We were happy to see that many Society members also wanted to talk about Palestine in psychoanalysis, with the space quickly becoming standing-room only. Our intention was to use psychoanalytic theory, practice and technique to highlight how the Palestinian narrative had been missing from psychoanalysis — some of us spoke to how that was not coincidental, particularly given the ways in which, historically, settler colonialism operated: the colonised does not have the luxury of a narrative. In fact, the colonised, as Frantz Fanon reminds us, is always presumed guilty. Our panel was one of many that sought to alter the psychoanalytic terrain such that, in this case, the silenced and presumed-guilty Palestinian narrative could find space and so that we, psychoanalysts and psychoanalytic practitioners, could provide witness.

The mere mention of Palestine instigated an ideological psychic break: approximately halfway through our panel, a middle-aged man wearing a white shirt adorned with the Israeli flag made his flagrant entrance into our room. He carried a large paper bag and exuded aggressive energy by locking eyes with me (the only woman, and only Arab, on the panel) and repeatedly flexed his biceps and cracked his knuckles, as if preparing for a fight. The irony was not lost on me that he also appeared to "warrior up" by wrapping his neck with what is traditionally a *kuffiyeh* (a black and white scarf that has become a symbol of Palestinian resistance). His version of the scarf, however, was adorned with Israeli flags. This man, a fellow SPPP member and psychoanalyst living in New York, blocked the doorway and only entrance to the room for the duration of the panel; he disrupted the panel continually, admonishing the panellists and audience with declarations such as, 'there is no such thing as Palestinians!' and 'Palestine has no place in psychoanalysis!' Despite several interventions from more senior clinicians, he continued his disruptive behaviour. When people exited at the conclusion of the panel, he forced pamphlets onto them that were entitled, '101 Lies that Palestinians Tell'.

The experience was a first for many people in the audience.[2] The attempts from senior clinicians were admirable and appreciated given the onslaught, yet largely relied on traditional psychoanalytic theory to offer readings of what may have been happening in the group process. What was largely missing from the interventions, however, was an acknowledgement of what was unfolding *in real time*, materially, or an analysis regarding the ways in which normative ideology was being actively weaponised. Indeed, hegemonic ideology is most threatened by changes that challenges its primacy. I understood what appeared to be this man's imperative as not only an attempt to silence dissenting voices, but also, to purposefully deflect and derail a reality-testing exercise that sought to bring Palestine to the forefront against the crushing weight of a dominantly entrenched Zionist ideology.

---

2   A video I took of the disruption is deeply troubling — a room full of clinicians, many of whom are "frozen", heads hanging, unsure of how to intervene. Many confided in me following the panel that they had been concerned the man was carrying a weapon; many women further commented to me about their sense of danger and feelings of being intimidated as well as their concern about confronting an aggressive, hypermasculinist male in a closed space with no escape.

If we are to call this an enactment, it is one that stems from the fear inherent in a changing of the tides. Indeed, the enactment appeared to be one that exposed a real-time disruption of settler-colonial reality bending (Sheehi and Sheehi, 2022). That is, the mere mention of *talking about Palestine* was so threatening as to cause a cavalcade of aggression, the primary intention of which was suppressing expression, thought, and witnessing. This act was not arbitrary, nor was it individual or individualised, but rather a logical extension of the violence of the settler-colonial state of Israel, a state that necessitates settler-colonial outposts everywhere — here at a conference — to sustain its myth. Further, in the context of psychoanalysis, it was a vigilante attempt to name what constitutes appropriate or pure psychoanalytic content — a practice that itself is deeply troubling and perpetuated by ideology. So, it comes to be that when we speak of Palestine, the ideological weight of Zionism as its alleged counterpart, as its reaction formation, as the salve perhaps for annihilation anxiety, collapses our ability to remain as much in the material space, as in the symbolic.

The Unspeakable P-word

This vignette, though perhaps more extreme than what typically unfolds on a listserve, might be familiar. Those of us who have long fought in solidarity with the right for Palestinian self-determination against the settler-colonial, Apartheid state now known as Israel have noticed, repeatedly, that something curious, if not entirely ideologically predictable, appears to happen with the mere whisper of Palestine within psychoanalysis. An unspeakable "p" word within a "p" word that transforms the symbolic into the real with one utterance: *Palestine*. Within our memberships, on our listserves, in our psychoanalytic conferences, the presence of Palestine renders a parallel process, the burden of which appears to be uncontainable; the affective response of which appears to be anxiety-ridden; the experiential space of which appears to be perpetually conflict-inducing. The curiousness comes because the word "Palestine" appears to hold a unique power within psychoanalysis. The taboo word swiftly conjures the most unbending ideological splits *despite* contemporary psychoanalysis' emphasis and insistence on fluidity in theory, technique and practice, and despite its growing willingness to address issues of class, race, gender and ableism.

As a psychoanalytic clinician, scholar and activist, I believe psychoanalysis has a critical role in speaking to and about injustices, liberation struggles, and the unconscious processes that may work to replicate systems of oppression. Of course, I am not the first to note this. From Freud to Fenichel, Fromm to Fanon, and more contemporarily, clinician-activists,[3] especially those from and in the Global South, and especially Palestinians, have urged clinicians to interrogate and centre the decided link between psychoanalysis and our sociopolitical world. Moreover, they have called on us as a field to embody the ethics of clinical work, to veer away from disavowing our responsibility in unpacking the distressing and demoralising material stemming from the systemic inequities beyond our clinics.

In the case of Palestine, however, we have seen that time and again, these ethical calls often turn to ether and are subject to a particular type of weaponised 'psychoanalytic rigor' such that, in Fanonian terms, one witnesses the materialisation of a 'racial distribution of guilt'. In *Psychoanalysis Under Occupation* (Sheehi and Sheehi, 2022: 61), we expand on this tendency and locate it within a phenomenon we term, *psychoanalytic innocence*. Ideology is intrinsic to the viability of psychoanalytic innocence and ideological misattunement (Sheehi and Crane, 2020) is a central, mechanical tenet of psychoanalytic innocence which allows for displacement and banishment of material reality and social conditions from the therapeutic space. Stephen Portuges (2009: 70) warns us about this misuse of psychoanalysis' hallmark principle, neutrality, which 'has turned out to be a technical intervention that obfuscates the recognition and elucidation of the role of ideologically constructed factors in the psychoanalytic theory of treatment that contribute to patients' psychological difficulties'. He reminds us that this ideological manoeuvre displaces the *embodiment* of social conditions and material realities within historically marginalised patients.

---

3   See for example, work by Nadera Shalhoub-Kevorkian, Rana Nashashibi, Fathy Flefel, Samah Jabr, Lama Khouri, Shahnaaz Suffla, Mohamed Seedat, Kopano Ratele, Guilaine Kinouani, Foluke Taylor, Robert Downes, Ian Parker, Erica Burman, Martin Kemp, Chanda Griffin, Leilani Slavo Crane, Annie Lee Jones, Kirkland Vaughans, Carter J. Carter, Nancy Hollander Lynne Layton Stephen Portuges and countless others.

Like neutrality, in making Palestine a four-letter word, psychoanalytic theory and practice, through psychoanalytic innocence, works in service of settler-colonial violence. For example, psychoanalysis' insistence on dialogue, reason, and working through, even with the mention of Palestine, without a sustained analysis of the material conditions of dispossession inflicted on Palestinians acts under the pretence not only of neutrality and objectivity, but also universalism, empathy as an endpoint of process, and the myth of safety. In this way, psychoanalytic innocence works in concert with the logic of settler colonialism and occupation, denying the everyday violence enacted on Palestinians and conveniently forgetting how this is also structured by the unconscious. Indeed, psychoanalytic innocence relies on the hegemony of what Lynne Layton (2006) has termed 'normative unconscious processes'. Deployed in this way, it is particularly insidious because it simultaneously forfeits psychoanalysis' supposition of unconscious process and structure, while also ignoring material reality.

I would also like to draw our attention to how liberal and humanistic psychoanalysis maintains this naturalisation, remaining complicit through forms of oppression by seeking to graph a universalised 'healthy' adaptability onto colonial and racialised subjects whose humanity and psychic interiority are negated. In a liberalised version of psychoanalytic theory, these colonial subjects, especially Palestinians, are only able to access 'empathy' from psychoanalysis when they occupy the position of 'victim', and surrender their rights to experience political and material realities in full alignment with their experience and social context — a psychological process that involves succumbing to 'colonial introjects', as I have noted elsewhere (Sheehi/Masri, 2009), or to what David Eng (2016) calls 'colonial object relations'. This does not happen intrapsychically, but rather, *structurally and systemically*, one part of which is when Palestine is treated as a four-letter word.

Treating Palestine as a four-letter word demands an unspoken, yet affectively felt, prerequisite for Palestinian and pan-Arab subjectivity: you must simultaneously open yourself to predominantly anti-Palestinian spaces, but do so *without claim to historical, and political specificity*, and, also commit to a fundamentally self-effacing *dialogue* while being aggressed upon. This dialogue is expected to happen without noting the visceral truth (what Fanon might say is felt on a cellular level) of how this feels and what it *means* materially, i.e., the *reality* of what Dorothy E. Holmes (2006) might call 'wrecking effects'. More specifically, we are not to speak of how this depoliticised dialogue about Palestine, whether in the clinic or professionally, replicates a particular social order that demands one's non-affect while itself being mobilised *through affect* — demanding to be *felt* but remain unseen, unacknowledged, and unpacked.

The discussion of Palestine is indeed circumscribed by entrenched ideological formations, particularly Zionism, that saturate, even unconsciously, our theory and practice as a psychoanalytic collective. While many in the field have long sounded the alarm of PEPness (Progressive Except Palestine) as one such hegemonic ideological formation alongside cisheteronormativity, patriarchy, etc. that enframe our field, practice and theory, the utterance of Palestine continues to cause a particular type of collapse of psychoanalytic process, technique and practice. In other words, the mention of Palestine appears to shut down psychoanalytic thinking and trigger an urgent fleeing into psychoanalytic innocence. My observation, then, is that the utterance of Palestine provokes a resistance against what otherwise might be spoken about and/or experienced as a natural reflex to psychoanalytic thinking. If we view this as ideological, it is also decidedly not coincidental. In keeping with psychoanalytic innocence, the utterance itself — Palestine — is seen as the aggressor.

The way I have witnessed this process to unfold — or perhaps better, collapse — is through a primarily unconscious internalisation of an ideological formation, which is itself supported by material, social, cultural, and historical conditions (i.e., the conditions that perpetuate the social relations in which we are reared and come to find identifications) (Layton, 2006; Portuges, 2009).

Fanon (1952, 1963) himself was aware of the potential for this doubled-edged sword of psychoanalysis. Armed with its tools and promises, he also alerts us to the dangers of dominant ideological formations within psychoanalysis itself and how they work to reconstitute themselves in the same breath they are being torn down. If Fanon is speaking of the power and force of racism and colonialism, I am speaking of Zionism as a settler-colonial ideological formation, a set of logics — psychic, political, economic and social, based on the negation of the Palestinian people.

The presence of this internalised dominant ideological formation in our psychoanalytic collective precipitates a splitting off of conflicting identifications in order to retain and maintain its structural coherence. This is the foundation from which normative unconscious processes (Layton, 2006) emerge. That is, the unbending identification instigates an expression of normative unconscious processes that necessitate the disavowal of other potential self-states, or identifications, that may contradict or threaten the integrity of the ideological formation. The anxiety of deviation, therefore, is so pronounced, though perhaps not conscious, that all attempts to hold true to the position are made. Due to its unconscious 'common sense' (Hollander, 2009) quality, this ideological formation is at once all-encompassing and can go on unchallenged if not acknowledged and unpacked by our community as a whole.

The countless examples of this collapse is an indictment of how psychoanalytic scholars and clinicians (even activists), are complicit in perpetuating ways of thinking and actions, professionally and clinically, that deny the humanity of the Palestinian people. It is also an indictment of how the mere mention of Palestine collapses analysable spaces *in service of a dominant ideological position of innocence in which psychoanalysis finds itself secure and privileged.*

Disavowing Israeli Apartheid

Many readers will be familiar with the details of how the International Association of Relational Psychoanalysis and Psychotherapy (IARPP) made the unconscionable decision to hold its 2019 conference in what is now known as Tel Aviv, Israel, as well as the years of 'negotiations' in the aftermath of this decision. This particular event was the lynchpin in solidifying my thinking about how entrenched psychoanalysis' ideological misattunement is, and what later cohered around the concept of psychoanalytic innocence (Sheehi and Sheehi, 2022).

Indeed, this example highlights how Palestine, after decades, continues to consistently emerge as a four-letter word not just within the clinic, nor on the individual level through the analytic dyad, but rather structurally and systemically. This debacle is also meant to urgently highlight how Psychoanalysis, through its insistence on apolitical, universal humanism causes undue harm and violence to Palestine and Palestinians on a *global scale*. I am hopeful that this will alert us to our field's responsibility in the suffering of others, as Layton (2019) reminds us.

I will primarily focus on how psychoanalytic innocence operates rather than deflect from the affective charge by exclusivising or essentialising this to IARPP as an institution. Indeed, IARPP's bad faith decision is helpful only inasmuch as it provides us with a very visible and archetypal example of how 'liberal' modalities of psychoanalytic practice betray what Avgi Saketopoulou (2020) also aptly refers to as 'whiteness closing ranks' within psychoanalysis, here when the issue of Palestine is raised.

Psychoanalytic innocence emerges as a powerful lens to read why the IARPP deliberately crossed an international picket line called for by more than 20,000 Palestinian social workers and psychologists (https://bdsmovement.net/news/palestinian-union-social-workers-and-psychologists-urges-colleagues-not-participate). This analytic is especially important if we are to move away from sanctimonious ad hominem attacks. The IARPP affair demonstrates psychoanalytic innocence, bringing into focus the mechanisms by which psychoanalytic associations and, indeed, practitioners, especially from the global North, not only disavow the comprehensive violence of settler-colonial systems, but also actively perpetuate and participate in this violence, by pathologising, in this instance, resistance to Israeli apartheid and by diminishing the value of Palestinian life and well-being.

Indeed, psychoanalytic innocence helps us account for the glaring contradictions in IARPP's positions, seemingly indecipherable to IARPP leadership. For example, without invoking psychoanalytic innocence, how else do we account for locating the conference in Tel Aviv with the theme 'Imagining with Eyes Wide Open: Relational Journeys'? This decision betrays the unconscious marking (Razack and Fellows, 1998) immediately naming whose relational journey is worth imagining. As I have noted elsewhere (2019), how does an organisation imagine a conference in the settler-colonial state of Israel without implicitly, if not explicitly, dis-imagining Palestinians? Or at least, a particular *type* of Palestinian? This was further highlighted in an absurd pre-conference roundtable discussion that aimed to speak about 'the absence of Palestinians to look at the obstacles to an Israeli

Palestinian encounter' — even here blatantly disavowing the countless Israeli-Palestinian encounters that happen under a brutal occupation. This same roundtable asked the seemingly innocent questions: 'can we create a dialogue about the absence of dialogue? Can we give presence in the absence of presence? Is the absence a powerful protest or a refusal to see another?'

We are able to see clearly through this example how the power of psychoanalytic innocence relies heavily on the ability to weaponise and abuse theory to gaslight those who engage in the politics of refusal, whether that be a patient, a supervisee, a student, an analysand, or in this case Palestinians and those who believe in their right to self-determination. The IARPP replicated the same strategies of innocence within psychoanalysis, with the organisation and its leadership appealing to abstract notions of "reason", "civility", and, of course, "dialogue" — all the while disavowing how these terms and notions are decidedly not neutral and, in fact, rely on racialised, classed and gendered codes to gain traction.

Psychoanalytic innocence here resembles Margarita Palacios and Stephen Sheehi's (2020: 295) exposé of white innocence, namely that, 'within its habitus of universal humanity, permits us also to consider how the flesh itself that is constituent of the "we" is not ideologically and socially same throughout this heterogeneity of the third-person collective'. In this way, IARPP provided the ideological valiance of "impartiality" and "openness" as the *operative structural process* of collusion with racism and settler colonialism.

What is especially important when considering psychoanalytic innocence are the ways in which the field brazenly deploys tropes of "dialogue" and "neutrality" to censure, while simultaneously deflecting from how these very concepts are also mechanisms for collusion, control and dominance. This perhaps was evident in IARPPs co-presidential statement:

> We will be extending invitations to Palestinian colleagues, and we will work to enable their presence with us. Rather than foreclosing those issues and silencing conversation, we aim to create within our relational psychoanalytic conference an open and safe space in which attendees across the political spectrum can engage and exchange views. We believe that dialogue, more than ever, is needed across divides.

While on the surface this might strike some as "reasonable", if we operationalise psychoanalytic innocence, and the way Gloria Wekker (2016) highlights how Edward Said's (1993) 'cultural archive' manoeuvres unconsciously. Most importantly, it is not reasonable if we attend to a sustained material analysis, at which point the statement emerges as an archetypal hybrid of liberal bad faith, combining the "white innocence" of the United States with the disavowal and nomenclature of soft Zionism. Even if Palestinian and non-Palestinian Arab clinicians had been willing to betray the Palestinian call for boycott, most were not able to travel to Israel, legally, as they would have faced criminal proceedings in their home countries. Finally, we know that even if they were able to receive "visas", the process is intended to be psychologically humiliating and subjecting Palestinians to such processes *just to be present* would be an unconscionable violation.

The weaponisation of language contrived to shut down, not create, space and legitimised explicitly non-Palestinian voices as the arbiters and protectors of Palestinian freedom of speech. Samah Jabr, a Palestinian psychiatrist and chair of the Mental Health Unit at the Palestinian Ministry of Health and her co-author Elizabeth Berger, hone in on such language, saying, 'leadership took ownership of the virtuous language of "dialogue", the "third", and "empathy" while asserting that Palestinians who decline their kind invitation might be indulging in the reprehensible language of "splitting", "non-inclusiveness", or "acting out"' (Berger and Jabr, 2020). In this particular example, the statement acts as testimony to the predetermined parameters of conversation or "dialogue", one that communicates little interest in material reality. In this way, psychoanalysts, and psychoanalytic organisations, quickly come to embody what Fanon warned were the ways in which clinicians act as agents of the State.

Further, IARPP not only egregiously attempted to derail an independent event called 'Voices of Palestine' held simultaneously to their NYC 2018 conference, but also, in what we already know is a surveillance state, hotel security was alerted of potential 'danger' posed by supporters of the event. Indeed, New York Police Department (NYPD) and Homeland Security were present in full and visible force during the Voices event, a presence that was deemed 'coincidental', despite proof from hotel staff stating otherwise. Here innocence is marked since, surely one could anticipate that a call to NYPD about 'concerns' regarding any activity in support of Palestine would be heard and read against anti-Arab and Islamophobic tropes that readily saturate the collective unconscious.

If we are not using psychoanalytic innocence as a framework analytic, we might be tempted, indeed seduced, into reading IARPP's response to the dissent of its members as a psychological 'enactment' of the irreparable violence between Zionists and Palestinians. What this reading misses, however, are the ways in which this response demonstrates a clear example of how psychoanalytic innocence ensures that psychoanalysis, as a field, ideologically and politically colludes with power — not as a byproduct or symptom, but as constitutive of its practice and theory. This is because collusion and complicity operate within a shared structural, systemic, and political tradition of whiteness that emerges out of coloniality and settler colonialism. What the traditional psychoanalytic reading also displaces is how calls for 'dialogue' and neutrality — mainstays of our practice — are weaponised, here insinuating that there might even be a 'safe-space' where dialogue can exist. In fact, this example demonstrates how dialogue itself can be a structural tool to disempower.

Again, perhaps if we were not attentive to the mechanics of psychoanalytic innocence, we would get mired in theories of displaced fear or misdirected hate, identification with the aggressor, etc. — all important theoretical readings, but readings that nonetheless do not account for material reality, let alone offer a sustained analysis of struggle in the context of settler colonialism or why Palestine consistently emerges as a four-letter word.

IARPP enacts and performs a betrayal of what, structurally, we as a psychoanalytic field have always relied on: the fantasy that we can exist outside of the material reality of power. Here, psychoanalytic power is literal in terms of credibility as bestowed by the psychoanalytic establishment, and the power we have to name another's process; it is also innocent, as an organisation like IARPP is given space to exist both as a perpetrator of political and social violence and still be received as non-threatening, afforded plausible deniability through the wilful unlinking of whiteness (and its violence) and coloniality from their organisational actions (even pleading with us to remember 'the good people' within its ranks — of course they exist, even if they become magically undone of their power to represent structures).

When it comes to Palestine — and by extension, perhaps all other 'unseeable', unanalysable spaces and issues (classism, sexism, transphobia, xenophobia), we first must acknowledge and examine our own collective complicity and investment in sustaining the structures through and by which oppression can continue to happen.

Oppression works best when the oppressed, here the Palestinian, becomes responsible for all suffering — theirs *and* that of their oppressor, while the oppressor, through collective complicity and hegemonic power is consistently exonerated and provided the magnanimity of innocence. The success of a dominant ideological formation, as distinguished from other types of ideologies, is predicated on the normalisation of its presence, the literal 'taking in whole', such that it is undetectable and results in a 'common sense' acceptance. Within our ranks, our own continued unwillingness to include the Palestinian narrative within our oeuvre as well as the foreclosed analytic spaces such as those described above normalise and, indeed, prioritize Zionism, while in the same breath demanding 'dialogue' (Sheehi, 2018) from those who express dissent.

Insisting on Presence

The act of refusal is a wilful act, a positive act, and a productive act — an act that, according to Glen Coulthard in *Red Skin, White Masks*, can also be encouraged and read as a 'disciplined maintenance of resentment' (2014: 108). We should not read this as a deflection from the depth work of psychoanalysis, but rather, as a contingency for vibrant liveability in the face of oppressive structures. Palestinian refusal, especially on the part of our Palestinian clinician colleagues, is an affirmative wilful disobedience and is a retooling not only of psychoanalytic theory and practice but also the ethics of care. To bring us back to Preciado (2021: 94), their 'position is one of epistemological insubordination'.

Our Palestinian colleagues and comrades are 'willfully disobedient', as Sara Ahmed (2014: 149) would say, the disobedience of an oppressed people to become an 'agent of [their] own harm'. Whether in the clinic, in supervision, or in the street, Palestinian clinicians validate Palestinian selfhood and Palestinian subjectivity in the face of brutal occupation. Their 'willful disobedience', especially in positions in which they are constitutively disenfranchised, radiantly expresses wilfulness as an act of affirming relationality, as a wilful act of affirming and standing with their patients, each other, their families and their community.

These positions by Palestinians are decolonial and feminist positions, ones that *reclaim feminism*, in Vergès' (2021: 17) words, and realise in their powerful simplicity, 'the way in which the complex of racism, sexism and ethnocentrism pervades all relations of domination'. While we are busy metamorphosing the mere whisper of Palestine into a four-letter word, our Palestinian colleagues are refusing, in the most beautiful Fanonian sense, to become agents of the state and to engage in carceral discipline of themselves or their patients. Rather, they are mutating psychoanalytic practice into a radical, decolonial feminist practice that operates on a revolutionary potential of attuned care.

In this way, Palestinian insistence on *presence*, even as psychoanalysis actively attempts its negation, embodies Preciado's call to us: 'drag the analysts' couches into the streets and collectivize speech, politicize bodies, debinarize gender and sexuality and decolonize the unconscious' (95).

Our Palestinian colleagues engage daily with revolutionary acts of refusal, which also embody autonomy — an autonomy that is social and communal rather than focused solely on the individual or limited to the clinical dyad. It is an autonomy that insists on indigenous presence in defiance of settler regimes, carceral logics and, most importantly to our field, their psychoanalytic proxies.

Our Palestinian clinician comrades *resist becoming a four-letter word* and, instead, highlight for us how their clinical work comes to be both a space for resistance for their patients and also an extension of their own resistance against settler-colonial hegemony; a collective practice, unified precisely through its engagement with creating and maintaining life and life-worlds, as well as political and historical realities, for Palestinians, by Palestinians.

Bibliography

Ahmed, S., *Willful Subjects* (Durham, NC: Duke University Press, 2014), https://doi.org/10.1515/9780822376101.

Berger, E., and Jabr, S., 'Silencing Palestine: Limitations on free speech within mental health organizations', *International Journal of Applied Psychoanalytic Studies*, 17(2) (2020), 193–207, https://doi.org/10.1002/aps.1630.

Coulthard, G. S., *Red Skin, White Masks: Rejecting the Colonial Politics of Recognition* (Minneapolis, MN: University of Minnesota Press, 2014), https://doi.org/10.5749/minnesota/9780816679645.001.0001.

Dadlani, M. B., 'Queer use of psychoanalytic theory as a path to decolonization: A narrative analysis of Kleinian object relations', *Studies in Gender and Sexuality*, 21(2) (2020), 119–26, https://doi.org/10.1080/15240657.2020.1760027.

Eng, D. L., 'Colonial object relations', *Social Text*, 34(1) (2016), 1–19, https://doi.org/10.1215/01642472-3427105.

Fellows, M. L., and Razack, S., 'The race to innocence: Confronting hierarchical relations among women', *Journal of Gender Race & Justice*, 1 (1998), 335.

Fanon, F., *Black Skin, White Masks* (New York: Grove Press, 1952).

Layton, L., 'Attacks on linking: the unconscious pull to dissociate individuals from their social context', in L. Layton, N.C. Hollander, S. Gutwill (eds), *Psychoanalysis, Class and Politics: Encounters in the Clinical Setting* (London: Routledge, 2006), pp. 107–17, https://doi.org/10.4324/9780203965139.

Palacios, M., and Sheehi, S., 'Vaporizing white innocence: confronting the affective-aesthetic matrix of desiring witnessing', *Subjectivity*, 13(4) (2020), 281–97, https://doi.org/10.1057/s41286-020-00106-9.

Preciado, P. B., *Can the Monster Speak?: Report to an Academy of Psychoanalysts*, vol. 32 (Boston, MA: MIT Press, 2021).

Portuges, S., 'The politics of psychoanalytic neutrality', *International Journal of Applied Psychoanalytic Studies*, 6(1) (2009), 61–73, https://doi.org/10.1002/aps.188.

Said, E., *Culture and Imperialism* (New York: Vintage Books, 1993).

Sakatopoulou, A., 'Whitness Closing Ranks', 2020, https://wp.nyu.edu/artsampscience-nyu_pd_blog/2020/06/30/whiteness-closing-ranks-avgi-saketopoulou/.

Sheehi, L., and Crane, L. S., 'Toward a liberatory practice: Shifting the ideological premise of trauma work with immigrants', in P. Tummala-Narra (ed.), *Trauma and Racial Minority Immigrants: Turmoil, Uncertainty, and Resistance* (Washington, DC: American Psychological Association, 2021), pp. 285–303, https://doi.org/10.1037/0000214-016.

Sheehi, L. and Sheehi. S., *Psychoanalysis Under Occupation: Practicing Resistance in Palestine* (New York: Routledge, 2022), https://doi.org/10.4324/9780429487880.

Sheehi, L., 'Disavowing Israeli Apartheid', *Middle East Report Online (MERO)*, 2019, https://merip.org/2019/06/disavowing-israeli-apartheid/.

Sheehi, L. (n.e Masri), 'Introjects in the Therapeutic Dyad: Towards Decolonization', Major Area Paper in the Completion of the Doctorate of Psychology', George Washington University, 2009. Unpublished.

Sheehi, S., 'Psychoanalysis under occupation: Nonviolence and dialogue initiatives as a psychic extension of the closure system', *Psychoanalysis and History*, 20(3) (2018), 353–69, https://doi.org/10.3366/pah.2018.0273.

Vergès, F., *A Decolonial Feminism*, trans. A. J. Bohrer (London: Pluto Press, 2021), https://doi.org/10.2307/j.ctv1k531j6.

Wekker, G., *White Innocence: Paradoxes of Colonialism and Race* (Durham, NC: Duke University Press, 2016), https://doi.org/10.1515/9780822374565.

Fig. 19 Anonymous, Tom Hurndall playing football in the Al Ruweishid Refugee Camp at the Jordan/Iraq border, photo taken on his Nikon camera, March 2003.

List of Illustrations

Index

About the Team

Alessandra Tosi was the managing editor for this book.

Caitlin Broadie and Melissa Purkiss performed the proofreading.

Lucy Barnes indexed this book.

Jeevanjot Kaur Nagpal designed the cover. The cover was produced in InDesign using the Fontin font.

Jeremy Bowman typeset the book in InDesign. The text font is Tex Gyre Pagella; the heading font is Californian FB.

Mihaela Buna wrote the Alt-text for the images in the book.

Cameron Craig produced the paperback, hardback, EPUB, and PDF editions.

Ross Higman produced the HTML and XML editions. The conversion is performed with open source software such as pandoc (https://pandoc.org/) created by John MacFarlane and other tools freely available on our GitHub page (https://github.com/OpenBookPublishers).

This book has been anonymously peer-reviewed by experts in their field. We thank them for their invaluable help.

This book need not end here...

Share

All our books — including the one you have just read — are free to access online so that students, researchers and members of the public who can't afford a printed edition will have access to the same ideas. This title will be accessed online by hundreds of readers each month across the globe: why not share the link so that someone you know is one of them?

This book and additional content is available at:

https://doi.org/10.11647/OBP.0345

Donate

Open Book Publishers is an award-winning, scholar-led, not-for-profit press making knowledge freely available one book at a time. We don't charge authors to publish with us: instead, our work is supported by our library members and by donations from people who believe that research shouldn't be locked behind paywalls.

Why not join them in freeing knowledge by supporting us: https://www.openbookpublishers.com/support-us

Follow @OpenBookPublish

Read more at the Open Book Publishers BLOG

You may also be interested in:

'Fragile States' in an Unequal World
Isabel Rocha de Siqueira

https://doi.org/10.11647/OBP.0311

World of Walls
The Structure, Roles and Effectiveness of Separation Barriers
Said Saddiki

https://doi.org/10.11647/OBP.0121

Democracy and Power
Noam Chomsky

https://doi.org/10.11647/OBP.0050

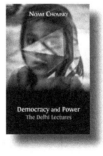

Ingram Content Group UK Ltd.
Milton Keynes UK
UKHW051820090723
424713UK00003B/10